PROMISE AND DELIVERANCE

S. G. DE GRAAF

PROMISE AND DELIVERANCE

VOLUME IV
CHRIST AND THE NATIONS

*Translated by H. Evan Runner and
Elisabeth Wichers Runner*

PAIDEIA PRESS
St. Catharines, Ontario, Canada

First published in Dutch as *Verbondsgeschiedenis,*
© J.H. Kok of Kampen.

ISBN 0-88815-010-5
Printed in the United States of America.

Table of Contents

JOHN: THE WORD OF LIFE

JOHN: WE HAVE BEHELD HIS GLORY

CHRIST'S WAY TO THE GENTILES

CHRIST AND THE GENTILES

CHRIST'S WORLDWIDE REIGN

CONSUMMATION

John:
The Word of Life

1: The True Light

John 1:1-34

The Word is the eternal Son of God, and as such He gives us God's communion. By Him the world was made. Thus the whole world was made to serve that communion between God and man, a communion established by the Word. This communion, which was present in the covenant of God's favor,* was broken by the Fall but was restored by the eternal Word in the covenant of grace. Thus the Word was life because life is nothing other than living in communion with God. This life is also the light of men. It has been shining from the beginning for there was a continuous revelation of the Word of communion. That light shone in the darkness and the darkness did not overpower it.

In the covenant of God's favor *before* the Fall, the communion between God and man depended both on the eternal Word and on Adam. In the covenant of grace *after* the Fall, however, the eternal Word, the Son of God, took it upon Himself to become Adam Himself, the second Adam. That happened when the Word became flesh. Now the communion between God and man depends solely on the Word which became flesh.

The Sanhedrin in Jerusalem sent representatives to John the Baptist to ask him who he was. Apparently this group consisted of Sadducees who first addressed John, and of Pharisees who questioned him afterward. Verse 24 should be translated: "There also were representatives from among the Pharisees."

The expression occurring in verses 15 and 30 means: He who comes after me has surpassed me, He has caught up with me and has gone ahead of me; He has put me in His shadow, because He was before me.

---

*See Vol. I, p. 29—TRANS.

Main thought: *The true light was coming into the world.*

The light shines in the darkness. In the beginning, when God created the world, He created it through His Son. The Son of God carried out the work of creation. He had taken it upon Himself to give God's love to the people who were going to be created. He would maintain the communion between God and man. When He created the world He arranged it in such a way that everything for man would be a token of God's love and everything would serve the communion between God and man.

Finally He created man and gave him God's communion in paradise in the covenant of God's favor. What a marvelous life man had then! That communion with God was the light of man's life.

But man rejected that love of God, thus breaking communion with God. As a result all the light went out of his life. Then the Son of God wished to restore that communion again; He wished to renew God's love to man. He accomplished this through the covenant of grace. But now God's love assumed a new dimension: it was a love through which God forgave man's sin.

What a blessing it was that God's Son continued to give man this new communion. He has done that throughout all ages. At first He gave communion to all of mankind and later, after the human race had twice turned away from Him, He gave it only to the people of Israel. But life in communion with God, which the Son gave, went on. There was still light in this world after all. That light continued to shine in the darkness of sin but the darkness could not overpower it. Though many turned away from God, the grace of God revealed through the Son was victorious time after time.

The Word became flesh. In paradise during the covenant of God's favor, communion between God and man depended both on the eternal Son of God and on Adam. God's Son was to give that communion and Adam was to receive it. When Adam rejected God's communion the Son of God promised to act as the Head of the human race, taking Adam's place. To do this He had to become man and do what Adam should have done plus make atonement for what Adam had done wrong. By replacing Adam He had the right to restore man to God's communion again.

Immediately after the Fall the promise was given that He would come to take Adam's place. Finally, after many centuries, the time had come: He was born a manchild in Bethlehem. For thirty years He lived quietly in Nazareth but then He began His ministry among the people. The Son of God appeared to give us God's communion. The whole world had been created by Him and yet, because of sin that world was alien to Him. It was sin that alienated us from God and that was why the world did not know Him.

Worse yet, His own chosen people did not receive Him, the people God had chosen to be His special possession and who were privileged to live in His covenant! Even though God had spoken to that special status nation for centuries, its people did not, when the time came, recognize God's Son!

Some among them did receive Him in faith; that was the result of God's work in their hearts. The Holy Spirit changed their hearts in such a way that they knew the Son of God and believed in Him. To them Christ gave God's communion. They were privileged to live in the light of God's favor as His children and were transformed into His image more and more.

How marvelous it was for His own to follow Him! Jesus showed them God's full grace and faithfulness. No one has ever known God on his own and no one can climb up to God to find out who He is. Instead, the Son of God revealed God to us again through His love. There is no knowledge of God's grace apart from the Lord Jesus Christ, God's Son.

That was the wonderful thing about the Lord Jesus for those who followed Him. God showed His grace through Jesus. The Son of God appeared as an ordinary human being, weak like us. Admittedly, He was without sin, but He nevertheless bore the consequences of our sins. He was also burdened with the yoke of our misery. He became flesh, a weak human being, a man subject to suffering and death, and thus took our sins upon Himself to atone for them.

Make straight the way for the Lord. Because the Son of God looked like any other man and because the world was so alien from God it wouldn't recognize His Son, God sent John the Baptist to introduce Christ as God's Son and our Redeemer.

Several months before the Lord Jesus began His ministry among the people, John had begun to preach that the Kingdom of heaven was at hand. He who would give us God's communion again and through that communion restore our life had come at last. This is what was meant by the Kingdom. God's grace would reign over us again and we would be glad to serve Him in life. But life in God's communion demanded a complete change in our lives. Our life without God had to die and a new life was to begin. That is why God sent John to baptize. Baptism signifies the death of the old life and the birth of the new. As a result, we receive forgiveness of sins, signified by the washing quality of water.

John preached and baptized at Bethany (Bethabara) in Trans-Jordan. Many came to him to be baptized, we are told. The elders of the people in Jerusalem heard about it and became quite concerned about John's influence because they were afraid the people might reject their leadership. They knew what John was saying was completely different from what they said. They taught that man must save himself while John said that God gives us His grace through the Lord Jesus. In their anxiety they sent some representatives to John to find out who he was and what he was doing.

Among these representatives were some Sadducees who believed that man needed only the light of reason, not, as John claimed, the light of God's revelation. They started the interview by asking John who he was, demanding whether he claimed to be the Messiah and wondering why he thought he needed a following. But John, unwilling to distract attention away from Jesus, dismissed their questions. The Sadducees thereupon wanted to know if he thought he was Elijah or some other prophet. Again, John's response was a denial.

Then they demanded he tell them who he was; they had to take some kind of answer back with them. John then pointed them to the Word of the Lord in which the prophet Isaiah had said a voice would be heard in the desert calling men to prepare their hearts and lives to receive Christ. He was that voice, he explained, nothing more. They should not, he said, focus on him, but instead direct their attention to the coming Messiah. If they were prepared to see God's grace coming in the Messiah they would receive His love into their hearts.

He stands in the midst of you. Among those representatives were also a few Pharisees. The Pharisees believed that life was meritorious; they had no further need of God's grace. It disturbed them greatly that John summoned everybody to be baptized. They were righteous in themselves and did not need any renewal of life or forgiveness of sins. They knew that when the Messiah came He would cleanse the people. But if John was not the Messiah, as he admitted, or a prophet returned to this world, what were his credentials for baptizing?

John explained he only baptized with water. He only gave the *sign* of the renewal of life. He could not give the renewal itself. The renewal would be given by Christ, the Son of God for He had come to restore the communion with God. Therefore He stood so far above John that John was not worthy to untie the thongs of His sandals. They should not think, he cautioned them, that the coming of this Redeemer was still a long way off; in fact, He was standing in the midst of them. He had already come and it was John's calling to introduce Him to the people.

Should John's message not have warned these representatives? God had sent His Son to restore the communion between Him and the people and, besides, He had sent someone to point His Son out to them. But the leaders of the people were not impressed. God's grace remained alien to them; they did not want God's communion.

See the Lamb of God! How did John know all the things he told those representatives? The Lord Jesus had come to him to be baptized. Jesus had to be incorporated into His people as their Head. After His baptism, the heavens had been opened and the Father had proclaimed the Lord Jesus as His beloved Son. Moreover, the Holy Spirit had descended upon Him in the form of a dove.

Throughout John had learned to recognize the Lord Jesus for

what He really was. As they were related, John of course knew Jesus, but he also knew that He was the Messiah. John learned about Christ's Messianic role when he baptized Jesus. He was the Son of God, filled by the Holy Spirit. Moreover, He united Himself so completely with His people that He agreed to undergo baptism and thereby take all their sins upon Himself. He was the true sacrificial Lamb who would atone for the sins of His people, and John knew all that.

The day after those representatives had come, John saw the Lord Jesus coming towards him. John pointed to Him and said, "See there the Lamb of God who takes away the sin of the world. He is the one. This is He whom I claimed would come after me. He has surpassed me and I must diminish for He existed before me. He is from eternity, the Son of God!" John further explained how these matters had been revealed to him through the sign of a dove.

Thus John focused people's attention on Christ, not on himself. It was pure joy for in the Lord Jesus he had seen the salvation of the world. To see Him and to point Him out becomes a real joy even though it takes us out of the limelight. Only Christ counts!

2: Confessors

John 1:35-52

The calling of the disciples in John 1 was different from the calling that took place later in Galilee. On that later occasion they were called to a specific discipleship but in the John 1 calling Christ brought them to a confession of His name.

Christ conquered and claimed them because He showed that He knew them. By His light they recognized what they were. Christ was revealed to them and that caused them to know themselves. He called all of them to confess His name and thus invited them to communion with His Father; yet He called each one of them in a personal way, according to each person's nature and disposition.

Main thought: *By means of His call, Christ brings us to a confession of His name.*

Andrew and his companion. The day after John the Baptist had pointed the Lord Jesus out to the people as the Lamb of God, he again saw Him walking around. Two of John's disciples were standing with him. One was Andrew; the name of the other was not recorded. It may have been John, the author of the gospel, and he may have omitted his own name intentionally. Again John the Baptist pointed the Lord Jesus out as the Lamb of God and announced Him as the atonement for our sins.

John's disciples did not fully understand their master's words, but now they knew, formally at least, that Jesus was the

17

Messiah. They wanted to go to Him and yet did not dare to speak to Him. They just followed along behind Jesus when suddenly He turned around and spoke to them. He asked what they were looking for.

They couldn't really answer that question. What indeed were they looking for? They did not quite know themselves. They wanted to be with the Lord Jesus, talk to Him, know Him, but they did not understand the yearning of their own hearts. They did not know what they wanted from Him just then or, at least, were not able to express themselves.

Embarrassed, they asked, "Teacher, where are You staying?" Perhaps they thought that if they could be in the same room with Him, they might be able to identify what they were looking for.

Unknown to them, the Lord Jesus had known them all along. He knew the Father had made them feel restless and lonely. He knew, better than they, that they were looking for contact with God through Him and that, as soon as they found God, they would also be in touch with life itself.

How delighted Jesus was when He recognized His Father's hand nudging these two men! He invited them to His place and because it was four o'clock in the afternoon they stayed with Him the remainder of that day. We do not know exactly what they talked about but we can be sure that He revealed Himself to them. He showed them that He sensed their loneliness and that He could fulfill their hearts' need. In His love God gave Himself to them. As the Son of God He brought them God's communion. This became such a marvelous thing to them that later they remembered the exact hour it had happened.

Throughout history, He rescues lonely people and leads them into contact with God and with life. He leads them to confess Him as the Christ, as the One who was sent by God to give us God's communion.

Simon Peter. Andrew was a brother of Simon. He went to Simon and confessed in public that he had found Jesus to be the Christ; he had come to know the Christ in Jesus. Andrew did not argue the point with Simon, but simply led him to Jesus. That is what we must do; it is still possible even though Jesus is no longer here on earth, for we have His Word and it is in that Word that He comes to meet us. We must give His Word to the people.

Thus Simon was led to Jesus. From the moment Jesus looked at him, He knew what Simon was like. Simon was an emotional man, often impetuous, which made him rather unstable; he rapidly changed from one mood into the next. But he wanted badly to change! God had made him dissatisfied with himself and now Jesus said to him: "You are Simon, the son of John; you will be called Peter, which means *rock*." How did the Lord Jesus know about Simon's desperate longing to become as firm as a rock?

Jesus promised Simon that he would someday be called Peter. Jesus not only knows us but by the power of His grace He also makes us what we should be. He is like a sculptor who can see the finished product before he starts to carve. He saw a stable Peter in the volatile, excitable fisherman called Simon. And what of us? What will He make us into?

If we surrender ourselves to Him and permit Him to work in us, He will refashion us after His own image. Let us diligently hear and read His Word. Then we will understand how He knows us and we will be pleased to entrust ourselves to His hands.

Philip. The next day the Lord Jesus wanted to return to Galilee. That morning He met Philip and invited him to return with Him. This had an entirely different meaning for Philip than a mere invitation to accompany someone. He had been asked by Christ, the Son of God! To Philip, it was a revelation! He knew that Jesus was aware of his desire to commune with God. Philip understood the honor of this calling and he promptly surrendered.

He was far from understanding everything about the Lord Jesus. That was evident from what he said about Him later. But he clearly realized that He was the One who had been announced by Moses and the prophets. He was the prophet whom the Lord would call out of Israel. He was the One who would redeem life and make known the will of the Lord's grace. He would assure us that God knows us truly and that our lives are to be spent following Him.

Nathanael. Philip met Nathanael and witnessed that he as well as Andrew and Peter had discovered the promised One in the person of Jesus. When Philip introduced Jesus as the son of Joseph from Nazareth, Nathanael, who came from Cana, a town close to Nazareth and constantly feuding with the people of Nazareth, mused: "Can anything good come out of Nazareth?"

We can imagine what was going on in Nathanael's heart. He had heard what John the Baptist had said and he wanted very much to believe that the Messiah had come to redeem His people. But he had his doubts, especially when he heard about Nazareth. It simply could not be true that the Messiah came from such a place. Today, many people have the same difficulty with the Lord Jesus. He is unimportant to them. Often they like to remain in their doubt, raising objections so they can continue to doubt. With Nathanael, however, this was not the case. The basis of his thinking and questioning was faith, even though he was not yet aware of it. Yet Philip did not start arguing in order to convince Nathanael; he merely said, "Come and see." That is how faith is. Faith trusts and knows that Jesus has the power to reveal Himself to everybody; He can be a Savior to everyone.

As soon as Jesus saw Nathanael coming towards Him He said, "Here is a true Israelite in whom there is nothing false." That statement proved to Nathanael that Jesus had seen into his innermost being! Though he doubted, his doubting was not insincere or hypocritical. He did not pretend he wanted to be freed from his doubt while in reality he loved it. Beneath his doubt lay concealed the longing of faith. Indeed, his longing proved his honesty. Jacob, the progenitor of the people, had also wrestled with God, and as a result had become righteous. Since then God had called him Israel. Nathanael was a true descendant of that Israel.

Amazed and touched, Nathanael asked Jesus how He knew him. The answer was totally unexpected: "Before Philip called you, while you were still under the fig tree, I saw you." Evidently while Nathanael was sitting under the fig tree he had been asking himself if it really could be true that the Messiah had now come. How completely the Lord Jesus knew him!

Then the Word of God took hold of his heart and he said, "Rabbi, You are the Son of God! You are the King of Israel!"

Nathanael professed a great deal about the Christ. He was the Son of God in whom the full love of God had come. Evidently he had heard that word from John the Baptist and was now saying "Amen" to it in faith. In that love of God He would reign over His people. Thus Nathanael's life was redeemed; he had been known in his doubt and had been freed from it. The Lord Jesus also frees us from our doubt in the same way if only we let Him speak to us through His Word.

Yet there was still something in Nathanael's life that threatened to darken his outlook. So much of his life had yet to be cleaned up and he ran the risk of becoming absorbed in his own life. We are often in danger of doing the same thing and as a result lose sight of Christ. This is why Christ directed Nathanael's attention to *His* glory.

The vision that Jacob had once seen in a dream would find its fulfillment in Christ. His disciples would see that there was daily communion between God and Jesus. The heavens would be opened above Him, the angels would carry His prayers up to God and bring Him God's answers. We can all see Christ in the light of God's eternal communion and by seeing Him thus in faith we are blessed.

3: Life's Renewer

John 2:1-12

Christ is the One who renews life. That is how He revealed Himself when He turned water into wine. He especially revealed how, by His grace, He renews life, turning it into joy.

Main thought: *Christ's revelation of Himself as the Renewer of life.*

What God's communion means for our lives. When Jesus returned from Judea to Nazareth He found that His mother, who very likely had already become a widow, had gone to Cana to attend a wedding. He also went to Cana and was invited to the wedding together with His followers. He accepted this invitation; together with those who had confessed Him as the Christ He went to the wedding feast and enjoyed life's joy.

That must have seemed very strange to the disciples of John the Baptist who denied himself every pleasure, lived in the desert and spent much time in fasting. But then John had to bring a different message, or rather, he had to show a different aspect of the same message. By his whole life he said and showed that we have forfeited everything by our sins. He was a preacher of penitence. The Lord Jesus, on the other hand, said and showed that He would restore everything to us by making atonement for our sins.

If we have been reconciled to God and have communion with

Him we may enjoy life in that communion again. He grants us again the joy of life. But that is then a complete joy, a joy for which we give thanks to God, a joy that is a thank-offering for what He has given us in His grace.

The hour of the Father. Because so many unexpected guests attended the wedding dinner, the wine ran out, a stunning embarrassment to a Jewish host. Evidently Mary knew the host well and shared his concern. She went to the Lord Jesus and whispered in His ear that they were out of wine. Wouldn't He, the Messiah, help out? How little Mary understood His calling. He certainly had not been sent simply to help people out with their occasional problems. He had been sent to restore the communion with God. That did not mean He would not help people with their problems, but then always with that primary purpose in mind. Thus He always had to wait for such opportunities as the Father provided for Him.

Just as Mary was foolish on this occasion, so we too often desire to be rescued from our difficulties, even though we do not long for communion with the Father. But that is not the way He helps. He therefore reprimanded Mary very sharply: "Woman, what do you have to do with Me? You may not push your way into the work that the Father has given Me to do. I must wait for the opportunity the Father gives Me." How He must have hoped, however, that the Father would give Him the opportunity to reveal Himself! How marvelously they would see here the power of grace!

Mary simply could not drop her concern. She wanted very badly to help in her own way and she wanted to enlist Jesus' help to provide her own solution. Accordingly, she told the servants to keep their eyes on Jesus and do as He told them. She was convinced He would find some solution. However, the Lord did not help in Mary's way, but rather in His own divine way, for He understood that the Father gave Him the opportunity to reveal Himself and at the same time to call the people to have faith in Him.

The sign. Jesus saw six empty stone water jars standing nearby, of the kind used for washing up. Each of these jars could hold from twenty to thirty gallons. He told the servants to fill the jars with water. When they had filled them to the brim He ordered the servants to take some water out and have the master of the ceremonies taste it.

In the meantime, by the power of His grace, He had changed the water into wine. Moreover, this was such excellent wine that the master of ceremonies asked the bridegroom why he had served the lesser wine first and saved the best for later!

What a tremendous miracle the Lord Jesus had performed! Of course, the Lord's grace governs all of nature and its powers. Grace can turn water into wine but it can also restore and renew our corrupted nature. Our depraved nature is governed by sin and succumbs in death; it does not know true joy. By the power of grace we are restored to the true joy of communion with God. Every day life becomes a feast. We can enjoy everything in life because we see it as a gift of God's grace.

The faith of the disciples. The Cana miracle was the first one Jesus performed. In it He revealed His glory, His dominion over all things through grace. His disciples had been in contact with Him for only a few days and already they had confessed Him to be the Christ. Now, through this concrete miracle, they saw His glory and gave themselves into His hands for life. They believed in Him.

His glory is still the same; if we see it we too give our lives into His hands. All of life becomes one big feast, a partaking of the banquet of God's love. And one day we will also partake of the wedding of the Lamb, the feast of God's love after this life.

4: The Kingdom as a Revelation

John 3:1-21

The Kingdom of God is a mystery hidden to the flesh. It must be revealed to us. Through this revelation we are born again. We must bear in mind that Christ is speaking here about regeneration in the broader sense of the word, so as to include the conversion of our life and all the ways in which that life expresses itself in our actions.* Such rebirth is brought about by the preaching of the gospel of the Kingdom. We may assume that regeneration in the narrower sense—without ongoing conversion—already had taken place in Nicodemus; otherwise he would not have come to Jesus.

Christ's reply to Nicodemus was: "Unless a man be born again he cannot see the Kingdom of God." This was a rejection of Nicodemus' whole attitude to life. But Christ rejected Nicodemus' way of life in order to save Nicodemus. Christ's answer also had to be instrumental in Nicodemus' conversion or sanctification.

The earthly affairs of the Kingdom are those things that take place on earth, such as faith and regeneration. Heavenly affairs are what lie beyond or behind these earthly matters, namely, God's love in Christ and the sovereignty of His grace.

---

*Today's usage generally distinguishes "regeneration," a once-for-all divine act of rebirth, from "conversion," the lifelong process of sanctification. In conversion, man cooperates with God by responding obediently to God's Word out of the new nature he has been given in the new birth (regeneration)—TRANS.

25

Main thought: *The Kingdom of God is a revelation to us.*

The revelation of the Kingdom works the new birth. When Jesus first began His public ministry He did not remain long in Galilee. Very soon He and His disciples were in Jerusalem. There He went to work with great power as the One sent by God. He performed many miracles in that city. This made a deep impression on the people, and many believed in Him. Although they believed, their faith did not always result in total surrender to Him. Jesus could not really count on their "belief," the result of a mere impression.

But there were also those whose hearts were genuinely touched by His teachings and practice. This was also true of a few of the leaders. It brought a good deal of conflict into their lives because what the Lord Jesus said was directly opposed to their own teaching. They believed they had to earn their own salvation and future. One day God's Kingdom would come in the way they imagined and they would have *earned* themselves a place in it. But Jesus came with the message of the Kingdom of *grace*. A Kingdom as a gift, not as something earned, a Kingdom in which everything is given freely through grace. We can receive this gift now and become citizens of the Kingdom. For the leaders to have believed that, however, would have necessitated a complete turnabout in their lives.

There was one leader of the people, a Pharisee named Nicodemus, who often reflected on Jesus' words. He did not yet understand the need for such a complete turnabout but he could not shake off Jesus' message. He did not immediately side with Jesus but wanted to know more about Him. Accordingly, he went to see Jesus alone, at night, because he had not yet come to any decision. He could not yet abandon the Pharisee world and life view. Therefore, no one was to know that he went. For the time being, at least, he was still ashamed of what he was doing.

Even in the night the Lord Jesus received him. Nicodemus got right to the point; he began by acknowledging Jesus as a teacher sent by God. The miracles were proof enough, and he pretended that his colleagues shared his opinion. Thereupon he wanted Jesus to explain the Kingdom further. Nicodemus thought that his whole outlook and life style could remain the same. He wanted to tack Jesus' message about the Kingdom of God on to what he already had.

Jesus' answer must have amazed him: "Unless a man is born again, he cannot see the Kingdom of God!" A total renewal, a complete turnabout, had to take place within him. This was the new birth. Only if the old life died could a new one arise.

Nicodemus didn't understand that at all. Surely, he thought, a man could not be born a second time? "No," the Lord Jesus answered, "new birth comes by water and the Spirit." He reminded Nicodemus of John's baptism which was a sign of dying and rising anew.

Such new life is wrought in us by the Spirit. It proceeds from God, though it comes through the preaching of the gospel of the Kingdom. Without this rebirth one cannot enter the Kingdom. This new birth was also necessary for a Jew, like Nicodemus, a son of Abraham, because everything that is born of the flesh is flesh. On account of sin the whole human race lives trusting in itself. We are even born that way. Therefore, every person has to be born of the Spirit so that we will trust solely in God's grace.

This should not surprise us. New birth is God's work and therefore unsearchable. We could perhaps compare it with the wind: we hear it but cannot tell whence it comes or where it goes. This applies to everyone who is born of the Spirit. New life cannot be explained as something that exists in man but has its origin in God.

The revelation of the Kingdom can only be known by faith. If it is true that new life has its origin in God alone, we cannot investigate it through our own wisdom; only faith can disclose what God tells us about it. Only then we shall get to know that work of the Spirit. However, Nicodemus was not ready to listen in faith. Full of doubt, he asked how new birth was possible.

He was a teacher in Israel but could not understand Jesus' teachings. What had he been teaching the people instead? Had he not told them of God and the power of His grace? No, he had not. He had always looked to men and taught the people to trust in their meritorious obedience to the law. He and his colleagues foolishly thought that wisdom could be found in themselves.

Instead, Jesus declared that He and John lived by what God had revealed to them. That gave them the right to proclaim. Yet Nicodemus and his colleagues had not accepted their witness; they had failed to see its wisdom because they boasted in their own foolishness. And if their foolishness blinded them to such essential Kingdom qualities as conversion and renewal, how would they ever understand God's love which makes conversion and renewal possible?

Did Nicodemus really think he could know anything about these matters on his own? He might have known that man cannot climb up to heaven to discover such truths. Jesus knew only because He had come down from heaven. In Him the fullness of God appeared on earth and God bestowed on Him whatever knowledge He had to have.

Accordingly, men were to look on Him as the One in whom God's grace had come to us. Just as Israel was healed by looking at the bronze serpents, we can be saved only if we look up to our crucified Savior. May we learn to look up to Him in faith and listen to His Word! The Kingdom of grace will be revealed to us and we shall enter into it.

The origin of the Kingdom is in God's love. How easy it should be to surrender to the Word of the Lord Jesus Christ and to believe in Him, for in Him God's love has come to us. What moved God to send His Son to establish His Kingdom here on earth other than His love for the world? He wished to love the world again in Christ; now He gave it what was most precious to Him.

Note well: God did not send His Son to *condemn* the world. That was something the Pharisees expected would happen. They believed that together with the Messiah they would defeat and subject "the other nations," specifically the Romans. However, contrary to what the Pharisees believed, God's Kingdom came with Christ in order that through Christ God's love would conquer the world. Admittedly, Christ's coming implied judgment, of course, but that judgment would strike, not just "the other nations," but anyone, Jew or Gentile, who did not believe that God's love had come down in Christ to *save* the world.

There are many who simply will not believe this! When we believe in that love, the light has come into our life; in that light of God's love our sins become exposed. Then we become ashamed of our sins and we shun them. However, many people love sin and cannot come to the light. People whose lives are governed by the truth of God's love want to walk in that light and begin to show the effects of regeneration through a renewal of life, which is a gift of God. They live their lives not by their own strength but by faith, God's gift of love.

5: The Bridegroom

John 3:22-36

John the Baptist pointed away from himself to the Christ, the Bridegroom of John 3. If we now were to focus on the Bridegroom's friend, we would be going contrary to John's intention. He was able to point away from himself because he saw the Bridegroom's glory and was able to bear witness to it. We must bear witness to that glory with John's message.

Main thought: *The Bridegroom receives the bride from the hand of the Bridegroom's friend.*

He must increase. After His conversation with Nicodemus Jesus left Jerusalem but did not yet go to Galilee. Near the Jordan in Judea, in Aenon, near Salim, John the Baptist was still preaching and baptizing. Jesus went to that region and started to baptize there Himself or, at least, He had His disciples do it. And many came to Him and were baptized by His disciples.

Intentionally He made His appearance in this area and thereby shifted the movement from John to Himself (John 4:1, 2). Had John, after all, not gathered the people together for Jesus? Had John not pointed the Christ out to them? Christ had now begun His own ministry, so John would have to retreat into the background.

For John's disciples this constituted a serious problem. With envious eyes they watched the shift. That was not all; John and his disciples spent much time in fasting and also kept the injunctions

30

of the scribes regarding the washing of hands and the like.* Jesus' teaching strongly emphasized that baptism was the sign of complete cleansing in His kingdom. Was washing still necessary? Some of John's disciples got into a dispute about this with the Jews. This issue was a sore point for John's disciples; upset, they complained that everybody was rushing over to Jesus.

"Haven't I told you," John answered, "that I am not the Christ, but have been sent before Him? At a wedding the friend of the bridegroom introduces the bride to the bridegroom. He brings the two together; he may not desire the bride for himself. On the contrary, he is full of joy when he notes the bridegroom's pleasure in his bride." Being the bridegroom's friend was John's role. He did not desire the people for himself; he brought them to Christ. It was a joyous role because he saw Christ's glory. How great people's joy when they meet their Savior! That is why John said, "He must increase, but I must decrease." He did not want to come between the Redeemer and the people. Similarly, everyone who preaches the Lord Jesus, if he but sees His glory, will never want to bind the people to himself.

He who comes from above is above all. John seized this opportunity to witness again of Christ. And how highly he extolled Him! Christ was from heaven, the Son of God. The fullness of the Godhead, of the divine love, dwelled in Him. And He became man that He might witness to us of God. His humanity was completely governed by this purpose and the Father revealed to Him everything that He needed to make this witness. Only through Him are we, or any prophet, able to bear witness. Otherwise we are only of the earth and do not know the truth. He who comes from above is above all. Before Him all the prophets will bow down. How marvelous is His testimony!

Belief in His testimony. John was not grieved by the fact that the movement shifted to the Lord Jesus. What did make him sad was that nobody accepted Christ's testimony. John said this even

*See Vol. III, pp. 237-241—TRANS.

while many people were having themselves baptized by Jesus' disciples. The people's leaders—and a great many with them—kept aloof. And did everyone who came to Him see that He was the Christ, the Savior of the world, and accept His testimony in this sense?

Those who accepted His testimony affirmed that God is true, for the testimony of Christ is the testimony of God. By the power of the Spirit, which was given to Him without measure, He bore witness. If anyone rejected the witness of Christ, he made God out to be a liar.

Christ, the Son of God, gives us eternal life through faith in Him. This power the Father has given Him. Did He not come to restore communion between God and us? In that communion is eternal life. Whoever does not believe in the Son of God will be destroyed by God's wrath.

6: The Gift of God

John 4:1-42

Living water, that is, clear, oxygen-rich water, was often called the gift of God. Christ gives us living water otherwise known as communion with God. That communion was obtained by His atonement and is ours through faith in His name. Thus Christ is also God's gift to man.

From the very beginning the Samaritan woman was impressed by His words. But time after time she tried to get out from under them. She feigned misunderstanding and sometimes used irony. She was like a sheep that is being driven into the fold, but each time deliberately bolts past the door.

Already here the Christ went beyond the boundaries of the covenant with Israel. The Samaritans lived outside of it. Bringing in the Sycharites prophesied the opening up of the covenant to all nations. But note that Christ expressly maintained the truth of the covenant with Israel in His words, "You worship what you do not know; we worship what we know, for salvation is from the Jews." The Samaritan woman was amazed that a Jew would even speak with her. The enmity between Samaritans and people of the covenant, however, was broken down in her by the display of His grace. The same happened to the Sycharites who confessed that He was the Savior "of the world," not just of the Jews.

The disciples were amazed that He talked with a woman since it was contrary to custom. Here too we have a prophecy of conditions under the new covenant: in Christ, there will be neither man nor woman. John 4 is a chapter concerning the true emancipation of women.

Main thought: *The Christ is the gift of God to all nations.*

Living water. The Pharisees in Jerusalem had heard that the movement was shifting from John the Baptist to the Lord Jesus. They were glad John was being upstaged but now the followers of the Lord Jesus became a far more serious threat to them. The leaders became fiercely hostile to Jesus but Jesus did not want to precipitate a conflict just yet. For that reason He decided to return to Galilee.

He did not take a roundabout way, as people did who wanted to avoid all contact with the Samaritans, but went straight through Samaria. Tired from the journey, He sat down by the Well of Jacob near Sychar, a well said to have been dug by Jacob himself. His disciples went off to the city to buy food.

While He was sitting there alone a woman from Sychar came to draw water. She came all by herself and at noon, the hottest time of the day. Why did she not come with the other women towards evening? Was she alone in life, an outcast?

After she had drawn water Jesus asked for a drink. She was utterly amazed! How could He, a Jew, ask this of a Samaritan woman? Jews despised Samaritans and, moreover, it was not the custom to address a woman in public. But there was no contempt in His voice. He had come to gather all peoples into His Kingdom and do away with the disparity between man and woman. He accomplished this through His grace, by which He reconciled the world to God.

Jesus also had used His thirst as an opportunity to speak to the woman. Did He not always seek out the lonely? In her answer He detected her bitterness about both the Jewish contempt for Samaritans and her own people's contempt for her, an outcast. Had He not come to redeem? Here He saw an opportunity which the Father was giving Him. Therefore He replied, "You call this streaming water the gift of God, but if you knew what it is that God wishes to give to men, and if you knew who I am, you would have asked Me and I would have given you living water." By this "living water" He meant the communion with God which He was able to give.

The woman was impressed by what He said and understood very well that He did not mean the water from the well. However, she was living in sin, and was embarrassed by Christ's helping hand. She pretended not to understand and somewhat mockingly pointed out the well was deep and He had nothing to draw with. Did He think that He was greater than Jacob, she heckled, the great patriarch who needed a well for himself and his cattle? Could He supply water without a well? Clearly, although apparently turning away from Him, she was still reaching out.

Jesus used her reply as a springboard for further discussion. In an apparently puzzling way He reminded her that everyone who drank of this water would thirst again and again, but that He could give her water that quenched her thirst forever. In Him that water became an ever-flowing fountain. Does not communion with God quench our thirst forever?

The woman understood that He meant something different than our physical thirst. She was becoming more impressed all the time but still she suspected a trap. She was like a sheep that bolted past the door of the fold time and again. Therefore she said airily: "Give me this water so that I won't have to come here again." She was impressed but still tried to make light of it.

It is I. Because she repeatedly tried to put Him off Jesus now wanted to take her captive by His word. The Father had revealed to Him what was in her heart and her life. He proceeded to show her that He knew her. He said to her, "Go, call your husband and come back here." She had every opportunity to go away and never come back but she was no longer able to resist Him. Her reply, "I have no husband," was probably a pathetic whimper betraying her despair and despondency. But she was immediately taken by surprise when Jesus told her she had spoken the truth. She had been married five times, He said, and each time had become unfaithful. Now she lived common-law with a man. He told her she had indeed spoken the truth.

Should she not have surrendered, knelt before His feet and confessed everything? Instead, she still stubbornly refused to enter the gate of salvation by confessing her guilt, even when she saw that gate opened up. Stubborn to the end, she tried again to deflect the conversation away from herself by raising another point. "I see," she said, "that You are a prophet. You say that we must worship God in Jerusalem while our fathers have taught us that Mount Gerizim is the place. What am I to think of that?" Why did she ask Jesus, a Jew, about this? Was it because she had never been able to find any peace, any comfort, in her own form of religion though she had made the journey to Mount Gerizim many times?

"According to the covenant," Jesus replied, "the Lord can be worshiped only in Jerusalem, not on Mount Gerizim. But you're wrong on another point as well. Soon people will be able to worship the Father everywhere. Then the service of the Lord will have nothing to do with Jerusalem. That time is coming soon; soon the Father will be worshiped everywhere in spirit and in truth. God is a Spirit, who turns Himself towards us completely in the fullness of His love. Now He does this by means of *symbols* in the temple; soon those symbols will mean nothing and He will live in our hearts. By faith we turn to Him completely and open our whole heart to Him. You have never done this; you have never given yourself to Him in faith, but have always held on to your sin."

The woman had been touched to her innermost being. Could there yet be redemption for her? Everything was still so dark. She knew that the Redeemer would come someday to show the way of salvation. How she, a prisoner of sin, sometimes yearned for that day! She sighed in dismay and confusion. Then came Jesus' answer, which must have caught her completely off guard: "I am the Redeemer." Suddenly she recognized the grace that had come to her. At last she was taken captive. God in His grace was very close to her and He had sought her out!

White fields. She had no time to reflect for just then the disciples returned from the city. They were surprised to find their Master talking with a woman but no one dared to ask Him what He had discussed with her. The woman hurried away, leaving her water jar behind.

As soon as she came to the city she said to the people: "There is a man who knows everything about me!" She was no longer ashamed to admit it but confessed her sins before her fellow citizens. The curse of being an outcast and her resulting bitterness had been broken. Her public profession relieved her even more. She had been redeemed by the mercy of Christ. Now she became the evangelist in her city. "Is not this the Messiah?" she asked.

The people were startled; they realized something special had happened to the woman. They had never known her to act in this way. They promptly went out to the Well of Jacob to see Christ.

Meanwhile the disciples had urged Him to eat some food. But He said He had food that they knew nothing about. Surprised, they asked each other whether someone had brought Him some food. But He answered that it was His food to do the will of Him who had sent Him, explaining that if He was permitted to reveal the grace of His Father, He would suffer neither hunger nor thirst.

He began to explain about the harvest. "It is common for a farmer to say, 'Four months yet and then comes the harvest.' But look!" Jesus pointed to the people of Sychar coming down the road and continued, "There is the harvest. Never mind the four months; the fields are ripe for harvest now! I am sowing now; in a little while I will also sow My own life. My life is the fruit-bearing grain of wheat. One day you will reap the fruit of My labor. That is what I'm sending you out for. One day, when the great harvest comes at the end of time, you will rejoice with Me. You will reap what you have not sowed, for there is one who sows and another who reaps."

The interim harvest. Meanwhile the Sycharites had come up to Him. God had given great grace to that woman, for through her word the hearts of many people from her city had been opened to believe in Christ. How was that possible? Did not the Samaritans have a very hostile attitude towards the Jews? But how strong God's grace is through Christ! His mercy for a sinful woman from among them won their hearts. If only God's Spirit is at work!

They urged Jesus to stay with them but apparently that had not been His intention. However, He quickly realized that the Father had prepared this field for Him. He stayed for two days and taught the people. They had first been moved by the testimony of the woman but now Christ's presence brought God's grace, grace for Samaritans who were despised by the Jews. Christ would unite all nations to be His people. The Samaritans believed because they had heard Him and experienced God's grace in Him. They now professed Him to be Savior of the world, not just of the Jews.

Because of their encounter with Jesus, brought about by the woman's testimony, the people of Sychar increased in faith. We also meet Jesus in His Word, though we may be led to that Word by others. Through His Word Christ gives Himself as God's gift. Thus He gathers the people of all nations into His elect.

John:
We Have Beheld
His Glory

7: The Opening Up of Galilee

John 4:43-54

When Christ spoke of His own country in which He received no honor, He could scarcely have meant any other place than Galilee. (See also His remark in Luke 4:24.) He nevertheless went purposely to Galilee to open that land up to the gospel. After He had His disciples baptize many people in Judea, and after winning the Sycharites in Samaria, He now directed His attention to Galilee.

Although the Capernaum official mentioned here was in the service of Herod Antipas, he must have been a Jew for Christ included him with the others when He said, "Unless you people see miraculous signs and wonders, you will never believe." Galilee had not been opened up to the gospel of grace.

When this official and all his household believed, it was a true faith in which a person surrenders himself to Christ for his entire life and with all that he possesses. Thus Galilee was being opened up to the gospel.

Main thought: *Christ opens Galilee up to the gospel.*

Closedness. Although the Word of the Lord Jesus bore much fruit in Sychar, He stayed there only two days. He had been sent in the first place to the people of the covenant. In Judea many had been baptized. Now He turned to Galilee. To work there would be a lot more difficult for that was where He had grown up. And it was He who said that a prophet is not honored in his own country. We are far more inclined to honor strangers.

41

When He arrived in Galilee, conditions seemed more favorable than had been expected, for the Galileans received Him with a certain expectancy. They too had been at the Passover Feast in Jerusalem and had seen the miraculous signs He had done there. Now they expected Him to do the same in their country but that was not the kind of expectation Christ desired. They only wanted the miraculous signs and they wanted to believe in His miracle-working power. Sensationalism was what closed their hearts to the gospel of salvation. But Christ wanted their hearts. How would the Father give Him the opportunity to reach their hearts with the gospel of grace?

Surrendering in faith. Jesus came again to Cana where He had performed His first sign. That sign had been observed by a private circle of friends and evidently was not widely known. Quickly rumor spread that He was in Galilee once again. It even reached Capernaum where He had already spent several days before going to Jerusalem. In Capernaum lived a royal official whose son was dying. This man also had heard about the miracles Jesus had performed in Jerusalem. Immediately he left for Cana, a journey of about five or six hours.

When he found Jesus, he begged Him to come with him to heal his son. Here was a direct request for a miracle. The Lord Jesus saw in his request the sinful desire of Galilee for miracles. People were prepared to believe only after seeing Him perform some miracle, Jesus complained to the official.

Was the official indeed motivated by a desire to see miracles? Was that the extent of his faith? Did not Jesus detect some deeper dimension in the man? At any rate, it had to be brought out in the open because Christ desired the hearts of Galileans, including the heart of this official, who was himself a Jew. Perhaps Jesus hesitated in order to teach him a lesson.

But the official did not let himself be turned down. "Lord," he said, "come with me before my child dies." To hold fast to Christ in this manner was quite unusual but even his insistence could have been born of his great need. Therefore Christ put him to the test by saying, "Go, your son will live." And the man left, believing Christ.

The man must have come expecting to see more than a mere miracle. He must have seen that Christ spoke with power and authority. And if he did, his faith must have been implanted by God. The official acknowledged Christ's calling and entrusted himself to His word. Christ had forced him to surrender in faith. This was faith without seeing, true faith—being assured of the things we do not see, of the grace we hope for (Hebrews 11:1). The official must have seen the power of God's grace. Would God be so gracious as to save his son's life? He believed that through the Word of Christ God's grace had come over his house even though he had not seen the "proof." Similarly, we must also hold fast in faith to God's grace even though it cannot always be readily seen in our lives.

The faith in the official's family. It was about one o'clock in the afternoon when this man had encountered Jesus. After his journey to Cana he could not return since it was the hottest time of the day. Very likely he could not travel at night either, forcing him to stay over until early the next morning. As he traveled home the next morning, his servants came to meet him with the happy message that his son had recovered. When he asked at what time he had taken a turn for the better, he learned that it had happened the day before, exactly at one o'clock. It had happened precisely as Jesus had said. What a joy for this whole family!

But still more happened. This family saw the miracle that had taken place but they also believed in the grace which they did not see. They believed in God's grace for Israel and for the whole world; they believed that this grace had appeared in Christ. The whole family followed the Lord Jesus in the spirit. Thus there was a family in Galilee, the family of an official of Herod Antipas no less, that believed. Galilee had been opened up to the gospel, no matter how barren that field had appeared to be. How the Lord Jesus must have rejoiced in this!

8: The Everflowing Spring

John 5:1-18

It cannot be determined which feast is meant in verse 1. At any rate, between Christ's former stay in Jerusalem and the present trip comes a period of work in Galilee.

In most of the manuscripts, including the most reliable, the last words of verse 3—"and they waited for the disturbance of the waters"—and all of verse 4 are missing. They were probably inserted later to explain verse 7. Perhaps we should think of Bethesda as an intermittent spring with healing powers. Then we can picture it this way: an invalid would have to get down into the water just as soon as the spring became active, because the water that rose and bubbled up mixed with the pool water and immediately lost its healing power.

But we should bear in mind that such a healing action of a spring is the work of God's grace which also governs the forces of nature. The real spring is the grace of God which does not go into action only at certain times but is ever-flowing. As Christ said: "My Father is always at work to this very day, and I, too, am working." Note that He is here speaking about the God of grace. God is constantly at work through His grace.

The cause of the man's illness, according to Christ ("Stop sinning, or something worse may happen to you.") was the man's own sin.

Main thought: *God's grace is an ever-flowing spring.*

Not knowing the spring. After Jesus had worked in Galilee for some time, He went up to Jerusalem again for one of the feasts. While there, He visited a facility for the disabled. He had come to reveal God's mercy; that is why time and again He sought out the suffering.

44

This facility, situated close to the wall of Jerusalem near the Sheep Gate, was called Bethesda, House of Mercy. Many sick people, blind, lame and paralyzed, lay there, for there was something very special about this place. At regular intervals the water in the pool would be stirred, apparently from an underground spring. That spring water evidently had healing powers. In order to be healed, however, one had to be in the water the moment the spring erupted. Once the spring water mixed with the standing pool water, it would lose its healing properties.

There was a man at the poolside, an invalid for thirty-eight years whose illness had proved to be incurable. Finally he had decided once more to seek a cure at Bethesda. But it was hard for him to move around and he was never able to be the first to get into the spring water. In fact, that hope was also cut off for him. There the man lay, like one bound not only by his affliction but also by the hopelessness of his situation. Look to Bethesda he did, but he could not see the grace of God that lay beyond. Moreover, he was bound by the guilt of his sin which was really the cause of his illness.

And yet, should Bethesda not have been a testimony to him of God's grace? Why are there still such healing powers in the world if not because God is gracious in Jesus Christ and desires to save the world? Such healing forces as these are also the work of His grace. Contrary to the Bethesda spring, God's grace is not a spring that flows only intermittently; it is a spring that supplies water constantly. Such grace heals us completely and forever. But this man did not see that spring. We all look hither and yon for help but do not see the complete salvation which God's grace gives us.

Healing through the spring water. Jesus saw the man lying there, and the Father pointed the man out to Jesus as an object of His saving mercy (see verse 19, 20). To this man, bound by his sin, Jesus could show the purpose of His coming to earth: He came to liberate us from sin and all its consequences.

He asked him a strange question: "Do you want to get well?" Who is there who would not want to get well? But hope had died in this man, and by His question Jesus wanted to awaken new hope and a beginning of faith in him. Would there still be mercy for him? Through this question, and by the way the Lord Jesus looked at him, a faint glimmer of light began to dawn on him. He addressed Him as "Sir," and poured out his troubles to Him. He began to look to Jesus with some vague sense of expectation.

Once Christ had awakened this hope in the man, He helped him. He said, "Get up! Pick up your mat and walk." Immediately the man was healed and he did what he was told. He had been plunged into the spring of God's grace and had been delivered. The doom of despair had been broken.

However, Jesus had something else to teach him. But that would come later; for now Jesus avoided the crowd. Otherwise the people would have flocked together and worshiped Him as a miracle worker. All those sick people would have wanted to be healed, and then He would simply not have been able to reveal that He had come for the redemption of life unto eternity.

Revelation about the Father. It was on a sabbath that Christ performed this miracle. The leaders of Jerusalem saw the healed man walking around, carrying his mat on his shoulder. That was not allowed, according to them, for they considered it work. They asked the man why he did it. He answered that he had been told to do it by the one who had healed him. When they asked him who that was, he replied he didn't know. He did not know the Lord Jesus. He had, of course, encountered something of God's mercy in Him, but did not know who He was. Dissatisfied, the leaders retreated.

Some time later the Lord Jesus found the man in the temple. Jesus was finally able to talk with him quietly. Jesus told him that his illness had been a consequence of his sins. He pointed him to God's mercy which had saved him. Henceforth, Christ told him, he should live by faith in God's grace and work to overcome his sins. If he refused, if he didn't accept the grace of God but fell back into his sin, something worse could happen to him. Thus Christ showed him the grace of His Father.

Glad that he now knew the Christ the man went to the leaders of the people and told them it was the Lord Jesus who had healed him. They would, he reasoned, be happy for him and acknowledge Christ's authority as the One sent by the Father. After all, if Christ healed on the sabbath, what could be the harm? It shows how little he understood the leaders! They constantly kept an eye on Jesus, always looking for an opportunity to put Him to death because, they charged, He broke the sabbath commandment. He healed on the sabbath and ordered a man to break the Law. If that persisted, He would undermine their authority. After all, they saw to it that the law was strictly maintained.

When they accused Jesus of breaking the sabbath, He replied, "My Father is always at work, through His grace, to this very day. His is an everflowing spring. For that reason I too am always at work to reveal that grace and its power. That is not a violation of the sabbath. What, after all, is the meaning of the day of rest? It is to assure you that you may rest in that grace of My Father. But since you refuse to rest in that grace you are also unable to understand the sabbath."

The leaders rejected His word; in fact, they were even more determined to kill Him because He called God His Father. The quintessence of faith, the fact that Christ is the only-begotten Son of God who reveals and gives to us God's full Fatherly love, the leaders dismissed as blasphemy! As a result of sin, that is how closed the human heart is to the truth!

9: The Bread of Life

John 6

I shall not discuss the whole content of this chapter. I will not deal with Christ's walking on the sea, because that was discussed earlier.*

Multiplying the loaves of bread revealed the power of *grace*, not just God's omnipotence. What we witness here is the power and the authority delegated to Christ by His Father. Just as in His grace God supports and directs all things through Christ, so by that same grace He also worked this miracle. If that were not so, Christ could not have linked His words "I am the bread of life" to this miracle. The grace that has been given to us in Him fulfills all our needs. Children must be made to see clearly the power of God's grace in this miracle.

Main thought: *Christ reveals Himself as the bread of life.*

The power of grace. After revealing Himself again in Jerusalem at the feast, Jesus returned to Galilee. In Jerusalem men had become hostile towards Him, but in Galilee He was followed by large crowds. The report of Jesus' presence went through the whole country.

Especially around the time of the Passover Feast huge crowds gathered around Him. They followed Jesus because of the many miraculous healings He performed. Now He wanted to withdraw from the crowds. He longed to be alone with His disciples and to pray on the hillside by Himself. The work was very burdensome

---

*See Vol. III, p. 92f.

because He saw that the people were not following Him because they believed that in Him the salvation of God had come but merely because He was a "special attraction." He felt the need to strengthen Himself in communion with His Father. He therefore took His disciples and sailed across to the opposite shore of the Sea of Tiberias (i.e. the Sea of Galilee). There He went up into the hills with His disciples.

But the people had seen Him sail away and they had a good idea where He would come ashore. They walked around the lake to meet Him on the other side. While the Lord Jesus sat on the hillside the first ones arrived. From then on a stream of people kept coming, until the crowd grew to a multitude of five thousand men. And He again gave them of His time.

While all this was happening the day passed and evening fell. The time of the evening meal had come and gone. How could all those people go home without being fed? Jesus said to Philip, one of His disciples, "Where shall we buy bread for these people to eat?" It was impossible to buy bread for such a multitude. Where would they find it in that region? Moreover, where would the money come from? The Lord Jesus knew the answer to these questions; He was thinking of something else. He saw that the Father was giving Him another opportunity to reveal Himself. But He was putting Philip to the test. Would it also occur to Philip that his Master wanted to reveal Himself in the power of His grace? Nothing was farther from Philip's mind. He replied that eight months' wages wouldn't be enough to buy bread for all these people. Although he had already experienced so much, Philip's vision was still extremely limited. With the other disciples it was exactly the same. One of them, Andrew, had been trying to find out whether the people had taken bread with them. There was a boy who had five barley loaves and two small fishes. But what could be done with that?

To His disciples and to the whole crowd the Lord Jesus wanted to demonstrate the power of grace. He therefore had the people sit down. There was plenty of grass around and it was early summer. There they sat, five thousand people. Jesus stood in front of them, took the loaves in His hands, thanked God for the gift of bread, and asked Him to bless it. Then He broke the loaves, and had His disciples distribute the pieces to the people. He did the same with the fishes. Bread and fish multiplied in His hands so that everybody was satisfied. The pieces that were left over were gathered up, filling twelve baskets. Thus there was even more left over than there had been to begin with.

A great miracle had taken place, yet such strangely wonderful things happen all the time. How, for example, does grain grow in the field? That also happens by the power of God's grace. Because He wishes to grant us His eternal communion in the Christ, God causes food to grow on the land. And He shows us that same grace in everything He does.

With this miracle the Lord Jesus wanted to show that God in His grace provides for all things; He takes complete care of our needs in order that we might surrender ourselves to His grace in faith. Then we are well provided for, both for this life and for the life to come.

Had the crowd understood the full thrust of Jesus' message? They certainly were deeply impressed by this miracle, saying He was the prophet who had been promised (see Deuteronomy 18:15-19), but they did not want to entrust themselves to Him. On the contrary, they wanted rather to manipulate Him. Although Jesus refused to play the role of Israel's king in order to liberate the people from the Romans, that was precisely what the people wanted of Him. They saw Him as a reincarnated David. They wanted to take Him to Jerusalem against His will in order to proclaim Him their king. But He avoided the crowd and went up the mountain alone to pray. The crowd still had not understood that He wanted to deliver them from their real enemies, namely sin, death and satan. They failed to understand because they were unwilling to surrender themselves to Him.

Whoever eats My flesh and drinks My blood. A large part of the crowd spent the night there. The next morning they hoped to see Him again. He had asked His disciples to go back with the boat but Jesus had remained on the mountain. There was no other boat, so the people concluded that He should still be there. However, He was nowhere to be found. Other boats were coming in from Tiberias but none of them carried His disciples. Finally they concluded that He must have left. Unknown to the crowd, He had indeed gone away during the night, and by His strange and wonderful power had walked on the sea and joined His disciples in the boat. Since the people could not find Jesus they finally boarded the boats from Tiberias and sailed back across the lake.

The people met Jesus again in the synagogue in Capernaum (see verse 59). Surprised, they asked Him how He had crossed the Sea. He did not answer them, for He had something else to tell them. He knew they followed Him around mainly for the miracles; they were not ready to accept Him and God's love given through Him. Accordingly, He admonished them not to become preoccupied with perishable food but to concentrate instead on the food that endures through eternity, the communion with God. While a man has to work for his daily bread it should not be his chief goal in life. That goal must be the communion with God, to know and honor Him in communion. Through that communion God will concern Himself for everything in our lives. He will provide for our every need, though we must continue with our daily task.

Thus Jesus summoned the crowd to believe in Him. Instead, they asked Him for a sign. Otherwise, they said, they would not be able to entrust themselves absolutely to Him. Had they then forgotten about the multiplication of the loaves and all the other signs? No, but they asked for a sign from heaven such as their fathers had been given, the sign of the manna that came down from heaven. Their fathers had believed Moses as a result of the sign and they now promised to believe Jesus if He would also accommodate them! Again Jesus had to dispute with them to teach them to believe. Moses, He pointed out, had not given their fathers the bread from heaven. That manna had simply been a proof of God's favor. God's grace is the true bread from heaven, and that grace had appeared in Him. He was the bread from heaven and needed no further sign.

Frustrated, they shrugged their shoulders. Was He then giving them Himself to eat? The Lord Jesus immediately confronted their wilful lack of understanding. He put it to them in even stronger language: they would have to eat His flesh and drink His blood. By this statement He foreshadowed how He was going to die for their sins and shed His blood for them. To eat His flesh and drink His blood means to believe in Him; it makes us one with Him, so that we are assured of our redemption and the forgiveness of our sins.

However, the crowd understood nothing of what He meant because they did not believe in Him. They were offended and turned away. "This," they said, "is impossible. Who can accept it?" And, admittedly, we can only understand it by faith.

The crisis. This was all part of Jesus' teaching in the synagogue. Grumbling loudly, the people left the building. Among them were many people who had otherwise followed Him. He still wanted to try to hold on to them and said, "Does it offend you that I said that I came down from heaven? What if you saw Me ascend to heaven?" He thus promised them they would see His glory if they believed in Him. To disarm them further, He said that to eat His flesh and drink His blood meant they were part of Him; and confirmed that they accepted by faith the grace of God which was given to them through His suffering. That grace and the Spirit of God's love came to them in His Word. They had to accept that if they were to share His life.

At the same time He warned them that some of His followers did not have true faith. Faith, after all, is a gift of God. If they did not bow humbly before the Father in order that He might teach them to have faith, and if they thought they could make a judgment about the Christ on their own, they would never know Him and have no part of Him. He said this because He knew that even among His twelve disciples there was one who would betray Him.

They refused to listen to His warning. Many turned away from Him and no longer followed Him. At that point the crisis had come. Had His work been a failure? He had tried to gather the crowd together in faith and this was the end result! Before long they would reject Him. He would die on the cross to atone for the sins of His people. Others would believe in Him. His message would most assuredly bear fruit. It would become clear that His work had not been in vain.

Nevertheless, their rejection was a deep disappointment to Him. He put His twelve disciples to the test by asking them if they also wished to leave but their response was of a different spirit. In the name of all Peter answered, "Lord, to whom shall we go? You have the words of eternal life. We believe and know that You are the Holy One of God.'' Here Peter professed that through faith they had seen God's favor come to them. They had recognized the bread of life in Him. For the Lord Jesus this was a great comfort. In those faithful men He saw the multitude of those who would one day believe in Him, the church that would be gathered through their word.

Yet He had to direct a warning even to them: ''Have I not chosen twelve of you? And one of you is a devil.'' He knew Judas would betray Him. Did Judas suppose that Christ's cause in Israel was doomed to failure? Did this moment mark the beginning of his betrayal? Did the Lord Jesus perceive Judas' thoughts? Whether Judas realized it or not, Jesus knew who would betray Him. And it was one of the Twelve, one of those whom He had received from the Father. Judas, however, had never fully realized or acknowledged the honor of that election; he had never seen or acknowledged God's sovereign disposition over his life. Thus his heart conceived to betray Him whose love had come so close to him. Especially when He comes so near to us in His Word we either acknowledge Him as the bread of life or we hate Him. This imminent betrayal, however, caused our Lord Jesus bitter anguish, a suffering He also had to bear for our sake. For by nature we all hate Him, which is why He constantly warns us.

10: Life's Joy

John 7

The Feast of Tabernacles was a commemoration of the journey through the wilderness, when Israel dwelt in tents. God had brought them into the land flowing with milk and honey. Now they dwelt, not in barren regions, but in a land where living water flowed. This joy they celebrated at the Feast of Tabernacles. They made themselves tents from leaves and branches and poured out water before God's presence as a thank-offering to Him.

However, the joyful celebration of this feast had deteriorated. Although the people rejoiced in the good things the land offered, this bounty was not seen as a gift or as proof of God's loving-kindness. Under such circumstances the true joy of living cannot be experienced. There was, instead, immoral abandon and licentiousness. Christ called a halt to such decadence. He gave the living water of communion with God and, through that, life's true joy. In any who receive communion through the Spirit, that joy becomes a fountain by which even others are refreshed.

Main thought: *The Christ gives life's true joy.*

His brothers' unbelief. In Galilee the people's hostility had reached crisis proportions. But it was still worse in Judea. Judean hostility was so intense that it seemed no longer safe for Jesus to be seen there.

The Feast of Tabernacles was coming soon. At that feast the Jews recalled their journey through the wilderness and thanked

God for the good land into which He had brought them. The crowds were already going up to Jerusalem. The younger brothers of the Lord Jesus were also preparing for the journey. They noticed that Jesus was not preparing to go to Jerusalem, so they asked Him if He was going. Secretly they were quite proud of His miracles and His great reputation. They regretted that the crowds in Galilee had begun to turn away from Him and that Jesus Himself was withdrawing. He should go to Jerusalem, they suggested, and perform a great miracle at the feast. Then the wavering Galileans would take His side again and His followers in Jerusalem would regain their courage.

They failed to understand that He wanted to be the Redeemer of the people and yet remain in the background. They failed to see that He had come for the truly spiritual redemption of His people. He also had to endure His brothers' misunderstanding. Because they did not believe in Him Jesus was now unable to give Himself to them. Later He would reveal Himself to them as well whereupon their faith would be awakened.

Jesus explained to His brothers that, since His time had not yet come, He could not accompany them to the feast. Unknown to them, Jesus was alluding to His suffering on the cross. He did not want things to come to a head in Jerusalem just yet. For that reason He would have to act discreetly, for in Jerusalem they hated Him because He testified constantly against legalism. However, He permitted His brothers to go; as they had not embraced Jesus, no one had reason to hate them. Later, when the feast had begun and the roads were clear, Jesus and His Twelve also went to Jerusalem.

The law for life. Once again He taught in the temple. The people had asked themselves where He was and whether He would come to the feast. They were divided on Him; some were for Him, others against, but no one dared to speak out publicly. Everyone noticed the hostility in Jerusalem but the Sanhedrin* had not yet pronounced any judgment.

Jesus' teaching astounded the people. How, they asked, did

*See Vol. III, p. 135, note—TRANS.

He know the Scriptures? He had never studied under the scribes. Jesus answered by pointing out that He had been sent: He had received His office from God and God Himself had taught Him. If, He challenged, there were any who desired to fulfill God's calling in their lives they would have to understand that His teaching was from God. They would know that He truly embodied the Word of God. Often we do not want to submit ourselves to that Word and therefore do not understand it.

His hearers did not submit themselves to God's Word. Instead, they boasted about the law of Moses which, incidentally, they did not keep as they were plotting to murder Him. Most chose to misinterpret Jesus and charged that He was possessed. They demanded to know who, according to Jesus, was trying to kill Him. Jesus ignored their shouting and pointed out that it was they who wanted to be rid of Him. He brought life itself, He said, the true life in God's covenant, and so fulfilled the meaning of the sabbath. (See Vol. I, pp. 34-35.) They hated Him because He brought them life and they preferred instead to cling to their own way of life that led to death. Their eyes were closed to the covenant and to the meaning of the sabbath within that covenant! To illustrate the inconsistency of their legalism Jesus pointed out that, according to the law of Moses, children were also circumcised on the sabbath. Why, then, were healing and forgiving sins excluded from the sabbath?

In the end, there was a difference of opinion about Him. Some openly vowed to get rid of Him. They were flabbergasted that He was even allowed to appear in public. They wondered whether Jesus had managed to persuade the leaders that He was the Messiah. Some elders heatedly denied this. Most leaders were convinced that when the Messiah came, no one would not know where He came from. The true Messiah, they claimed, had mysteriously been among them for a long time and would some day appear quite unexpectedly. But they knew that Jesus was from Nazareth. Jesus replied that they did not know where He was from because they did not know that the Father had sent Him.

Opposition hardened. Many wanted to lock Him up then and there. Many hated Him intensely yet nobody laid a finger on Him. How could that be? The time of His suffering and death had not yet come; so the Father was watching over Him.

Streams of living water. Tension increased. Many common people said, "Would the Messiah be able to do more miraculous signs than this man has done?" They began to believe in Jesus, a fact that alarmed the Pharisees and drove them into an unholy alliance with the Sadducees. Having decided to kill Jesus they sent their servants to arrest Him at the earliest convenience.

Jesus' enemies were all around Him. The decision had been made; the die was cast. He would go to God whence He had come. The people would look for Him in vain. They would look for a Redeemer, a Messiah, but fail in their efforts because they refused to acknowledge that Jesus had been sent by God.

Most Jews made no effort to understand. Mockingly they asked if He intended to go abroad to win support. They realized very well that this was not what He was talking about, they kept wondering for He had made them restless.

On the last day of the feast the excitement reached its peak. The people rejoiced in the good land in which they lived. It became a feast of wantonness. They did not see the good things as a sign of God's favor in His covenant. They did not enjoy God's communion in that covenant. As a result, they were hostile to Jesus who preached that communion and wanted to give it to them. Again Jesus invited them to share God's communion: "If a man is thirsty, let him come to Me and drink." He offered living water, the true joy of communion with God, communicated by the Holy Spirit. That Spirit would open up the entire creation to believers. They would enjoy the whole world as proof of God's loving-kindness and covenant faithfulness. Through this joy in life they would also become a blessing to others, because joy would become an everflowing fountain within them.

Again dissension arose. Some claimed He was the prophet they had been waiting for. Others said He was the Christ. Still others contradicted both claims by arguing that the Christ was to come from Bethlehem, not Galilee. The atmosphere became so charged with recriminations that some wanted to seize Him. However, nobody could lay a hand on Him, for the Father's time had not yet come. However, in the end they rejected Him because the Word of God had not made them thirsty for the living water He wanted to give.

Self-sufficiency. The delegation of servants (temple guards) returned to the Sanhedrin without having accomplished its mission. When asked why they had not brought Him in, they admitted that they too were deeply impressed by His teachings. Furious, the Pharisees asked if they too had been led astray. They were told to go by what their superiors, none of whom believed in Him, had instructed them. The elders certainly were self-sufficient and had no need of Jesus. With arrogant self-sufficiency they looked down upon the crowds which did not understand the law and therefore threatened to cross over to Jesus. The haughty Pharisees cursed the common people while Jesus reached out His hands to them.

Fortunately there was one Pharisee who thought differently. That was Nicodemus, who on an earlier occasion had gone to the Lord in the night. Evidently his heart was being opened more and more to the Word of life. He ventured to oppose his colleagues, asking them if it was in accordance with the law to condemn a person without a hearing.

Now they turned their fury on Nicodemus. Go ahead, put yourself on the side of the Galilean! they sneered. Had a prophet ever come out of Galilee? they chuckled. Their pride became apparent in the contemptuous way they saw Galilee, ignoring the fact that God often prefers the humble. Without accomplishing anything the elders went home. God's time had not yet come. Yet for many Pharisees the time of grace was running out; in their self-sufficiency they had vowed to reject the living water Jesus offered.

11: Come to Save

John 8

I am not going to deal with the authenticity of the first part of this chapter.

The woman caught in adultery was deserving of death, according to the law. However, Christ did not put Himself in the place of the authorities which had to pronounce sentence. He did not deny that, according to the law of Moses, this woman should be stoned but He opposed the spirit in which her accusers brought her to Him. On the surface, their charges were consistent with the law. It was their arrogant legalism and impersonal hatred for the woman that Jesus objected to. They lacked a knowledge not only of their own sins but also of God's mercy. Accordingly, they could not show any mercy either but showed, instead, a satanic pleasure in her death. They were no longer concerned about maintaining God's law. They wanted to triumph over this sinful woman and thereby boost their opinion of themselves. Their hearts were filled with murderous thoughts.

That the death-penalty should have been imposed was consistent with the injunctions of the old covenant. Through such severe punishment the strictness of God's justice had to be revealed. However, Christ would redeem life from the curse of the law and His merciful treatment of the woman was a prophecy of the forgiveness that would be a mark of His Kingdom. Sanctification of life has to come through faith in the forgiveness of sins.

59

Main thought: *The Christ came to save our life.*

The legalistic authorities. Early one morning, while still in Jerusalem, Jesus stood in the outer court of the temple. He was teaching the people who came to Him when suddenly a group of scribes came in, dragging behind them a woman who had been caught in a criminal act. According to the law of Moses this woman had to be stoned. Jesus had often shown Himself a friend of tax collectors and sinners, so they brought her to Him to see what He would say. Would He now go against the law of Moses?

The Lord Jesus saw right through them. In their arrogance they had passed judgment on this woman, as if they were without sin! They wanted the woman executed in order to make themselves appear law-abiding and righteous. They were unable to temper divine justice with divine mercy because there was nothing divine about their cold, calculating legalism. Thus in their hearts they were murderers, no matter now technically correct the sentence might have been.

But scribes and Pharisees do not have a corner on arrogance and legalism. How we enjoy passing judgment on others to make ourselves look comparatively righteous!

Writing on the ground. How was the Lord Jesus to answer them? He had not come to abolish the law of Moses, but neither was He the authority with legal jurisdiction. If the Pharisees hoped to lure Him into that trap, He would not give them the pleasure. Therefore He bent down and wrote on the ground, acting as if nobody had asked Him anything. It was not His task to judge, nor should they have tried to force that role on Him.

He did not remain silent because He was at a loss for an answer or because He was unconcerned either about the law or the woman. The problem pained Him, even as He was scribbling in the sand. He perceived their malevolence and hypocrisy and His wrath was kindled against them. And how clear it was to Him that He had to make atonement for the sin that existed in the hearts of all men. Even while His wrath was kindled, He also took the guilt of sin upon Himself and suffered under its burden.

If any one of you is without sin. That He was not at a loss for an answer was evident when they insisted He say something. Standing up, He said to them, "If any one of you is without sin, let him be the first to throw a stone at her!" He confronted them with their own sins and shamed their hypocrisy for wanting to pass judgment on this woman. He left no doubt that He saw right through them.

His words struck home. They all came to their senses and admitted to themselves that they were in no sense without sin. Nobody dared to take up a stone; one by one they retreated, beginning with the eldest.

For most of them this could scarcely have been a true confession of guilt; they were, perhaps, embarrassed by Jesus' perception. Only if we are genuinely shamed into humility by God's grace and stop proclaiming our own grandeur can we humbly confess our sin before God and receive forgiveness.

The Son of man will set you free. While the accusers were drooping off Jesus again wrote in the sand. Finally no one was left but the woman. When He asked "Woman, where are they? Has no one condemned you?" she answered, "No one, sir." He declared, "Then neither do I condemn you. Go now and leave your life of sin." The grace of God burst into the woman's life. She was an outcast; she had deserved to die. However, the Lord Jesus revealed to her that we are all under the guilt of our sins, but through God there is forgiveness.

Did Jesus not put the law of Moses aside after all? He had not come to abolish that law, but rather to fulfill it. Why was it that in the Old Testament God had placed such a severe punishment on this kind of transgression? It was to teach Israel what strict demands God's righteousness makes and how His judgment will come upon our sins. The Lord Jesus had come to suffer this judgment and to reinstate the divine justice that had been violated. In the law of Moses the death penalty was required for several sins as a sign that, because of our sins, we deserve to be banned from God's fellowship forever. This purpose of the law of Moses has been fulfilled by Christ's cross. There we see what we deserve because of our sins, but there He also chose to make atonement for those sins.

By atoning for our sins and desiring to bring us to a knowledge and confession of them, He wants to set us free (see verse 32). Thus He gives us the forgiveness of sins and destroys the power sin has over us. Of these things He spoke later in the outer court of the temple (verse 20). But because of this the elders became angry with Him. From whom did He intend to set them free? They were not slaves, they argued, but free sons of Abraham. They did not see that they were slaves of sin and of the devil.

The devil, a liar from the beginning, deludes us into believing the lie. The devil prevented the elders from understanding the truth about their sin and the grace of God. The Lord Jesus reproached them for that. They did not hear or recognize His voice because they did not know the Father. Jesus is the Truth and reveals the Truth to us. If we listen, we are put to shame by His words! But only then can we understand that He came to save the world, not to condemn it. The doom of the world lies in the fact that it does not believe in His Word of grace.

12: Come for Judgment

When Christ in verse 39 said that for judgment He came into this world, He was not denying that He did not come to condemn the world, as He said elsewhere. He came to save the world but everyone who does not believe condemns *himself*. In this way Christ brings judgment.

Verse 39 makes it clear that verse 41, "If you were blind, you would not be guilty of sin" is to be understood as follows: "If you would admit to your blindness, you would believe in Me and not be guilty of sin, not lay the sin of unbelief upon yourselves." But the Pharisees were saying, "We see," and therefore remained in the sin of unbelief.

The disciples, proceeding from the notion that particular individual sins are the cause of particular judgments, were confronted with a mystery in the case of the man born blind. They could hardly believe that he would have been punished like this for a sin of his parents. But was it possible for a person to commit a sin before his birth or perhaps for his soul to do so in a previous existence? Individual judgments, however, frequently are revelations of God's wrath upon communal guilt. The great works of God that were to be revealed in this man born blind are His works to remove that guilt.

As appears from this entire chapter, the healing of the man born blind had as its aim to reveal Christ as the One who causes us to walk in the light. Thus the manner of healing had a symbolic significance. Christ put mud on the man's eyes to remove any illusion that he was able to see. The name of the pool of Siloam was also symbolic, as now appears, for Siloam means "Sent"; it symbolizes the One sent by the Father.* In His communion we receive our sight.

---

*A reference to archeological discoveries which connect the pool of Siloam with the work of King Hezekiah described in II Kings 20:20. See Vol. II, p. 372. Cf. Isaiah 7:6—TRANS.

63

Main thought: *Through the Christ the blind receive their sight and those who see become blind.*

The disciples' enlightenment. The previous discourse of the Lord Jesus with the leaders of the people had ended in the greatest of tensions. They had wanted to stone Him, but He had slipped away. His hour had not yet come. As He and His disciples left the temple, they saw a beggar who had been blind from birth. Apparently he was well-known and the disciples knew that he had been born blind. The disciples were not under such tension that they failed to see this man. They were convinced that behind such a judgment as this man's blindness there must always be a particular sin. Now the question arose among them whether in this case the man's disability was the result of his parents' sin. They could not believe that. But was it then possible that this man had sinned *before* he was born? They had many problems with the question of sin and its power. That came from their association with the Lord Jesus. As long as sin is kept in the dark it has power. Jesus came to uncover and remove sin. It was understandable, therefore, that the disciples took their question to Him.

He gave them an answer that was very revealing. The cause of this man's blindness was not a sin that either he or his parents had committed. There is a communal guilt, which makes itself manifest at one point in one of God's judgments, and in another somewhere else. The Lord Jesus came to take this guilt away. These are the great works God wished to accomplish through Him, and they would result in the removal of all misery. This had to be displayed in this man's life.

Over and over again He wanted to teach His disciples, and us too, about the grace that had appeared in Him. And the Father showed Him opportunities to reveal this grace, this time in the healing of this man. He added that He did this work with great joy. As long as He was in the world He was the light of the world. He was permitted to do His work to enlighten the world. Soon, with His death, the night would come in which He also could do no work. True, He would arise from the dead and be at work in the new eternal morning for the enlightenment of the world, but that task would be based on the work He had finished on earth. That is why He worked hard and found joy in all that He did.

Opening the man's eyes. After He had said this, He spit on the ground, made some mud with the saliva and put it on the blind man's eyes. This was very strange. Why did He do that? Sometimes you cannot tell if a man is blind. By this action He made it abundantly clear this man was indeed blind, for He wanted to point out something to them. We are not aware of our blindness, that we lack the light of God's favor. That is what we must begin to understand. That is what He wanted to say by putting the paste on the man's eyes.

Then He told him to wash in the pool of Siloam. Siloam means "Sent." It was not unintentional that He had this man wash himself in that pool. The Lord Jesus is the One sent by the Father. In communion with Him we receive our sight. All the details of this healing imply communion with Him.

At this point the man had not grasped the full meaning. But everything Jesus did was calculated to arouse his expectation. And he believed; that is, he believed that a miracle could happen to him. He had probably heard something about the Lord Jesus already. He was led to Siloam, washed himself and received his sight.

Again a miraculous act had taken place. But it was not just the Lord Jesus' intention to help that man. As well, He had to reveal Himself as the One who makes us walk again in the light of God's favor.

Spiritual glimmering. The blind man who had been healed did not return to thank the Lord Jesus but went home full of joy because he was healed. He forgot his benefactor. Obviously he did not recognize in Him the Savior of the world.

When his neighbors and other acquaintances saw him they could not believe he was the same person. Some said he was a double. But he confirmed his identity and, when they asked, he told them how he had been healed. All he knew was that Jesus had done it but he did not know what had become of Him.

This healing had also taken place on a sabbath and the Pharisees again intervened. They brought the man to them and he repeated his story. They didn't know what to do about it. This Jesus could not possibly be from God, because He did not keep the sabbath, some reasoned. But others said that if He was not from God He could not have performed such a miracle. Finally they asked the man himself what he thought of Him. The man replied Jesus was a prophet; beyond that he had no idea.

The Pharisees wanted to deny the whole miracle. Deception, they agreed, had probably played a role in it. They stuck to their guns and called for his parents. They confirmed that he was their son and that he had been born blind. But that was all they said. They said nothing in support of Jesus for the elders had already threatened to throw out of the synagogue anyone who confessed the Lord Jesus as the Messiah. The parents were not prepared to commit themselves further.

For the second time the Pharisees called the man and told him God had healed him and urged him to give God the praise. Jesus had had nothing to do with it, they lectured, for He was nothing but a sinner; of that they were convinced. But their opposition only brought further spiritual growth to the man. He began to have doubts about the authority of the Pharisees instead! He was not at all sure that Jesus was a sinner; the fact that he had been healed was beyond doubt.

Hoping they would find something to benefit their investigation, they asked him to tell them once more how it all had happened. At this point, the man even began to mock them. He asked them why they wanted to hear it again. Did they want to become His disciples too? At that point they lost their tempers and started to hurl insults at him. He was a disciple of Jesus, they hectored, but they were disciples of Moses. Moses was from God, but as for this Jesus, no one knew where He came from.

This continued badgering led to the man's further spiritual growth. God can also use opposition to illumine our mind. The man found it strange that no one could say where Jesus had come from, while He yet performed such miracles. He concluded that one evidently had to believe in Him in order to know Him and to know He was from God. The man was being drawn closer and closer to the Lord Jesus. He testified before the elders that his benefactor had to be from God, for God does not listen to a sinner. The man began to see a sparkle of light; would he come to see the eternal light in the Lord Jesus?

Furious now, the Pharisees accused him of being a sinner for otherwise, they reasoned, he would not have been born blind. Roughly they threw him out of their meeting, forcing him to suffer scorn for Jesus' sake. That too must have brought him closer. He was compelled to choose with his whole life even though that choice would bring him the hostility of his people. Yet he thought it was worth it.

Those who see and those who are blind. However, the man was still groping. Jesus heard what had happened and went to find him. Without telling him yet who He was, He asked him if he believed in the Son of man. The man must have suspected it was his benefactor who was meant, but he still did not know that the Son of man was actually standing in front of him. When he asked who the Son of man was in order that he might believe in Him, the Lord Jesus revealed Himself to him. The man answered, "Lord, I believe," and, falling to his knees, he worshiped Him. Now he believed in Him as the Savior, the Son of man, who had been sent by God. His whole life was bathed in light; Christ had revealed Himself to him as the light of the world.

Christ also said something to the man in connection with the struggle he had just had with the Pharisees. He should not be surprised, Jesus said, that things had gone as they had, for Christ had come into this world for judgment. Those who thought they saw, such as the Pharisees, would become blind and completely lose their way; full of hostility, they would resist to the end. Those whose blindness Christ would uncover, and who would admit to being blind, would receive their sight. That is how the polarity, the antithesis, would come into the world.

Some of the Pharisees heard Him say this and asked whether, in His opinion, they were blind. If He claimed to have come to give sight to the blind, was He implying all men were blind, including them? Once again the Lord Jesus tried to dislodge them from their self-assuredness and their own way of reasoning. If only they would admit to their blindness and acknowledge their dependence on Him, He would be able to heal them! Such a confession would remove their sin of unbelief. But now they continued to insist that they could see and therefore they persisted in their sin of unbelief. When Christ becomes a light to us He teaches us to admit to our blindness. Without Him we are completely in the dark.

13: The Good Shepherd

John 10

Christ does not use a parable here, but speaks in an allegory. Repeatedly He uses various figures of speech when He refers to Himself. In this case He mixes His metaphors, meaning there are two different, though not unrelated, ideas. On the one hand He calls Himself the Good Shepherd and, on the other, the gate through which the sheep pass. As I said, they are not unrelated because the shepherd often slept at the entrance to the sheep pen, thus acting as the gate protecting the sheep.

Main thought: *The Christ is the Good Shepherd.*

My sheep listen to My voice. The tension between Jesus and the Pharisees had greatly increased following the healing of the man born blind. He now continued His conversation with the Pharisees, using a figure of speech which He took from the life of a shepherd.

In the evening shepherds drove their flocks together into one communal sheep pen. Throughout the night one of the shepherds guarded the gate against wild animals. In the morning the remaining shepherds returned. The watchman-shepherd allowed them to enter the pen. Each shepherd stood at the entrance and called his sheep out. They all knew his voice, left the pen and waited for the shepherd to lead them to pasture.

A stranger would not be admitted by the watchman. Imagine someone wanted to steal some sheep. He would have to

68

come at night and climb over the fencing of the pen. Whatever his reasons for invading the pen, it's safe to say he was up to no good.

Contrast that with the good shepherd. Full of trust the sheep follow him even when he leads them through rough places and along precipices. They gain trust and feel safe because of the shepherd's familiar voice. They would never willingly follow a stranger.

By "stranger" the Lord Jesus was referring to the Pharisees and the other false leaders of the people; by the Good Shepherd He was alluding to Himself. Those leaders came with wrong intentions, seeking their own advantage. The flock did not know them; when they spoke the sheep did not hear the voice of God's love and therefore they could not follow. But when Jesus spoke the sheep heard a voice they could trust. That is why those who were truly God's people, like the man blind from birth, ended up following Jesus.

The door for the sheep. The Pharisees understood nothing of what He said. Their hearts must really have been closed for the message was quite clear. The simplest things become obscure to us if our hearts are unwilling to understand. That is why Jesus continued to talk with them.

He literally said that all those who had come before Him, pretending to lead the people but actually tempting them away from Him, were thieves and robbers. They had come to destroy. Only through Him could the leaders become a blessing to the flock and lead the sheep into the safety of the pen or take them into pasture.

He was the watchman-shepherd who admitted the shepherds to the flock and let the flock go in and out. Such a watchman was like a door to the sheep pen, which is why He said, "I am the door." In the evening He let the sheep enter the pen and in the morning He let them out.

Without the Good Shepherd all their sheepherding was in vain. Yet that's exactly how it had been. Every shepherd acted on his own, motivated more often than not by his own self-interest. Predictably, this was detrimental to the sheep. Only if a shepherd spoke for Christ and was motivated by Him could he genuinely serve the interests of the sheep. Through Him the flock would have life and abundance, for only He could give true life in communion with God. Through Him we never lack a thing.

The shepherd puts his life on the line for the sheep. A good shepherd is one who will sacrifice his life for the sheep. A hired hand thinks only of his wages and cares nothing for the sheep. When a wolf comes he abandons the flock to save his own skin. A good shepherd, however, has a stake in his sheep and will risk a life-and-death struggle.

In a much loftier sense the Lord Jesus would give His life for His sheep. He would lay down His life to reconcile and save His people, impelled by a love that far exceeds any human standard of love. His love for His people can only be compared to the love between Himself and His Father. That love between Father and Son is the basis for the Son's love for His people.

Jesus would give His life not only for His people in Israel but also for people from among all the nations of the world. From among those nations the Father had given Him many who at that moment had never heard of Him. According to the Father's decree they were already His sheep even though they were from another flock than the people of Israel. All of them, however, would be gathered together into one flock under one shepherd. And today we see this flock of which Jesus then spoke, and for which He gave His life.

Giving His life for His sheep would be a voluntary deed; no one would take His life from Him. If He had not willed it He would not have died at the hands of His murderers. He voluntarily laid down His life for His people; the Father had given Him authority to perform this act of redemption. And for the purpose of remaining the Good Shepherd He also received authority to take His life up again. He would rise to lead His people to salvation.

This entire work He did out of a love unparalleled among men. All human love falls short while His love is all in all. No wonder men did not understand Him when He spoke this way. Some judged Him demonic and lunatic though others were deeply impressed and said, "These are not the sayings of a man possessed by a demon and, moreover, He healed a man who had been born blind.'' They were all confronted with the love of God which is far beyond our comprehension. But a fierce hatred was kindled in many others.

I give My sheep eternal life. The Feast of Tabernacles was followed by several months about which John tells us nothing. Perhaps Jesus went back to Galilee to teach during that time. In the month of December He was back in Jerusalem for Hanukkah or the Feast of Dedication, that is, the feast commemorating the restoration of the temple. On that occasion the Jews recalled how Judas Maccabeus had cleansed the temple after its desecration by Antiochus Epiphanes (165 B.C. See I Maccabees iv and Josephus, *Antiquities* xii.7.6).

Jesus was walking in the covered colonnade on the east side of the outer court which was called Solomon's Court. There the Jews surrounded Him and demanded that He tell them plainly whether He was the Messiah. They warned Him not to beat around the bush. They demanded whether He would free them from the Roman yoke and also restore the temple as Judas Maccabeus had once done.

He could not give them a straight answer. They expected a different kind of Messiah, a political Messiah. Instead, He told them what they already knew but this was not good enough. Why did they not believe, although His works bore witness to Him? They did not believe because they did not belong to His fold; their hearts were not open to Him. Only His sheep knew His voice and only to them was He the Messiah.

He began to tell them what the true Messiah does and who He is. He gives His people *eternal* life, not, as they expected, a political solution. He also preserves His people in that eternal life of communion with God, so that no one can snatch them out of His hand or out of His Father's hand. The people He gathers are also God's most precious possession. He could only secure that life of communion with God because He was one with the Father. For He is both the Son of God and God Himself. In Him God's full love has come to us.

When the Jews heard Him claim to be God's Son they picked

up stones to crush Him. Completely calm, He stood there facing them. He asked them for which of His works they wished to stone Him. Confused but still enraged, they answered it was not because of His works but His blasphemy, specifically because He had claimed to be one with the Father. He calmly pointed out to them that in the Scriptures people are sometimes called 'gods,' for example those to whom the Word of God came and who spoke in His Name. Had He been wrong to call Himself Son of God, seeing He had been sent by the Father into the world? The fact that the Father had sent Him was clear, surely, from the miracles He performed. He gave them a choice and they promptly made themselves guilty of rejecting God's revelation in Him.

His words were too much for them. By now they were infuriated and tried to seize Him. They hardened their hearts and did not yield to the Word of God's love, the Word of the Good Shepherd. But then, for His love to capture us our hearts have to be opened.

He escaped their grasp and went back across the Jordan to where John had been baptizing earlier. John's efforts there had been blessed, for now many people believed in the Lord Jesus. They realized that all John had said about Him was true. This is a sign to us that John's mission was true. Even though many rejected Christ, His work of gathering His flock went on.

14: The Resurrection and the Life

John 11

The raising of Lazarus does not refer only to the temporary restoration of his life on earth; rather it highlights the revelation of Christ's power over death. Christ has that power because He restores true life in communion with God. In the power of His grace He reigns over death. That is how He talked about it with Martha.

We do not know where and in what state Lazarus was while he was dead. Was this so-called "soul sleep" or did Lazarus really experience blessedness, which was erased from his memory after he returned to this life?

Main thought: *The Christ is the resurrection and the life.*

That God's glory might be revealed. The Lord Jesus and His disciples were staying on the east side of the Jordan River where they found rest and safety. While He was there a message reached Him that someone in Bethany was seriously ill. That person was Lazarus, brother of Mary and Martha. Jesus wanted badly to go to their home, for He had a very special relationship with these people, as is shown in the nature of their message: "Lord, the one You love is sick."

Mary and Martha must have thought Jesus would come immediately to heal Lazarus since the sickness had evidently taken a sudden turn for the worse.

When Jesus got the message all He said was that this sickness would not end in death but was for God's glory. He calmly stayed where He was and made no hasty preparations to leave. His reply and attitude must have baffled Mary and Martha for when the messenger returned, Lazarus had already died. What had Jesus meant by those words? In their deep sorrow they must have tried to cling to those words in faith, but the meaning of the message was too deep for them. Death and the painful loss spoke too strongly. They had no other prospect than that He would come in His own good time to comfort them, but Lazarus had been lost.

Yet Jesus knew what He was doing. The Father made Him see the purpose of this sickness and death of Lazarus. One of the greatest and most miraculous signs would take place here, close to Jerusalem, in order that Jesus would again be revealed to the Jews. This miracle would precipitate the crisis. Either they would believe in Him or they would reject the salvation which had appeared in Him.

He who walks by day will not stumble. For two more days He remained east of the Jordan River. Then He announced to His disciples that they were going back to Judea. But the disciples drew back in horror. They had repeatedly experienced hostility in Jerusalem and they knew how great the tensions were there. They felt sure the Master was walking to His death.

He answered that He was walking in the way of His Father; He was always, therefore, in the light. Then no harm could befall Him; His obedience, unto death, the Father would turn into an eternal blessing. If He did not do the will of the Father, He would be like someone who walks by night and stumbles. But walking by the Father's light He would do the Father's will to the end. If only His disciples could see what He saw they would also be in the light. But for that they would have to surrender completely to Him and to His Word in faith.

Then He told them their friend Lazarus had fallen asleep and that He was going to wake him up. When the disciples naively remarked that the sleep would do him good He finally told them plainly that Lazarus had died. He added that He was glad He had not been there to restore him to health, as now they would witness a great miraculous sign. More than ever before they would see the power of His grace, so they might have a still greater faith in Him.

However, the disciples could not perceive what Christ saw. Thomas, the most pessimistic of the Twelve, warned that Jesus' life would be in danger. However, they could hardly let Him go alone. There was nothing they could do but die with Him if necessary. They did not understand that Christ, living in communion with God, had power over death and therefore always stood in the light and knew what He was doing.

He who believes in Me will live. When He arrived in the vicinity of Bethany the news of His coming had already gone before Him. In the house with Mary and Martha were many visitors to offer their condolences. Many had come from Jerusalem. Apparently, Lazarus had many acquaintances there. Jerusalem was only a half hour away from Bethany and when Martha heard that Jesus was near she immediately went out to meet Him.

Martha told Jesus her brother would not have died had He been there. This was less a reproach than an affirmation of her faith. God had decreed it thus, and she knew that Jesus always did the will of His Father. Realizing that, she could again surrender to Him in trust. Therefore she added, "But I know that even now God will give You whatever You ask." By that she expressed the hope that what was broken might yet be restored. It was as though she struggled to reach beyond the limits of her faith. The way she phrased the statement shows she believed, though not without some hesitation. And yet, if she did not fully believe what she said, could she really believe that God's grace, as it appeared in Jesus, in fact restored communion with God and also conquered death? Could she not faithfully expect to see that victory over death before her very eyes?

But she had not yet reached that level, for when Jesus tried to bring her to such faith by saying that her brother would rise again, she replied, "I know he will rise again in the resurrection at the last day." She could accept the resurrection as a future fact but to hope against hope for the resurrection *now* was too much for her. She could not see Christ's power, though He was standing right in front of her. Then, by way of revealing Himself completely to her, He said, "I am the resurrection and the life." He added that whoever believed in Him would live, even though he had died, and that whoever among the living believed in Him would never die. Death had no power over those who believed in Him because death had no power over Him. On the contrary, He who regained communion with God for us was victor over death. Whoever could see Him in that light could expect to see the victory over death, present and future.

He wanted to bring Martha to that level of faith. He asked her, "Do you believe this?" Her answer affirmed her total surrender: "Yes, Lord, I have come to believe (Greek perfect tense) that You are the Christ, the Son of God, who was to come into the world." Once again she entered His immediate presence and went on to expect all things.

At His request she called Mary. Mary got up quickly to go to Jesus by herself. But the guests thought she was going to the grave and they followed her. Behind them came Martha too. The Lord Jesus had stayed where He was. Mary repeated what her sister had said but He did not repeat the discussion he had already had with Martha. He was very deeply touched when He saw Mary and the Jews who were with her weeping. He saw the power of death and the misery it had brought. His wrath was kindled against that suffering. So completely was His life caught up in His desire to overcome death that He almost wept.

Victory over death. "Where have you laid him?" He asked and they led Him to the grave. Then He could not hold back His tears. He shared in the grief of the human race and all its suffering under death's power. While experiencing that suffering, He also took the guilt, which was the cause of it, upon Himself. The Jews pointed out to each other that He was weeping. Annoyed, some of them asked whether He could not have healed Lazarus. They did not believe in Him and saw nothing of the glory which would be revealed.

Deeply moved, He came to the tomb, His wrath kindled

against the power of death. He ordered the stone taken away from the tomb. Even now, Martha still did not see that the miracle was about to take place right there. She was still not ready for it. So she replied that the stone couldn't be moved since her brother had already been buried four days. Gently reproaching her, He said: "Did I not tell you that if you believed, you would see the glory of God?"

When they had rolled away the stone, He thanked the Father that He had heard Him, that He might demonstrate the power of grace. He added that He had not doubted the Father would hear Him. Did He not always have the same intentions as the Father? He had already prayed, however, perhaps in the Trans-Jordan, that He might perform this miraculous sign and He thanked His Father aloud so the crowd might hear how He and the Father were one and He had come to do His Father's will.

Then He called Lazarus to life, revealing the victory over death. He would atone for sin and thereby break the power of death. He brought the eternal life of communion with God. Raising Lazarus was a sign of this communion, and also a prophecy of the salvation and restoration of the life of believers. Amazed at His raising of Lazarus, many of the Jews believed in Him.

It is expedient for you that one man die for the people. Some of the eyewitnesses gave a report to the Pharisees. How would they react in the face of this powerful miracle? The Pharisees and the chief priests called a meeting of the Sanhedrin. Something had to be decided, and at once. Action could no longer be postponed. Following such a miraculous sign everyone would believe in Him.

They said to one another, "If everyone believes in Him, He will cause a rebellion against the Romans; that will become a disaster and whatever is left of our national independence will then be lost as well. Jerusalem will be destroyed, together with the temple." Did they believe what they were saying? The fact that He was not the Messiah they desired was precisely the reason for their panic. They were more afraid of losing their control over the masses than anything else.

The chairman of the meeting, the high priest Caiaphas, was

especially vehement. He reproached the members for their cowardice. They would now have to resolve that Jesus of Nazareth be eliminated, for it was better that one man should die for the people than that the whole nation should perish. What Caiaphas said was true, of course, but not as he meant it. His spirit was hostile to Christ and yet the Holy Spirit was at work here. The high priest Caiaphas, in spite of himself, became a prophet. For it was indeed true that Christ would die for the salvation of the people.

In that session of the Sanhedrin the members decided that Jesus should die. The only thing left to decide were the details. The treachery of Judas would take care of that. For a little while yet the Lord Jesus withdrew for His hour had not yet come, although it was getting close. He went to a region near the desert, to a village called Ephraim, on the border between Judea and Samaria. There He remained in hiding for some time. By His cross and resurrection He would soon be fully revealed as the victor over death.

15: The Reproducing Kernel of Wheat

John 12:20-33

The Greeks who wanted to see the Lord Jesus could have been from Galilee and hence could have known Philip. Perhaps they were not proselytes but just pious people who wanted to worship the true God. Yet they remained aloof, not prepared to be incorporated into the covenant.

We do not know whether those Greeks ever had a chance to speak with Christ. The time for that had really passed, for now Christ would be revealed on His cross. The crucifixion as revelation must have been contrary to the expectation of the Greeks. Yet in the Christ they must have been looking for the qualities of a beautiful life. He put an end to that expectation by speaking of the kernel of wheat which dies in order to produce much fruit.

Main thought: *The Christ is like the fruit-bearing of wheat.*

The desire of the Greeks. After raising Lazarus Jesus withdrew. Before the Passover Feast, which was now at hand, the people wondered whether He would attend the feast. Six days before the Passover He returned to Bethany. The following day (Sunday) He entered Jerusalem to the shouts of the masses. This shouting made the elders all the more bitter. During those first days of this (final) week they shadowed Him constantly. In the

79

course of those days the Lord Jesus still had much to say.

Toward the end something extraordinary happened. Some Greeks wanted to see Jesus and speak with Him. They did not dare ask Him directly, so they turned to Philip, one of His disciples. Philip was equally reluctant to trouble Jesus under the circumstances. The elders would be all the more incensed if they discovered that Jesus fraternized with Gentiles. Therefore Philip first discussed it with Andrew. Together they decided to ask Jesus to talk to the Greeks.

What sensations Jesus must have experienced when He heard that request. Those Greeks were Gentiles who had come to the feast to worship the God of Israel. They had not allowed themselves to be incorporated into the covenant of the Lord and for that reason were only permitted to come into the outer court of the temple. In spirit too they still stood afar off. By this request the Lord Jesus saw in the spirit how before long many Gentiles would be asking for God; He saw how He might lead them to the covenant of the Lord through faith in Him. Then they would no longer be standing afar off, but would experience full communion with the Father.

The law of God's Kingdom. But why did the Greeks want to see Him? The time for quiet conversation had passed; the tension had reached a peak and His suffering was at hand. What were they looking for? Evidently they had heard of Jesus, of His wonders and His works. Did they desire to hear new wisdom from Him, anxious as Greeks were for new scraps of wisdom? Did they desire to see a life of beauty, full of harmony and inner peace? They would certainly not find the ideal in Him! There was indeed wisdom and beauty in the Lord Jesus, but these were revealed quite differently from what they—or we—expected!

Therefore the Lord Jesus began to tell of His glory. He would be glorified, and the time for His glorification had come. It would come about on the cross, for by dying for the sins of the people He would save many. That must have rocked those sophisticated Greeks but Jesus went on to explain that it would be with Him as it is with the kernel of wheat which falls into the ground and must of necessity die before it can bear fruit.

The life cycle of a kernel of wheat is analogous to the law in the Kingdom of God. This law applies not only to Jesus but also to all who belong to Him. If a farmer, for whatever reason, keeps his grain in the barn, it will remain infertile; but if he scatters it on the field where it will perish and die, he will receive much fruit. Likewise, the Father has delivered up His Son to death in order that He would bear much fruit. Similarly, the believer must give his life as a sacrifice. If, for whatever reason, he wants to keep his life for himself, it will also remain infertile, a single seed that will not bear fruit. When he gives it to the Lord and, for God's sake, to his fellow-man, he will bear much fruit. Through the germinating seed his life is saved. The germinating seed God will honor, just as He honored His Son.

The glorification of God's name. To talk about His imminent death was extremely difficult for Jesus for the manner of His sacrifice was grievous, even to Him. His sacrifice would involve suffering on the cross and, worse yet, being forsaken by God. He became deeply agitated in the course of the discussion. Briefly the thought cropped up whether there might be another way? Aloud He asked Himself, "What shall I say? Father, save Me from this hour?" Immediately, however, He understood there was no other way than the way of the cross. No, it was for this very reason that His life had been led to this point and that there was so much tension in Jerusalem. One thing only He wanted to ask of His Father—that He would glorify His name in Him, whatever the outcome. For that purpose He surrendered Himself unto death. And when He knew that His sacrifice would serve God's glory, He felt reassured and comforted.

This comfort and reassurance the Father wanted to give to Him. A voice from heaven, the Father's voice, confirmed that Christ had glorified God's name through His suffering and would do so again. How gratefully the Lord Jesus accepted this comfort even though He was all the more certain that the cross was near.

To that glorification of God's name Christ surrendered Himself. He had to die in order that God's name might be glorified in the many fruits He bore. We too must surrender ourselves to the glorification of God's name. God may do with us as He sees fit if only His name is glorified and we bear much fruit for Him. The strength for this we receive by faith in the Christ.

Much fruit. The crowd that was gathered around Him had also heard the voice, at least they had heard a sound if not the words. The disciples may have heard the words. Some people credited it to thunder while others said an angel had spoken to Him. But few understood the words. It takes faith to understand God's words, even today, for without faith we do not hear God's voice in the Bible and do not understand what He has to say to us.

Jesus told the people that the voice was for their benefit. He had no need of a voice for He knew throughout that God was in control. The voice had come purely for the sake of the crowd, in order that they might be prepared for the decisive events about to unfold. While this sign would not make a believer out of an unbeliever, those with perceptive eyes and receptive hearts might come to understand what was going to happen.

Now, by His suffering, He would overcome sin and triumph over satan. By atoning for the sins of the people He would take away from satan the right to hold the people in his grip. Satan, who had become the prince of this world, would be driven from his throne. And when, by His resurrection and ascension, the Lord Jesus was lifted up from the earth, He would through His Holy Spirit bind and draw to Himself all those whom the Father had given Him. Then it would be apparent how His life had produced abundant harvest.

John:
Love to the End

16: Love to the End

John 13:1-17

The first verse of this chapter is in essence a superscription not only above this passage but above the whole passion narrative. Yet it especially refers to the washing of the disciples' feet.

Christ's "love to the end" is a love unto death. Thus the phrase "to the end" does not have just a temporal meaning. Christ was willing to be utterly used up for His own people. He gave His all and yet received nothing in return that He had not Himself first given.

His love was being stretched to the limit. This refers to the love of His human heart which was based on His divine love, supported by it, and thereby raised to the highest peak.

We have to distinguish a threefold significance of the foot-washing. First of all He broke the barrier of human pride by taking the lowest place. Thus, He performed for the world His act of liberation. Second, the foot-washing is a symbol of the washing away of our daily sins. And, finally, Christ set an example.

Main thought: *In the foot-washing the Christ reveals the full extent of His love.*

85

His humiliation. The Lord Jesus' suffering was now close at hand. Once more before His passion He wanted to give Himself fully to His disciples. It was as if His love grew stronger as His suffering drew nearer. His divine love increased the love of His heart to the ultimate. He wanted to offer Himself to His disciples at a communal meal before His death.

The mood at the start of that meal seemed anything but suitable. When He had entered the upper room with His disciples, a basin with water and a towel were there but there was no servant to wash their feet. Who was to do this? Would one of the Twelve wash the feet of the others? They considered that beneath their dignity. They argued rather about which of them was most important. Was it not appalling that they quarelled while Christ burned with love for them?

No one washed Jesus' feet either. They reclined at the table with unwashed feet and grumbled peevishly. The discordant mood was disturbing in view of Jesus' imminent death and suddenly Jesus knew how best to teach them a lesson of the Kingdom. He saw His disciples—indeed, all men—all trying to be first because they refused to bow before God and settle for second or last place. Unless that pride was broken, the human race could not be saved. As yet, not one of the Twelve was ready to take a back seat to the others. Then the Christ knew the hour had come to perform His act of redemption.

He also spotted Judas, the one who would betray Him, reclining at the table. Faced with that betrayal His love reached out all the more. If He did not break the power of sin by His love, they would all be lost like Judas. He realized to the full His calling as Savior. The Father would give Him authority over all things to save the world. That authority He obtained through His humiliation. For the purpose of earning authority He had come from God, and for the purpose of receiving that authority He would return to God.

Driven by a love that was prepared to die for His own, He got up, removed His outer garment, took the linen towel, poured water into the basin and began to wash the disciples' feet. He then dried them with the linen towel He had wrapped around His waist. Stupified and ashamed the disciples stared at Him. By this act of humiliation He broke the power of selfishness.

A love that was prepared to give everything while expecting nothing in return enabled Him to make this sacrifice. Such love does not exist among men but such love was in His heart. He not only broke the power of sin but also took the lowest place among all men so that He could save all men, including the most abject among them.

The washing away of sins. He washed the feet of one after the other until He came to Simon Peter. This disciple could not stand the embarrassment any longer. Would the Lord humiliate Himself for him? He blurted, "Lord, are You going to wash my feet?" Peter was clearly shocked by Christ's self-humiliation, as we should be shocked when we recall that it was necessary for Christ to humiliate Himself.

Yet, Peter had first to bow his head, as do we, even though what Christ did may seem strange to us. Understanding will come afterwards, as Jesus pointed out to Peter. But Peter protested, "You shall never wash my feet!" The Lord dislodged Peter's stubborn pride by saying, "Unless I wash you, you have no part with Me." But being part of Christ was what Peter wanted desperately, he said, "Lord, not just my feet but my hands and head as well!"

Then Christ taught him what this foot-washing meant. "Someone going to a dinner somewhere usually bathes beforehand. On the road his sandaled feet become covered with dust but once they are washed the whole body is clean. Likewise, you have earlier been cleansed from your sins, much like bathing at home. God has forgiven you forever. Yet your daily sins—the dirt you pick up on the road—stain your conscience and interfere with your communion with God. I will always be at work to remove these sins over and over again in order that you may live in full communion with God. And now you are clean, though not every one of you." For He knew who would betray Him. What would the Lord Jesus say if He were here on earth today which, in fact, He is . . . ?

The example. Back at the supper table He asked if they had understood what He had done. "I have hereby set you an example," He said. "If I, your Lord and teacher, have washed your feet, you also should wash one another's feet for a servant is not greater than his master, nor is a messenger greater than the one who sent him. And you are My messengers into the world." That applied to the disciples and it applies to us as well.

Washing another's feet is not the same as doing an occasional good deed. We must be able to serve and learn to be the least. It is, above all, the disposition of our heart which determines our acts of service. We must always be ready to forgive and thus to break the power of sin in the world.

Jesus ended by saying, "Now that you know these things, you will be blessed if you do them." But how can we learn to humble ourselves? Our pride, for one, must be broken. His love enabled Him to humble Himself and He has sent His Spirit to enable us to do the same.

17: The Rock

John 18:11-27

John does not give us a report of the official hearing before the Sanhedrin, but of a provisional one by Annas and Caiaphas. It was probably during this hearing that the Sanhedrin was called together.

Perhaps the houses of Caiaphas and Annas were situated on the same inner courtyard but on opposite sides, so that even after Christ was brought to the house of Caiaphas, Peter could have been standing in the same courtyard, together with Caiaphas' men.

In this provisional hearing Christ rejected their charges of having plotted in secret. The gospel of the Kingdom is for the redemption of the world; it is therefore a public matter. Only "the flesh"* fears it as something hidden and dangerous.

Main thought: *In His suffering the Christ is the rock on which we may build.*

His surrender. The time of Jesus' suffering and death was not determined by His enemies but by God. That is how He knew the time of His death had come. In the night before His suffering He went to Gethsemane where He was arrested. There He fought His spiritual battle, at the end of which He surrendered willingly to the soldiers of the Sanhedrin.

That His surrender was voluntary was evident from the fact that the troops fell to the ground when Jesus said, "I am He." They could not lay a hand on Him unless God permitted it.

---

*For the biblical meaning of this term see Vol. III, p. 16—TRANS.

When He made Himself known for the second time, He said, "If you are looking for Me, then let these men go." He threw Himself into the breach for His disciples. In the same way He gave Himself for us, in order that we might go free.

What a mockery His surrender made of the soldiers! They came with torches and weapons as though expecting to find Him hiding in the bushes and preparing to fight it out! His whole life was in the open, as was His death. This openness made His work the foundation for life. It was not the work of darkness, done with subterfuge or force.

Peter's fall. First the soldiers led Jesus to the house of Annas, father-in-law of Caiaphas, the high priest. Caiaphas was also present. Together they gave Him a provisional hearing. In those days the whole Sanhedrin had to be called into session for the official conviction. Annas and Caiaphas planned to interrogate Jesus so that they could later charge Him officially before the whole assembly.

In Gethsemane the disciples, including Peter, had all fled. Jesus had warned them of that ahead of time. When Peter had said He would never desert his Master, the Lord Jesus had predicted he would, in fact, deny Him three times. Although Peter had protested vehemently, he fled too. Yet he immediately felt ashamed and turned back.

There was an unidentified disciple, known to the high priest, who had also entered the house of Annas. He spoke a word on Peter's behalf so that the girl guarding the door let Peter in.

This girl probably knew that Peter was a disciple of the Lord Jesus and presently went up to Peter and asked him if he too was one of the prisoner's disciples. That shocked Peter. He had ventured into the lion's den and now he did not dare admit he belonged to Jesus. He blurted a denial.

Now he had denied his Master. Earlier Jesus had captured his imagination and his spirit and had told him that he would be called Peter, a rock. Jesus knew how unpredictable was Simon, son of Jonas. Simon had wanted to show more firmness of character and Jesus had predicted that it would come true. What had become of that promise? His bubbling self-confidence had resulted in treacherous denial. He was still the same old Simon.

Only by faith could Simon become a Peter. He had not acted in faith but in self-esteem.

The faithful confession. Meanwhile the provisional hearing of the Lord Jesus by Annas and Caiaphas had begun. They questioned Him about His disciples and His teaching. What kind of secret doctrine, jealously kept from outsiders, was He teaching? Who were the other conspirators? They were sure Jesus and His disciples had been plotting something sinister.

What could Jesus say? He could not, surely take them seriously. On the contrary, He rejected conspiracy charges by saying that all His teaching had been in places open to the public; He had taught nothing in private to His disciples. And because He had always appeared in public everyone also knew His disciples. The high priest did not have to question Him, Jesus pointed out, since His hearers could testify to what He had said.

The Kingdom of God is not something hidden in the world; it is not open only to insiders. It is for the world because it is out in the open. Everyone who believes will know it and see it. Such a person also belongs to His disciples and finds in the gospel of the Kingdom his life's foundation. But those, like Annas and Caiaphas, who are disobedient to the gospel fear it as a secret plot to overthrow the social order.

That is how Jesus professed His work at the hearing. He did not deny His calling even though one of His own was meanwhile denying Him. It looked as if His work had been done in vain. And yet it would not be in vain. In himself Peter was not the rock; it was Christ who was the rock. Jesus made His profession in His own divine strength. Because of that profession He would also die and atone for the sins of His people. Thus He would become the rock on which life is built.

But that life is built on the rock by faith. Only by faith would Simon become Peter. As well, through faith our lives are anchored in the rock.

Immediately, Jesus was called on to suffer for that outspoken profession. One of the servants struck Him in the face barking,

"Is that any way to answer the high priest?" Jesus simply replied, "If I said something wrong, tell Me what it was. But if I spoke the truth, why did you strike Me?" The honor of His Word and work as well as the sacredness of His Father's calling was at stake, not merely His personal dignity.

Fallen and saved. After this provisional hearing He was led to Caiaphas' house to be tried officially by the Sanhedrin. The house of Caiaphas was on the other side of the same courtyard. Peter was still in the courtyard, standing around the fire. There he denied his Master two more times, once to his superiors and once to a relative of Malchus, the high priest's servant whose ear Peter had cut off in Gethsemane.

The first time Peter did not come to repentance. Confused in our sin we go from bad to worse. What else can possibly save us but Christ's love? We may deny our bond with Him but He does not deny His bond with us. He did not deny it before the high priest and He does not deny it now. Time after time He seeks us. To bring us to repentance He can use means of all kinds. Thus the crowing of the rooster reminded Peter of the warning he had received. Peter now recognized Christ's love conveyed to him in that warning. Through that love, which is stronger than anything else, Peter came to repentance. And through that love he learned to love with a power stronger than death itself.

18: Not of this World

John 18:28–19:16

That Christ's Kingdom is not of this world does not mean it would not be revealed in our history and enter into our life in this world. The original Greek text says the Kingdom is not "out of" (Greek, ek) this world. The Kingdom does not have its beginning (origin, roots) in this world which pretends to be self-sufficient since it has broken away from God. Rather, Christ's Kingdom has its origin in the grace of God. In every kingdom having its origin in this world, self-preservation is the dominating factor. If Christ's Kingdom were "of this world," His servants would of necessity have fought to prevent His arrest.

I do not mean that every earthly kingdom has its roots in this world. Government authority as such is of God and has its origin in the grace of God. If both government and subjects acknowledge this truth, such a kingdom is not "of the world" but can be of service to Christ's Kingdom. Of course, a government can be in Christ's service only with the limited authority it has been given. Nevertheless, an earthly kingdom is not necessarily in conflict with the Kingdom of God. National defense and law enforcement do not conflict with the spirit of the Kingdom of God. If only the weapons are used for the maintenance of God's justice and not for self-preservation!

Main thought: *Rejecting Christ means rejecting the Kingdom of heaven.*

The Kingdom of truth. An official session of the Sanhedrin subsequent to the provisional hearing by Annas and Caiaphas sentenced Jesus to death. In the early morning hours He was led

through the streets of Jerusalem to the palace of the Roman governor Pontius Pilate. He was in town for the festivities. The
Sanhedrin wanted to deliver Jesus up to Pilate so he would
sentence Him to die in the Roman way (crucifixion). They were
not allowed to stone Him to death, so they delivered Him up to the
Gentiles.

They did not enter the palace with their accused, possibly
because there was leavened bread present. If they entered the
palace they would become defiled and would not be able to
celebrate the Passover. Pilate accommodated them and came out.
When he asked about the charges they insolently replied, "If He
were not a criminal we would certainly not have handed Him over
to you." They asked Pilate to endorse the sentence they had pronounced. They preferred not to hold another trial before Pilate
because their accusation probably would have meant little to him.
But Pilate did not quite see it that way. "Why don't you take Him
yourselves and judge Him by your own law?" Then they admitted
they had already pronounced the death sentence and needed Pilate
to carry it out. Jesus had predicted this sequence of events long
ago; all this happened according to His foreknowledge and in
compliance with His voluntary self-sacrifice.

They informed Pilate of the specific accusation: He had called
Himself King of the Jews. Pilate had Jesus brought inside and
asked Him, probably with heavy sarcasm, if He was King of the
Jews. How could Jesus answer the question? He was, after all,
King of the Jews, though not in the way Pilate would understand.
Therefore He answered by asking another question: "Is your question genuine, are you serious, or are you only playing their game?"
Haughtily, Pilate answered that he was not a Jew and knew
nothing of the quarreling that was going on among them. Under
no circumstances would he be interrogated by a convict. He insisted Jesus tell him what He had done. In doing so the governor
repelled the Lord's attempt to make him hear the gospel of grace.

In spite of Pilate's rejection of Him the Lord Jesus continued
to proclaim the gospel to him. His Kingship was not of this sinful
world in which everybody seeks himself, otherwise His servants
would also have fought out of self-defense. Their refusal to fight
was proof that His Kingdom was not of this world. It had its origin
in God's grace; it was the Kingdom of heaven.

Baffled, Pilate asked, "So You are a king?" Solemnly the Lord Jesus answered that He accepted the title, although not in the sense in which Pilate would understand. He had been born and had come into the world as King of a Kingdom of truth; God's grace must conquer and reign over the people. Everyone who was born again of that truth would listen to Him and acknowledge Him as King. Such a person would find the fundamental certainty of life in that Kingdom.

What could these words possibly mean to Pilate, a man who had abandoned truth and inner certainty? Pilate took life as it came and did not look for the light of God's grace. So he shrugged his shoulders and sighed, "What is truth?" And, indeed, no one will understand the truth and the Kingdom of truth except him to whom it is revealed. But how the Lord Jesus suffered under this contempt for His Kingdom. In the eyes of the Roman governor His Kingdom was a delusion.

Power given over the Christ. Pilate led Jesus out of the palace and declared that he had not found Him guilty of any crime. This caused such an uproar among the Jews that the governor retreated; tentatively he handed the Lord over to be flogged.

But Pilate still made an effort to save Him from the angry Jews. He went outside and told the people he would have Him brought outside once more. Jesus came outside wearing a crown of thorns and dressed in a purple robe, props designed to mock His alleged royalty. Pointing to Him, Pilate said, "Here is the man. I find no crime in Him." If Pilate counted on the Jews' sense of compassion he was badly mistaken. Their thirst for blood was fully aroused; they demanded that He be crucified. Pilate wanted to disclaim any responsibility, so he said they would have to take responsibility for this crucifixion upon themselves as he found no basis for a charge against Him. The Jews answered that they took full responsibility, for according to their laws He was deserving of death since He had called Himself the Son of God.

The Jews expressed what Jesus had already alluded to when He said His Kingdom was not of this world. Pilate was shocked by these accusations. Again he took Jesus inside and asked Him where He came from. Was He a son of the gods? Superstitious

fear had taken hold of Pilate. But he received no answer. The Lord
Jesus never refused an answer to someone who was desirous of
salvation but He would not cooperate with someone who tried to
dishonor Him. How this humiliated Pilate. But how this charade
of words and double meanings made Jesus suffer!

Puzzled, Pilate asked why Jesus did not answer. Didn't He
realize, Pilate asked, that he had the power to crucify Him or to set
Him free? "You would have no power over Me," Jesus replied,
"had it not been given to you by My Father. I am in your power
only because the Father decrees it. As King in the Kingdom of
God's grace I shall now be condemned by you that by My suffering
and death I might give that Kingdom its foundation. Some day
too, all the kingdoms of the earth will be ruled by My Kingdom.
Temporarily, however, I am in your hands." He surrendered
Himself willingly to the power of the temporal authority. In the
same way His own people will yet have to suffer oppression and injustice. But the suffering will only consolidate the Kingdom of
God's grace.

Pilate did not understand at all. The reason, of course, was
his sin and the sin of all Gentiles; the nations had forsaken God's
covenant. But the Sanhedrin and the high priest had the greater sin
because they had knowledge of God's covenant.

We have no king but Caesar. After this conversation, which
had made a deep impression on the governor after all, Pilate made
several attempts to set Jesus free. However, he was not successful.
The Jews threatened to write the emperor in Rome about the incident. The Lord Jesus had claimed to be the King of the Jews.
Therefore He was a rebel and an enemy of the emperor. He deserved to be executed.

In the face of their blackmail Pilate caved in. He brought
Jesus outside and sat down on the judge's seat. He pointed to the
Lord Jesus and said, "Here is your King." But they shouted,
"Take Him away! Take Him away! Crucify Him! We have no
king but Caesar." With that they betrayed not only their hopes for
political independence but also the Kingdom of God. Instead they
chose the status quo dominated by the Sanhedrin, a kingdom of
this world . . .

Finally Pilate handed Him over to be crucified and the soldiers led Him away. Thus the King of the Kingdom of God's grace was condemned and rejected. Fortunately this suffering only served to gain the victory for that eternal Kingdom. By His suffering He wanted to make atonement for the sin of rejection of which we are all guilty.

19: The Love Offering

John 19:17-42

John describes some events that were not mentioned in the other gospels. Only these events will be dealt with in this chapter. The sacrifice Christ made in love is in the foreground here.

John purposely does not deal with the severest suffering, His being forsaken by God. However, he does mention that Christ, before He declared, "It is finished," also said, "I thirst." His thirst gives us some insight into the suffering He had already endured. He had not mentioned His thirst earlier; He had simply suffered it willingly. His thirst symbolized His spiritual thirst for communion with the Father and other human beings, a communion that was denied Him.

Main thought: *Christ brings His love offering.*

Throwing dice for His undergarment. When the soldiers had led Jesus to Golgotha they crucified Him between two murderers. Above His head Pilate had ordered an inscription that read: *"Jesus of Nazareth, the King of the Jews."* With this sign Pilate mocked and avenged himself on the Jews because they had forced his hand in this conviction.

Before Jesus' very eyes the soldiers divided His clothes into four bundles. They had already finished with Him and could proceed to divide His belongings. However, His undergarment was something special, a garment woven in one piece without a seam. It had been someone's gift of love to honor Him. The soldiers did not want to tear it, so they rolled dice for it. This too had been foretold in Scripture (Psalm 22:18).

Jesus willingly surrendered this token of love in order to earn for His own people the right to love Him and, through Him, to love God also. Through His suffering many would come to honor Him with the gifts of their love.

Dear woman, here is your son; son, here is your mother! Several women were standing near the cross, among them His mother Mary. His disciple John was also nearby. They were grief-stricken by the crucifixion. Jesus suffered all the more because of their suffering, especially that of His mother (Isaiah 53:4). He knows our suffering in the flesh.

In addition, He now had to end the personal relationships of thirty-three years of His life. Following His victory, He would go to another life. Admittedly that life had its own relationships of a more sublime nature but He would be known primarily as Head of His people; the personal tie with Mary would no longer exist. She would no longer be His mother, but simply one who had been blessed through His sacrifice, one who would have her own place among the people whom He had purchased with His blood. Therefore He had to say goodbye to Mary as His mother. He realized how ending the mother-son relationship would affect her because she was as yet unable to see the higher order of relationship which His sacrifice would bring. And Jesus suffered under it because He was far from enjoying this higher relationship. Just then He only felt bereaved and forsaken.

But even as He said farewell He provided solace for His mother. He gave her John as her son, as someone who would take His place in caring for her and He appointed Mary to be John's mother; a new relationship had been born, one that was treasured by both as evidence of Christ's love for them. Yet the Lord Jesus sacrificed something of immense value by doing this. He now entered even greater loneliness. Yet He obtained for Himself the right to establish those higher, eternal, spiritual relationships.

While on earth we always experience the severance of relationships. However, if these ties are sanctified by Jesus' love the inevitable breach is not permanent. On the contrary, the relationships we have on earth are transformed into relationships of a higher order.

I am thirsty. For hours Jesus suffered on the cross. We will never be able to realize fully what He suffered. Both God and man turned against Him. He experienced the hell of forsakenness. His bodily suffering contributed to this; the excruciating pain made Him aware that everyone, especially God, had turned away from Him. That, for Him, was painful reality. Unbearable thirst compounded His suffering. How long it had been since He had had something to drink! His thirst added to all the other anguish He had experienced since His arrest, from the merciless beatings to exposure to the cruel sun. And there was no relief, not even a cup of water to quench His thirst, not a single word from God to soothe His terror. More than His parched throat thirsted for water, His soul thirsted for communion with God. But both were withheld.

Yet He suffered willingly. If we have water in abundance, it is because He suffered thirst. And our comfort in communion with God we owe to Him who obtained communion for us. If, on the other hand, we lack something here on earth, we should not say that we want above all else to enjoy life. Jesus voluntarily gave up all pleasure in order to obtain for us the communion with God. That communion, therefore, must be our main focus in life. For whatever else, besides communion, He wishes to give us here on earth we must wait upon the Lord and thankfully receive whatever He gives. One day our sanctified desires will be fulfilled to perfection.

A soldier dipped a sponge into a jar of wine vinegar, impaled the sponge on a stalk of hyssop and reached it up to His lips. Jesus accepted because He knew that His most terrible suffering, being forsaken by God, had ended. The battle had been fought and the sacrifice made. He had not loved Himself more than God but had given Himself to regain the world for God. That is why He now said, "It is finished."

Everything needed for the redemption of the world and mankind had now been accomplished. We are not required to make a contribution of our own as, for example, our good works. His love was perfect and so too was His love offering. All His own are saved completely by that sacrifice.

Thereupon He "gave up His spirit" and surrendered His love offering to God as full payment for our sin. Thus He bought our freedom.

None of His bones will be broken. It was already Friday afternoon. At sunset the sabbath would start. Moreover, this was a special sabbath, for it was Passover. Condemned criminals, considered accursed, could not be left hanging on the cross until evening, for in that case the land would be defiled. Therefore the Jews asked Pilate to have the crucified men killed and buried. Pilate granted their request.

As a rule, criminals who were crucified were killed by breaking their legs and spearing their hearts. Breaking their legs was yet another torture. This procedure was followed in the case of the two murderers but the Lord Jesus had already died.

To make sure of that one of the soldiers thrust a spear in His side and pierced His heart, bringing a sudden flow of blood and water. God intentionally decreed this. He had John, an eyewitness, write it down in his gospel for us, so that nobody would ever be able to doubt whether the Lord Jesus had really died. He sealed His love offering with His death.

He also was saved from having His legs broken and His body was laid in the grave unbroken. This too was the fulfillment of a prophecy. No bones were allowed to be broken of the Passover lamb that was eaten; it was served whole. Through this sign the Lord promised that His people as a whole would be saved. As a unity they would be restored. The unbroken body of the Lord Jesus prophesies to us that His spiritual body, that is, His people, will remain unbroken and will one day be restored to unity. We expect this prophecy to be fulfilled in glory.

That His side was pierced also recalls the verse from Scripture: "They will look on the one whom they have pierced." That promise too will be fulfilled. Believers of all ages have admitted that they were the ones who really put Christ to death. Those who do not believe will also be confronted with Him whom, in their enmity, they persecuted and killed.

His burial. Joseph of Arimathea got permission from Pilate to bury Jesus' body, as was the family's right. The murderers were probably given a simple burial, possibly in a mass grave, but God granted the Lord Jesus a burial which prophesied of things to come.

Joseph of Arimathea was a disciple of Jesus. However, because of his fear of the Jews he had never openly admitted it. Now by this deed he confessed it publicly for the body was laid in his family grave, which was nearby. Moreover, there came another secret disciple, Nicodemus, a member of the Jewish Sanhedrin. He brought a wealth of myrrh and aloes, thus openly declaring his love.

It would have been easy for these prominent persons to remain hidden at this time. There was no longer any reason to deny anything. And yet, just at this time, they came into the open, more quickly even than the rest of the disciples. Jesus' love was the cause of these professions of faith. His love caused them to witness publicly. This certainly was proof that His life had not ended. In the hearts of His own He had not been buried; in them His love was alive. By His burial He obtained the right to dwell within the hearts of His people forever.

John:
Love's Victory

20: The Resurrection of Love

John 20:1-18

Especially in this section we should focus our attention not so much on the disciples and Mary as on Christ. With Him love has arisen too. He seeks His own and causes love to be born in them.

When John saw the condition of the shroud in the grave he understood that the body had not been "stolen." Accordingly, he believed. He suddenly remembered Christ's word about the resurrection. But his faith was still weak and evidently he did not yet dare to discuss the body's absence with Peter. Until now they had not understood from Scripture that Jesus had to rise from the dead (verse 9). Even now John's faith was not yet based on the full scope of Scripture.

Mary's faith was still based too much on her experience of the mercy that the Christ had shown her. For that reason her faith was too dependent on His presence. Christ's death had confounded her utterly. When she recognized Him, she expected the restoration of the former relationship, as is shown by the way she addressed Him: Rabboni! However, faith cannot be based merely on seeing Christ; faith embraces the whole Word of God. The appearance only confirms that the Word is true.

Main thought: *In the Christ love has arisen.*

Mary sought. After the burial the women who had known Jesus were very agitated. Immediately after the sabbath, at dawn on Sunday morning, they went to the grave, hoping to tend to the body, which they had been unable to do on Friday. When they came to the tomb they found that inexplicably, the stone had been removed. One of them, Mary Magdalene, thought the body had been stolen. This upset her so much that she immediately walked back to Jerusalem to warn Peter and John. Without sufficient proof she said, "They have taken the Lord out of the tomb and we don't know where they have put Him!"

Mary had always had a very special bond to the Lord Jesus. He had cast seven devils out of her. Her life had been imperiled because she was controlled by powerful spirits. Only Jesus could bind those spirits. From that time on she had been guided by His love. She followed Him constantly and could not do without His presence. Yet she relied too much on that single experience and too little on the full scope of His Word. Faith in His Word can be very much alive even when He is not visible; that was why, when she no longer saw Him, she was utterly confused.

Yet the tie between Jesus and Mary remained. That was very evident from her presence at the grave; somehow she was drawn to it. What was it but Christ's love that drew her? Did this not prove that Christ and His love were alive? Christ's love drove Mary to seek that very love, something she had hitherto failed to understand. Similarly, Christ forces us to search, though we often do not know exactly what we are looking for.

Peter and John drawn. Alerted by Mary, Peter and John also went to the tomb. John did not despise Peter for his denial of Jesus. John recalled his own loss of courage and he also knew the forgiving love of the Lord Jesus. How Christ lived within them even though He had died! His love had not died but had risen to new power.

Uncharacteristically, Peter walked more slowly than John. Shame about his denial was no doubt the cause of this. John first took a quick look into the tomb, though his love made him hesitant to go in. Then Peter went into the tomb, followed immediately by John. He saw the shroud all neatly rolled up. This orderliness ruled out the possibility that the grave had been desecrated. John was suddenly reminded of what the Lord had said about His resurrection. Did the neatness in the grave remind him of Christ's attention to details, such as in His great miracles?

However, John's faith was still weak. Earlier he had never understood the Scripture's message about Christ's death and resurrection. Even now his faith was not grounded in the Scriptures. Jesus would yet have to teach His disciples the full scope of Scripture. Failing to understand, John dared not discuss it with Peter. Yet the hope that he would yet see Christ in His glory had begun to dawn on John. Christ's love was alive and would conquer the world. If we believe these things on the basis of the Scriptures, we also receive the power to witness.

Peter had not come that far yet. Between him and faith stood his denial. He could not believe that one day everything would be well again, and that he would hear from Jesus' lips there was forgiveness for his sins. Jesus had to claim Peter, which He proceeded to do. We cannot believe in the resurrection and not have it liberate our whole life. If belief in the resurrection of the Lord Jesus does not free our lives, we cannot truly believe.

Jesus' love claims Mary. Mary went back to the grave and stayed behind alone. What else could she do? She bent over to look into the tomb and saw two angels inside. She saw them only now; for the Lord had suddenly opened her eyes. She was becoming aware of God's presence. But that presence was still remote, which was why she was unimpressed by the presence of these angels. When they asked her why she was crying she replied, "Because they have taken my Lord away and I don't know where they have put Him."

Even then she had the feeling that someone was standing behind her. Turning around, she saw Jesus. His love had not died. His love had conquered death by atoning for our sins, for it was divine, not merely human love. His human love was borne by His divine love and was therefore omnipotent. Now His love sought Mary. And it sought her first because of all Jesus' followers Mary was furthest from His love.

But Mary did not recognize Him, partly as a result of the

glory He had received through His resurrection but largely because she failed so miserably to recognize His new glory. She was so much blinded by her grief that she failed to understand the glory of His Word. In her ignorance she took Him to be the gardener and asked Him if He had carried away the body on orders of Joseph of Arimathea.

Jesus said only: "Mary!" His love went out to her. He showed Mary that He understood her grief. He brought her to His merciful love. At the same time she confronted herself and recognized her grief as a form of unbelief.

Wheeling around, she cried, "Rabboni!" and rushed forward to hold Him. Now that He had returned to her she never wanted to let go of Him again. She addressed Him by the title she had used so often before. She thought the past had now been restored, but that was not to be. She would have to learn to accept His Word as her daily bread, for soon He would leave His followers. He was going to ascend to His Father, marking the start of His reign of love through the Holy Spirit. But through the Spirit of His love He would be closer to Mary than if she were to hold on to His feet. Therefore He told her not to cling to Him. He would ascend to His Father, whom Mary would know as her own Father, His God whom Mary would know as her own God. His presence with the Father would bring us into communion with God.

By faith based fully on His Word she would proclaim the message that Christ would ascend, start His reign of love and, through His Spirit and our faith, bring us into communion with God. Through faith Mary relayed this message to the disciples. Similarly, through faith in the triumph of Christ's love our hearts are filled and impelled to witness.

21: Christ, the Son of God

John 20:19-29

Faith in the resurrection of the Christ is grounded not in His appearance, but in the Word of God. The appearance only confirms that the Word of God is true. This is how all the disciples, even Thomas, experienced it. The same thought is found in the words, "Blessed are those who have not seen and yet have believed."

It is not possible to have merely a historical faith in Christ's resurrection. Faith in His resurrection also involves the resurrection of the life of the believer. This was one of the reasons why the disciples, and particularly Thomas, at first could not believe. They did not believe that life had won the victory; they kept redemption at a distance. It was such a great thing for them, they could not believe it.

So we should not explain Thomas' unbelief by his pessimistic disposition. At worst, pessimism contributed to the disciples' unbelief. Accordingly, Christ did not treat Thomas' unbelief with psychological therapy but declared him guilty of unbelief. In showing up unbelief as sin He conquered it.

Christ repeatedly showed the marks of His wounds. By doing so He not only made His disciples see He was risen in the flesh, He also made them realize His suffering had been voluntary. For He was victorious. In this way His suffering had been an offering for sin. Thus His blessing—"Peace be with you!"—received its full meaning for them. Now they too were risen.

If they believed, they could also be sent out. For this mission Christ gave them His Holy Spirit, the Spirit by which they would bring the Word of God into the world. By that Word they would forgive or not forgive sins. The sins of everyone who believed in that Word would be forgiven. The church is now the bearer of that Word. Itself created by that Word and subjected to it, the church by that Word must now also forgive sin.

109

Main thought: *The revelation of the Risen One as the Christ, the Son of God.*

Resurrection. Later on resurrection day the disciples gathered together. Mary Magdalene, among others, had seen the Lord Jesus and spread news of the resurrection. This had brought the disciples together again. They hoped sincerely that Mary's message was true but they could hardly believe it. If it was true the Lord Jesus was risen, their lives were also redeemed. In fact, the whole world was redeemed. It was too marvelous for them to believe. Would God have performed such a miracle?

They still could not believe it. Thus they had not become victors yet. The entire Jewish world remained hostile, a power to be feared. That they would conquer the Jewish and Gentile world in Jesus' name was not yet something they could imagine. They still lived in fear of the Jews so they kept the doors locked. As such they were unprepared to go into the world. First they would have to awaken to faith.

Then, quite suddenly, He was standing in their midst. Apparently He had opened the door unnoticed. "Peace be with you," He said to them, His former greeting. He showed them His hands and His side; they saw the marks of His suffering. They perceived not only that it was really Jesus risen in the flesh, but by faith they saw His triumph over suffering and death. They saw that He had known all along about His resurrection. Evidently that suffering had been a voluntary act, a sacrifice for the atonement of our sins. Now He distributed to them the fruits of His sacrifice. He had won the victory over death for them. They were now privileged to share in that victory. They too had conquered sin and death. Their life in communion with the Christ and through Him with God would never die even though they still had to die. Complete happiness came upon them when they saw the Lord. They believed the word of the resurrection which He had spoken to them earlier.

Again He said to them, "Peace be with you!" They had to realize fully the peace which He brought them through His resurrection. The greeting was not a casual one; peace was actually communicated to them. If we believe in Christ as the risen Lord, we have peace because we share in the victory over sin and death.

Mission. Now that they believed and were awakened to new hope, the Lord Jesus could send them out into the world. They were no longer overcome by fear. They would take the message out to everyone. Therefore He said, "As the Father has sent me, so I am sending you" (vs. 21; cf. John 17:18). From His own mission He derived the power to commission His disciples. It was His commission that gave them boldness and confidence. That same commission gives us a task in the world.

The commission of the disciples, however, was a very special one. For one thing, they were the first. For another, the Lord put His Word directly into their mouths through His Holy Spirit. Therefore He said to them, "Receive the Holy Spirit!" As proof of the fact that He gave them the Holy Spirit, He breathed on them. Because of that sign it would be easier for them to open their hearts in faith to receive the Holy Spirit. Even this special working of the Holy Spirit, which would become their portion, would have to be received by faith. Whenever they would proclaim the Word of God by the Holy Spirit, men and women would either be freed from their sins by that Word or be condemned all the more. The Word would either liberate through forgiveness or doom man to his chains.

Fortunately this word of the apostles, the Word of God, has not been lost but has been preserved in the Bible. The church now has to be the bearer and proclaimer of this Word. Through proclamation the church either forgives or condemns. To those who believe the church proclaims that man's sins are forgiven; to those who reject the Word the church proclaims that man remains in bondage to sin.

Rebuke. That evening Thomas was absent, perhaps because he could not share the others' excitement about the resurrection. He didn't believe a word of it, nor could he accept the fact that there was redemption and that life had won a complete victory. It was especially hard for him because of his negative disposition.

Later the other disciples told him the Lord Jesus had appeared in their midst but he did not believe it. They must have imagined it, he concluded. If he could not put his finger in the nail marks in Jesus' body he could not believe the story. He only trusted his own sense of sight and touch. Had he not believed Jesus' earlier message about His resurrection? Thomas still could not grasp that; he could not imagine that sin and death could be conquered. It was shameful that he should trust his own sense of sight and touch but not the Word of the Lord Jesus. Do we ever come to faith through our sense of sight or touch? Believing always involves trusting the Word that the Lord has spoken.

The next Sunday the disciples were together again. This time Thomas was with them. Again the Lord Jesus suddenly stood in their midst and said, "Peace be with you!" Then He told Thomas to put his finger in the nail marks and convince himself. Jesus knew his unbelief! How humiliating a rebuke this was for Thomas! Probably it was unnecessary for him to put his finger in the nail marks. He recognized his shameful unbelief, but he also saw the confirmation of Christ's Word. By faith he saw Jesus as the victor over sin and death. He had won that victory because He was the One sent by the Father and was, indeed, God. Worshiping Him, Thomas said, "My Lord and my God!" He reigned over all things, even over sin and death; He was truly Lord. And that was possible only because He was also God.

But Thomas confessed Christ only because he shared in Jesus' victory. That is why he said, "My Lord and my God!" If we believe in Jesus' resurrection, we are also saved.

Thomas needed Christ's appearance in order to believe in the Lord's Word and Jesus rebuked him for this even after he believed. How many people, He told Thomas, would have to believe without ever seeing. That was still more wonderful and more God-glorifying. And how blessd are they who believe God's Word! It is God's right that we should take Him at His Word.

22: His Bond to this Life

There is a difference between "to appear" and "to reveal oneself." In this chapter we read repeatedly about Christ's "revealing Himself" (R.S.V.). The appearance was intended to confirm the word of resurrection. But when Scripture speaks of Christ "revealing Himself," something more is intended. In the forty days after His resurrection Christ revealed what He would always be for His people after His ascension. Therefore everything that took place by the Sea of Tiberias also has a symbolic and prophetic meaning.

Main thought: *After His resurrection Christ continues to be bound to this life.*

His blessing on our work. A few weeks had already passed since Jesus had risen from the dead. The disciples had returned to Galilee, because the angel and Jesus Himself had said they would see Him there. But where and when would He show Himself to them? They had to wait for further instructions.

Thus seven of the disciples were together by the Sea of Tiberias. Among them were Peter, Thomas, Nathanael, John and James. Feeling lost and helpless, Peter told the others he was going fishing. His former trade appealed to him again, as it did to the others. There was nothing wrong with that for the Lord Jesus can find us anywhere, even at work. In fact, it's there He wants to find us; for it is precisely in the activities of life that He has a message for us.

113

That night they caught nothing. Did they blame their failure on adverse conditions? Probably. They should perhaps have thought of Jesus, the risen One, who had the power to bless their efforts.

The next morning they saw someone standing on the beach. He called: "Would you have something to go with my bread?" They could only see him faintly in the dawning light. As well, they could hear him because they were no more than a hundred meters from shore. They called back, "No." They were disappointed that their labor had been in vain. The stranger then told them to cast their net on the other side of the boat. Could he have seen a school of fish that far away? In any case, they agreed and when they tried to haul it in they found it over full.

The stranger on shore had not identified himself. Should they have recognized him? In fact, there was only one who recognized the risen One, their former Teacher, by His deeds. The fish, after all are in His hand too. It was John who recognized Christ and he informed Peter. His great love for Jesus made him the most perceptive. One can imagine John standing on the forward deck of the boat, shading his eyes, staring at the figure on the shore with eyes focused by love.

Peter was of a different nature than John. As soon as he heard it was Jesus, he quickly wrapped his outer garment around him, jumped into the water and swam ashore. That was characteristic of Peter, unwilling as he was to be separated from his Lord.

In the meantime the others came more slowly in the boat. They saw a fire with fish roasting above it. Why then had Jesus asked them for fish? Now He asked them to bring some of the fish they had just caught. Again Peter was first; he dragged the net ashore, and together the disciples counted the fish. There were 153 large fish in the net, too heavy a load for the net and yet the net had not torn.

Such blessing for their labor! And such truth Jesus taught them through this mighty deed! The risen Lord has all things in His hand; in the sovereignty of His grace He rules over all creatures. If He is against us all our labor is in vain, but with His blessing our work will prosper. Apart from Him our whole life is vanity. But He wants to give us His blessing; even now, He is no farther removed from us than when He stood with His disciples on the beach. Sometimes He withholds His blessing to make us pay attention to Him and recognize His hand in our lives.

Strictly speaking, He does not need the fruits of our lives any more than He needed the disciples' fish. And yet He asks for them. And just as with the fish in the net, all the fruits of our life's work will be counted. Nothing of what we do for the Lord escapes Him.

Enticing love. After the fish had been prepared, Jesus invited His disciples to have breakfast. Sitting in a circle on the beach in their workclothes, they had breakfast with Him. It was, it seemed, just as it had been in former days; yet it was very different. The resurrection had taken place. His glory had just been revealed to them again in this miraculous catch. His resurrection had elevated Him to such heights that He almost seemed beyond their reach. By His resurrection He had demonstrated beyond doubt that He was the Son of God (Romans 1:4). He was so close to them and yet so far! Nobody dared ask Him, "Who are You?" It was not necessary for they knew He was their Lord. Yet the questions burned in their hearts: "Who was He to them? Could they still love Him? Would they be allowed to love Him? Was He not too far above them?" Throughout the meal, while the Lord Jesus handed them the bread and the fish, the questions bothered them. It did indeed look as if He gave them His love, but they hardly dared to accept it.

At the end of the meal a surprising thing happened. He turned to Simon Peter and asked, "Simon, son of John, do you love Me more than these?" He now called him Simon, son of John. All the apostolic dignity disappeared for a moment. Had Peter followed Jesus because of the splendor of the office? But did Peter the man, the son of John, love Jesus? Would he still boast of his own strength and brag of his uncomparable love for Jesus, a love greater than that of the other disciples? The question was penetrating, incisive. Yet there was something else in it too. At the time He asked for Peter's love and challenged him to give it, He was immensely far above them, truly the Son of God. And even then He asked for the love of a human being. Simon was allowed to love Him, as would the others. Jesus was not too remote for the love of a man; instead, He asked for it. He still does so today; we too may love Him!

The Lord asked Simon if he loved Him with a love that could give everything. But stated in that way Peter could not answer the question. He no longer wished to say he had more love than the others. He didn't even feel he had the right to speak of love anymore, and Jesus, he knew, knew what was in his heart. So he replied, "You know that my heart yearns for You, that there is a bond between You and me." Peter gave himself, for the Lord had led him to profess his love.

Then the Lord Jesus said, "Feed My lambs." The Lord restored his commission. By his denial, Peter had forfeited the office of disciple and apostle; publicly the Lord reinstated him in this honor. Peter would feed the flock if he remained true to this love, a love prompted by Jesus' love.

After some silence the Lord again asked, "Simon, son of John, do you love Me?" This time the Lord left out the words, "more than these." He simply invited Peter to love Him. Simon had to repeat it over and over, to anoint Him with his love. The Lord asks this from all His people. They may indeed love Him, and He longs to hear them say so. Peter's response was the same. And again the Lord commissioned him with supervision over the flock, "Take care of My sheep!"

Then the Lord put the question to him the third time. Now He employed the words Peter had used: "Does your heart yearn for Me?" This made Peter sad. Did the Lord doubt that he loved Him? Peter may have doubted his right to speak of love, but did Jesus not know there was more in his heart than his earlier denial? He replied, "Lord, You know all things; You know that I love You." Again the Lord said, "Feed My sheep."

This conversation was analogous to Peter's triple denial. Three times the Lord asked for a profession of his love as He reinstated Him in his office of disciple and apostle. But this conversation really concerned all the disciples. They were all permitted to love Him and Jesus asked for their love, just as a bridegroom asks for the love of his bride. And it was God who did this; for Jesus is God, the fullness of God's love. In the same way God in Jesus asks for our love. And what will be our answer! Will we answer as spontaneously as Peter, irrespective of our sins?

Sovereign rule over the lives of His own. The Lord gave Peter an emphatic warning that, although he had always acted in complete freedom, when older, others would lead him against his wishes and bring him where he did not want to go. This passage was written after Peter's death as a martyr for Jesus. The passage predicts Peter's death.

What did these words mean for Peter? He was someone who liked to be in the front lines. He was disposed to leadership. The Lord knew this and for a time, Peter was to give leadership. But eventually it would be different; he would be led and compelled to follow. He would be forced to withdraw to the background. That thought must have appalled Peter! And yet, withdrawal to a lesser role would sanctify him all the more. Often God's guidance goes completely against our grain. He gives us a heavy cross to bear. But the Lord knows what He is doing better than we do ourselves.

This became clear right away. Jesus said to Peter, "Follow Me." Evidently He wanted to discuss something privately with Peter. At the same time this call implied that Peter's entire life would be spent following the Lord. John was afraid the Lord would suddenly disappear again and he followed Jesus and Peter at a distance. Peter turned around and saw him coming and asked Jesus what part John was to play. It demonstrated Peter's impatience, for John's part was something hidden in Jesus' sovereign control over all things. Jesus replied, "If I want him to remain alive until I return, what is that to you? You are to follow Me." Thus the Lord turned away Peter's curiosity.

Yet Jesus' answer was of the greatest importance to John. The Lord had not really said that John would remain alive until His return yet this became the rumor. Peter had misunderstood Jesus once again, and probably so had John. John had to reckon with the possibility he might have to live until Christ's return. It ran contrary to John's wishes for he wanted to be with Jesus. In a certain sense John did live until the Lord's return, for it was to him that the Lord revealed the end of all things, the book of Revelation. May we all give our lives into the hands of the Lord Jesus! He glorifies us and leads us to our appointed end.

With this event the gospel of John ends, which does not, of course, mean that everything Jesus said and did has been committed to writing. Never will anyone be able to describe completely the revelation of Him who is the life. That life is new for us every day.

Christ and the Jews

23: Exalted as King

Acts 1:4-14

The acts of the apostles are really the acts of the exalted Christ through His apostles. After His exaltation the gospel of the Kingdom goes out to all the nations. The whole world will come to serve Him. The covenant is opened up to all peoples, making the people of Israel become one nation among many. In this manner the reign of Christ over the entire world becomes manifest.

Only gradually was the church brought to accept the fact that salvation was for all the nations. In the book of Acts we are told first of the spread of the gospel among the Jews. Secondly, events are shown in which the church was led to the preaching of the gospel among the Gentiles. Finally, the course of the gospel among the Gentiles is described, until it reaches Rome. In this book we see the driving force of the Spirit, reaching all the nations with the Word of God. In Rome the hub of the world was reached. The covenant was opened up to all the nations. Christ is sovereign Ruler of the world.

He exercises His sovereignty through His Spirit, the Spirit of love and communion, sent for that very purpose.

Main thought: *By His ascension Christ is exalted as King.*

121

The promise of the baptism with the Holy Spirit. Forty days had passed since Jesus was raised from the dead. Several times He appeared to His disciples. He revealed Himself only to them, not to the world. But repeatedly He disappeared from sight and even the disciples would not know where He was.

This, they all felt, was only temporary. Something would have to happen in the world; salvation would have to be fully revealed. This tension became more and more a part of their lives. On the fortieth day after the resurrection He appeared to His disciples again in Jerusalem. Evidently this appearance had been planned because all eleven disciples were together. He stayed with them longer than the other times. They even walked through the streets of Jerusalem together. They went out the gate, through the Kedron Valley and then climbed the Mount of Olives. It was like the days from before His death.

Jesus told them they should not leave Jerusalem, but wait there for the fulfillment of the promise He had given them. Very soon they would be baptized with the Holy Spirit. In that connection He reminded them of the baptism by John the Baptist. That baptism was now to receive its complete fulfillment. Through the Holy Spirit we die to sin in order to give ourselves to the Lord in a new life. Through the Holy Spirit life is sanctified to a perfect sacrifice. That was now going to happen very soon.

The disciples' expectation. How this promise aroused their expectation and increased anticipation! That was evident from the question they put to the Lord Jesus. "Lord," they asked, "are you at this time going to restore the kingdom to Israel?" They hoped that the promise spoken by the prophets would now be fulfilled. The kingdom of David and Solomon had been so glorious! That kingdom would be restored with even greater glory when Christ, anointed by the Father, would reign through His Spirit.

Did the disciples not see how rebellious and hostile Israel really was? They had thought of that, but they had also heard the promise Christ had given them concerning His Holy Spirit. Would that restoration be too wonderful for the Spirit? Would He not be able to renew Israel spiritually so that she would recognize Christ as King? The disciples believed so. Moreover, they remembered the prophetic promise that God would turn again to His people (for example, Jeremiah 16:14, 15; 30; 31 and Ezekiel 37-39).

We must also believe what they believed. The fact that all nations rebel against the Lord Jesus Christ is in conflict with His Kingship. Would God through His Spirit not be able to renew the life of the nations today? We must believe that He will and must continue to pray for it. For we have the promise that He will be called God of the whole earth.

The times and the seasons of the Father. At the same time, God is sovereign as to the time and manner in which He will fulfill His promise. We cannot say that it must be done at a particular moment and in a certain way; we must acknowledge God's sovereign freedom. Jesus answered His disciples: "It is not for you to know the times or the seasons which the Father has set by His own authority." The Lord's ways are always a surprise; they are different from our ways.

The disciples were simply to carry out their calling. They could not foresee the end of God's ways. They were told to focus on what lay immediately ahead—their calling and the power of the Holy Spirit which they would receive to fulfill that calling. They were to witness about Christ in Jerusalem, Judea, Samaria and among all the nations. Through their testimony God would fulfill His promise. Thus the Kingdom of Christ would be established among the nations by way of the miraculous change the Holy Spirit would bring about. Their duty was to preach the gospel.

Taken up into glory. The disciples often remembered Jesus' words, spoken just prior to His ascension. For although Christ's ascension may have tempted them to ignore their earthly calling, Christ's teaching had been addressed to their calling in the world!

In the meantime, they had arrived on the slopes of the Mount of Olives. He stood in their midst and, even as they were looking at Him, He departed. His feet left the earth and before their eyes He ascended to heaven.

He ascended to inherit the heavenly glory. The angels received Him with shouts of exultation. How He had longed and prayed for that glory! The ascension completed His being. We will never be able to imagine His joy, but one day we may hope to see Him in His splendor.

At that moment He took His place at the right hand of His Father, the Kingdom of His grace began to extend to all nations. As glorious and firmly established as are the heavens, so also is His Kingdom. And as the heavens extend over the whole earth, His glorious reign extends over all nations.

Moreover, by His ascension He is not separated from us in the sense that we are deprived of His blessing. On the contrary, His ascension has opened to us the treasures of heaven. All the fullness that heaven holds for the earth He wished to unlock for us. For us too He inherited heaven's glory.

The cloud that removed Him from their sight. That fullness we understand only by faith, for He is no longer visibly present among us. While the disciples gazed after Him, a cloud drifted by making Him invisible. From that moment life would be lived by faith. We do not see Him, and yet we know He reigns in heaven over all things. He involves all nations in the Kingdom of His grace. Although nations "liberate" themselves from Him and appear to forget Him, He does not forget them. Through His grace He wrestles with all those nations in order to save them for His Kingdom. That will happen only at the time chosen by the Father. A remnant will be saved. God will glorify Himself in the saving of the nations.

All this we believe; we do not see it. Seeing will come only upon Jesus' return on the clouds of heaven. Accordingly, the disciples' attention was directed to that day. While they stared after Christ, two angels dressed in white appeared beside them. They warned the disciples not to expect to see Him again for the present. It was time for them to begin their missionary work; as well, it was time for God's grace to go out into the world. But one day He would return in glory, just as they had seen Him go up into heaven. All their labors on earth were predicated on Christ's return.

Suddenly through faith they saw more than when they climbed the Mount of Olives with Him. Therefore they could return to Jerusalem with joy. The eleven disciples gathered in Jerusalem, along with certain women and Mary, the mother of Jesus, as well as His brothers who had learned to believe in Him. Daily they prayed for the fulfillment of the promise that they would receive the Holy Spirit. They implored the ascended Christ that they might see their path on earth clearly before them and remain in communion with Him, and that He might become glorious in His Kingdom among all the nations on earth.

24: The Organization of the Church

Acts 1:15-26

The election of Matthias was not a mistake, otherwise we would have to conclude that Peter erred in his appeal to the Old Testament. If Peter saw Judas' end so clearly prophesied in the Old Testament, he rightly concluded that the instruction, "Let another take his office," (Ps. 109:8) now had to be carried out by them. Although nothing is later mentioned about Matthias' activity, there is no reason to think that a mistake was made. We hear nothing of the work of most of the apostles. Neither is there any reason to conclude from the later calling of Paul that a mistake was made. The twelve apostles first of all had to bring the gospel to the Jews, while Paul was called immediately and especially for the preaching to the Gentiles.

From the election of Matthias it is apparent that the apostles considered the apostolate not only a gift but also an office. When Judas fell, no one claimed that only the remaining eleven had the apostolic gift. They saw a vacancy in the office which they had to fill. Evidently still more people had apostolic gifts for two names were proposed. Only one, however, was put into office. As a matter of fact Peter made specific mention of an office when he said, "Let another take his office."

Peter here names the requirements for the office of apostle. An apostle must be able to witness to Christ's resurrection. Therefore the office of apostle was only a temporary one.

The apostles became busy with the organization of the church while awaiting the outpouring of the Holy Spirit. The expectation of the Spirit and the organization of the church are thus not in conflict with each other. On the contrary, we can expect the work of the Holy Spirit only if we strive to organize the church in accordance with the Word of the Lord.

126

Main thought: *The working of the Holy Spirit can be expected in organizing the church according to the Word of the Lord.*

The ascension and the organization of the church. Before His ascension the Lord Jesus had promised His disciples they would receive the Holy Spirit in Jerusalem. While they waited, they prayed for although they had the promise, they still had to pray regularly for its fulfillment.

Nevertheless, they understood that awaiting the fulfillment was something other than waiting passively. In addition to prayer, there was work to be done. What did the Lord, who had ascended to heaven and entered upon His full reign, want of them? As King of the church He had given them the authority of office. However, Judas had fallen away. The first organization of the church, instituted by Jesus Himself, had been assailed by sin. They knew this breach would have to be closed.

One day, when a hundred and twenty persons were gathered together, Peter stood up and spoke to them. Because they desired to do the will of their King in heaven, the Scripture of the Old Testament was opened up to them. In it they saw the will of their Lord.

"Judas' deed," Peter said, "was already prophesied in the Old Testament. God ordained it that way in His eternal counsel. That does not remove Judas' responsibility. He had received high honors from Jesus, but he betrayed the Master in return. We know what judgment has come upon him for his betrayal. He hanged himself and when the rope broke he fell to his doom. The blood money was used to buy the burial plot called 'field of blood.' Everybody knows Judas died in disgrace. In fact, it had been prophesied in Scripture. But Scripture also states that another must assume his office. We must elect someone who was with Jesus during His life on earth, in other words, someone who is acquainted with every detail of His life and who can testify especially to His victory in His resurrection."

They were of one mind and readily agreed. Through the Spirit they lived close to their Lord and He revealed His will in Scripture. There was a vacant position, an office which Christ, as King of the church, had endowed with authority. For the Lord's honor the breach in the organization of the church had to be closed. Our love for the Lord arouses our concern for His church. In church matters, too, we must obey His will, a will He makes known to us through Scripture.

Organization of the church and the outpouring of the Holy Spirit. The disciples knew two men who were especially suitable for this office, namely, Joseph and Matthias. The King of the church would Himself have to decide which one He wanted placed in office. In those days the Lord often made His will known by special means. Therefore they prayed that the Lord would point out, by the drawing of lots, which of the two He had chosen. Judas had gone his own way and had perished. In order that the Lord now might choose someone who would give himself in obedience to this calling, they cast the lot. It pointed to Matthias; unanimously the participants agreed to place him in the apostolic office.

In this way the apostles had closed the breach in the church's organization. In those days, while they were awaiting the Holy Spirit, this was not a thing of small importance. If, within the church, they did not live in complete accordance with the will of their Lord, the Holy Spirit would not be able to do His work. The Holy Spirit must be our main focus. That Spirit has to create new life within us and in the world. In the church, however, we have to be obedient. Only then can we expect the powerful working of the Holy Spirit throughout the church. We can never expect this if we go our own ways, for although the Holy Spirit has been poured out on the church, we still must constantly expect His increasingly powerful activity. Our life too continues to be a patient awaiting of the Spirit.

25: The Spirit of Communion

Acts 2

With the New Testament came the indwelling of the Spirit in the people of the Lord. This Spirit is one of communion with God in His covenant. Through the Spirit Jesus poured God's love into our hearts. For Jesus is the One who brings about the communion between God and us.

It is difficult to determine the difference between the work of the Spirit in the Old Testament and that in the New. The new birth, faith and the entire renewal of life were just as much the work of the Holy Spirit in the Old Testament. But in the Old there was not yet the indwelling of God in the heart by the Spirit. That indwelling had so far only been symbolized and prophesied by the presence of God in the temple. The governing of the heart by the Spirit had only occurred from the outside. In the New Testament, through the Spirit of communion with God, the people of God received a principle of life all its own. This Spirit will nevermore depart from the people. In the dispensation of the covenant, the new and eternal testament has come. This dispensation of the covenant will not be followed by another, even though at the return of Christ our life will enter upon a higher glory. There now has come a communion with God through the Spirit which will remain forever.

The Spirit of communion with God was poured out in the congregation, in all of God's people, not in individual persons. The New Testament does not bring individualism. On the contrary, the unity of people in Christ, the Head, has been confirmed and strengthened through the indwelling of the Spirit. Whereas each individual shares in that life-principle of the church, the life of individuals within that fellowship stands out more clearly.

There is still another aspect to this transition which we must equally keep in mind. During the Old Testament period the church had been separated from the life of the nations, whom God had allowed to wander in their own ways. Now the church is going to be gathered out of all nations and all nations will be saved in the covenant. The covenant with Israel has not been broken, but has been opened up to all nations so that Israel has become one of the many, no more and no less than any other nation. The people of the Lord who are being gathered out of all the nations now have a claim on the world again; they have a claim on life in all its fullness, and the right to make use of the world.

In Old Testament times, isolation was, in many ways the demand of God's law. Israel was separated from the other nations. The world and life were actually unclean, as the laws regarding ritual cleanliness were meant to teach Israel. The commandments on fasting taught people that the world's resources had been forfeited. But now comes another dispensation. The church is being gathered out of all nations. Through the indwelling of the Spirit in His people, God again adopts the whole world and sanctifies it, so that in principle the world's uncleanness is purified. Through the redemption in Christ the people of the Lord obtain again the right to make use of the whole world. His people now enjoy Christian freedom. In this respect too the Kingdom of God has come.

Because the new and eternal dispensation of the covenant has now come, the end of this age has been brought closer. This fullness of the Spirit cries out for the complete glorification of life. We now live in the last days. Therefore in the prophecy of Joel the renewal of heaven and earth is directly connected with the outpouring of the Spirit.

A number of arguments can be brought forward for the idea that on the day of Pentecost the disciples spoke one language, the language of the Spirit, and that this one language was heard by the various people as their own language. Thus there is a miracle of speech on the part of the disciples, and a miracle of hearing on the part of their hearers. Concretely, there is, on the one hand, a wonderful revelation of unity through the Spirit, while on the other hand it appears that the renewal brought by the Spirit touches the ordinary and richly varied life of this world, because the Word of the Spirit is understood by the hearers in their native tongues.

Main thought: *With the Holy Spirit the love of God is poured out in the hearts of His people.*

Waiting for the Spirit. After the ascension the disciples awaited the fulfillment of the promise that they would receive the Holy Spirit. Daily they came together to pray. As yet they were unable to face the world; they needed the Spirit of communion with God. That would give them an invincible power. As well, the world was unprepared for their mission since God had allowed the Gentiles to stray from His light, seeking their own ways. Not until God readopted the nations and included them in the saving blessing of His covenant could the apostles preach the gospel of salvation to the world. Without the Spirit promised by Jesus they were unequiped to go into the world.

Ten days after the ascension the Jews celebrated the Feast of Pentecost. Jerusalem was filled with people in a festive mood celebrating the end of the wheat harvest. The first loaves of bread baked from the new flour were brought before God's presence. Thus the people acknowledged that the harvest was the Lord's and that He sustains life. They also meditated on the institution of the covenant of God with His people at Mount Sinai, on the law of the covenant through Moses, and on Israel's honor in being called to be the people of the Lord.

On the feast day the disciples also were gathered together in Jerusalem. No doubt they wondered whether the Lord would now fulfill His promise, and whether they would now be permitted to gather in the world's harvest. They wondered if the world would finally be opened up to them. Would they see how their life was sustained and made fruitful by the Holy Spirit? Was this the inauguration of the covenant dispensation which would far surpass in glory the covenant God had made with His people at Mount Sinai? Such thoughts must have been in their hearts, for they were living with such great expectation.

The coming of the Spirit amidst signs. Precisely where the disciples were gathered together we do not know. In any case, it was in a room large enough for their number. While they were together there, they suddenly heard the sound of a mighty wind which seemed to burst into the room. The sound filled the whole house. That was a very special sign, because there was no storm outside and the sound lasted for only a moment.

They soon discovered that the sign was accompanied by the Holy Spirit. God wished to make His coming known also by external signs. By such means the disciples, and we too, would more easily believe and understand what we possess. How wonderful and compelling this sign was! It symbolized the force the Spirit applies to our hearts, formerly closed to Him and resistant to His influence. Nothing can hold back this power of the Spirit which everywhere works invisibly. The Spirit conquers the most hardened heart.

Having recovered from the initial shock they saw flames above each other's heads, much like they were on fire inside and flames flickered above their heads. Of course, they really were on fire inside. The Spirit of God's love had come to dwell in them. He made of their hearts and lives a sacrifice unto Himself. Their whole being became a living sacrifice. And because it was sanctified to the Lord, it was also purified. They were now joined to the Lord by the perfect bond of the Spirit. Offering themselves to God as a sacrifice, they were privileged to know Him in His perfect love in the Lord Jesus Christ. And having come to know God through Christ they were suitably equiped to proclaim His salvation. Thus they became a light in the world.

Immediately the consequences of this indwelling of the Spirit in their hearts became manifest. They saw things they had never seen before. By the Spirit they saw something of the depths of God, of the magnitude of God's love, of His eternal love in His Son. They also received words to express what they saw. They glorified God for that love in words they had never known existed. This far surpassed their former life. It was the miracle of the Spirit. Yet in the New Testament it is normal for a man to be on fire for his God, on fire out of love. That he has insight into the depths of God's love testifies to this love. Unfortunately, this normal level is lowered so much by our sin! However, it is only through this love that a person attains his worth and is truly human. We may not be content if we love and proclaim less than the disciples. Even though the external signs are lacking, our life must be just as much a sacrifice.

The multitude taken by surprise. Many non-Jewish travelers, converts to Judaism, were in Jerusalem for the feast. Probably there were also many Jews, born and raised in the Dispersion, who had come to Jerusalem to pass the last days in the vicinity of the temple and be buried in holy soil. They were very devout people who sought the God of Israel. Evidently many of them were near the house where the disciples were gathered when the Holy Spirit was poured out on them. At the sound of the wind the crowd flocked together; there they saw the disciples and heard them speak.

They were amazed, because they heard the disciples speak their native language. How could those disciples speak those different languages? Probably the Holy Spirit caused the disciples to speak one language, the language of the Spirit, but at the same time caused the listeners to hear it as their own. It was a miracle of the Spirit which gave forceful expression to the fact that the Holy Spirit created a unity among peoples.

The multitude was deeply moved. They heard the most secret and most wonderful things of God's grace in their own tongue. It was not the sacred Hebrew language of the law and prophets as might be expected; the deepest issues were brought home to them in their own speech. They were directly confronted with God's grace.

It astonished them completely and yet they were devout people who attended the sacrificial offerings and regularly discussed Scripture and therefore might have expected the fulfillment of Scripture's promises! However, that was far beyond their expectations. But will God's grace not always encounter stunned disbelief? Their hearts were so unreceptive to salvation that some admitted they didn't know what to make of it while others mocked the disciples for being drunk. That is how by nature we react when confronted with the work of the Spirit.

Entered upon the last days. Peter then addressed himself particularly to the crowd and admonished the people for thinking they were drunk. They were not under the influence of wine but of the Spirit of God. They were witnessing, he explained, the fulfillment of prophecy.

"Remember," Peter said, "what Joel prophesied. Through him God promised He would pour out His Spirit, not just on a particular group of people, but on both men and women, old and young, masters and servants. Through this Spirit they all would be one, Joel wrote, for they would all know the Lord and witness to His grace. God would reveal Himself to them through the Spirit."

Imparting the Spirit would usher in the end of the world. The Spirit's message calls for the renewal of heaven and earth, a renewal begun at Pentecost. Pentecost inaugurated the new and eternal dispensation of God's covenant. That is why Joel could have the prophecy of the end of the world follow immediately upon the prophecy of the outpouring of the Spirit, no matter how much time would elapse between the two events. The sun will be turned into darkness and the moon into blood. Then the Spirit will break through into the whole creation and God will appear to His world.

That breakthrough, however, is given in principle with this outpouring of the Spirit; now the day of the Lord has come. The whole world has reached a state of crisis. Everyone is now confronted with the decision. Whoever will call on the name of the Lord in faith, trusting His Word, will be saved in this day of the Lord.

Christ's Spirit of Life. Peter proceeded to tell them about how the living Lord Jesus Christ had poured out His Spirit. Though handed over to death on the cross, He had been raised according to the counsel of God. God had guided the event of Christ's death in order that He might raise Him from the dead. Had Christ's death not been prophesied in Scripture? David had sung that God would not leave him in the kingdom of the dead or allow his body to decompose. David could not have said that of himself. David had been buried; his grave was in their midst. David had prophesied of Christ, who, according to the promise, was His descendant. That David's prophecy was fulfilled was witnessed by the disciples who had seen Christ after His resurrection.

Similarly, Christ's ascent had been prophesied in Psalms: "The Lord said to my Lord, sit at my right hand until I make your enemies a footstool for your feet." This Jesus, whom they had killed, had been exalted by God to be Lord and Christ. He reigns in the Kingdom of grace, and woe to them who do not subject themselves in faith to His grace.

Such was the preaching of the gospel on the day of Pentecost. That preaching proclaims God's gracious acts, thereby declaring us guilty for we have all rejected Christ. We must now trust the Lord, who has made atonement for our sins.

Conversion. Many were smitten by what they heard. They saw what God through His grace had done, and what, by contrast, they had done. What would become of them? Was there still deliverance for them? "Brothers, what shall we do?" they asked. Peter urged them to repent, to turn back to the God whom they had scorned when they had trusted in themselves. He encouraged them to put their hope in His grace and receive forgiveness for their sins. Peter offered to baptize them as a sign of God's forgiveness. They would receive the Holy Spirit and be able to testify to God's wonderful grace, just as the apostles did.

They had, as the people of God's covenant, received the promise that salvation in Christ was for them. He urged them to accept and believe the promise. It was for the purpose of their salvation that God reached out to them. Why reject His offer of salvation? They should not, Peter warned them, harden their hearts against the Lord as their ancestors had done.

Of those present, many believed. With joy they accepted forgiveness for their sins and were baptized. At least three thousand were baptized into a new community of faith motivated by the Holy Spirit, separated in principle from so many fellow Jews who continued to trust in themselves.

The new fellowship. (Compare Acts 4:32-37.) They practised orderly fellowship: in the morning they came together in Solomon's Colonnade in the temple where the apostles instructed them in the knowledge of the Lord and of His grace; in the evenings they met in smaller groups in members' homes to strengthen one another in faith, to celebrate the Lord's supper and to pray. "And the Lord added to their number daily those who were being saved."

The Word the apostles preached was confirmed by many signs; they saw the healing of life by the Holy Spirit.

To this fellowship belonged many poor people who were no longer supported by the synagogues to which they had belonged. These people now had to be supported by the believers, who did so with joy. If there was any shortage someone would sell a field or a house and give the proceeds to the poor. They formed a community of sharing and service which is still the hallmark of a congregation even though such sharing does not preempt private property.

They praised God and enjoyed the favor of all the people who were not hostile to the believers. The Lord worked His miracle of conversion in the hearts of many, so that daily believers were added to their fellowship.

This marked the first congregation or fellowship of believers, the mother church in Jerusalem. From there the community of believers would be extended over the whole world. There was still much to be done before this goal could be realized. However, this beginning was a miracle of the Holy Spirit, a miracle that would continue to this very day. It is a miracle that there is a church of the Lord Jesus Christ at all! It is through the proclamation of the Word that the Holy Spirit wishes to accomplish this miracle.

26: Revealed to Jerusalem

Acts 3–4:31

In the book of *Acts* we see the gospel go from place to place: from Jerusalem to Samaria, Antioch, Asia Minor, Europe, Rome. But in this passage we see the revelation of Christ to the people of Jerusalem.

This revelation occurs through the Holy Spirit, who awakens in Peter and John as well as in the crippled man the faith necessary for healing.

Peter's speeches to the people and before the Sanhedrin (see Vol. III, p. 135) were also inspired by the Holy Spirit, as was the shaking of the place where the disciples were gathered. This tremor is a prophecy of what the Holy Spirit will do in the last days when heaven and earth once again will be shaken (see Haggai 2:1-9, and compare Exodus 19:16-18 and Hebrews 12:18-26, esp. vs. 26).

Main thought: *Christ is revealed to Jerusalem as the One who is alive for evermore.*

The power of His resurrection. Already a crowd of three thousand persons had come to believe, but they were from all parts of the world. The Feast of Pentecost had come to an end and many had left town again. How many of those three thousand lived in Jerusalem? Would they have to go underground? Would the movement, which had such an auspicious beginning, come to a halt in Jerusalem? No, that could not happen, for the gospel had to be proclaimed to all the nations. The disciples must have waited in faith for the further guidance of the Lord Jesus and of His Spirit.

137

One day, at three in the afternoon, Peter and John went to the temple for prayer. They too wanted to take part in the prayer of the entire nation for the God of Israel to reveal Himself to His people. Peter and John also wanted to pray for this revelation, but then as a revelation of God through Jesus Christ. They still went up to the temple even though the whole temple service had been fulfilled by the work of Christ. Now one could worship God anywhere but the disciples still held to the regulations and practices of the Old Testament as much as possible. Eventually, this outward form would come to fall away.

After crossing the Court of the Gentiles, the disciples had to pass through the Beautiful Gate to the actual temple area. In front of that gate sat a beggar, one who had been lame from birth. Every day he was carried to this spot to ask for alms. Peter and John had probably seen the man sitting there several times before, so he was a familiar figure. Suddenly, however, their attention focused on him. Through the power of the Holy Spirit they saw him as the object of God's good pleasure. God wished to reveal to that cripple the power of Christ's resurrection. Through the Holy Spirit they saw the will of the Father, just as Jesus had so frequently seen it during His lifetime.

The beggar had seen nothing of that will. When Peter and John came by he asked alms of them as well. The Holy Spirit first had to awaken faith in the man. He did so by means of Peter's words and actions. As Peter and John both looked straight at him, Peter said, "Look at us," and added, "we have no gold or silver but something much better: in the name of Jesus Christ of Nazareth stand up and walk." Saying this, he took him by the hand and pulled him up. Instantly that man's spirit was changed. If it pleases Him, the Holy Spirit doesn't need hours to do His work. Through Peter's word and touch faith in the name of Jesus was awakened and he was healed. Jumping up, he stood on his feet and walked.

Thus the power of Jesus Christ was revealed to him. Peter declined to give him alms because he had something greater to give him: the restoration of his life. Healing was tantamount to restoring life. He was normal and strong like others. By healing him the Holy Spirit called him to give his restored life to the Lord. Then he would truly be healed, for the restoration of life lies in communion with God. This is the restoration the Lord Jesus wants to bring us. He often declines to give us alms, that is, things we think we need, because He has something better for us. The complete restoration of our life is the fruit of His resurrection. He has arisen to full communion with God, and He wants to share that with us. Someday this communion will result in the complete restoration of our life in ultimate glory. That power of Christ's resurrection was now revealed in the healing of this cripple.

The cripple probably recognized his healing as a gift of God's grace and came to communion with God. In any case he followed the apostles into the temple, jumping and praising God.

He has risen, according to the Scriptures. Not only did the cripple have to be healed, but the Lord Jesus Christ had to be revealed to all of Jerusalem as the living Lord. And that was precisely what happened because the man kept following Peter and John, all the while praising God. The people who saw him recognized him as the crippled beggar. When they learned what had happened, they were awed. Jesus of Nazareth had done such miracles! But surely Jesus of Nazareth was dead . . . The leaders immediately feared that the people might think Him alive. But that was exactly what the Holy Spirit wanted to tell the masses.

Judging from the crowd's astonishment it was time for Jesus to be revealed to Jerusalem. Peter proclaimed: "We did not make this man walk by our own power and godliness. Here is the revelation of the God of our fathers according to the covenant He made with our fathers. His Son Jesus, whom you delivered up to die on the cross, was raised from the dead. We are witnesses of His resurrection. He is the sovereign Lord of life. The power of His resurrection has been revealed in this man because he learned to believe in Him.

"Brothers, you were not fully aware of what you were doing when you killed Him. Through your crime God fulfilled His Word that His Christ would suffer to atone for sin. It is not too late for you yet. Turn to God and believe in Jesus Christ in order that you may receive forgiveness of sins and eternal salvation through Him. It will bring new hope for the nation. Was His coming not prophesied of old? Well, the time has come. Jesus Christ is now in heaven, leading His people on earth to the time when He will make all things new in His Kingdom.

"All the prophets urged you to listen to the One sent from the Father. To you He was sent first, for you are the people of the covenant and of the promise. If you believe, you will become, according to the prophecy given to Abraham, a blessing for all the nations, for you may make known to them the message of His resurrection. But everyone who does not believe will be completely cut off from His people."

Through the marvellous healing of this crippled man and Peter's address, Christ was revealed to Jerusalem as the living Lord. Many believed in Him, and the small number of believers in Jerusalem soared to five thousand. Christ had begun to subject Israel to His reign of grace.

Conflict with the Supreme Council (Sanhedrin). While Peter and John addressed the people, the priests, the captain of the temple guard and the Sadducees joined them. Sadducees did not believe in the resurrection of the dead, but now they heard it proclaimed that Jesus had arisen from the dead and had conquered death for all who belonged to Him. It made them livid. They arrested the two apostles and put them in prison until the next day.

Next day the Supreme Council met. It also included a number of Pharisees who believed in the resurrection but hated Jesus with a passion. Naturally, they were loathe to see stories about Jesus' supposed resurrection published abroad. Not surprisingly, the whole Supreme Council was united against Peter and John.

The Supreme Council interrogated the apostles, demanding by what authority or in whose name they had performed their miracle. To them the whole incident had been some sort of trick. The apostles had to confront their prejudice with a straightforward message about Jesus Christ as the living Lord. Of course, that meant indicting the council.

Filled with the Holy Spirit, Peter said, "Since this is a court of law, we will give you a full account of what happened. There was no trickery or magic; Jesus Christ, whom God raised from the dead, made this man well. By your crime He was prosecuted and crucified. Through you the following prophecy has been fulfilled:

there will be a stone rejected by the builders but used by God as the cornerstone. On that stone God is now going to build a new world in His Kingdom, for there is no other name under heaven given to man by which we must be saved.''

The members of the Supreme Council were enraged at the impertinence of the apostles. They were only disciples of this troublemaker Jesus and peasants to boot! But what of the man who had been healed? He was standing right there! Thus the Holy Spirit and power of Jesus Christ was shown to the Sanhedrin. Confused, they could do nothing about it. Nevertheless, they closed their hearts; they did not want to humble themselves before God or His Christ. They would never subject themselves to Him in faith! How intransigent can be our unbelief!

After dismissing the apostles they discussed what they should do, for they could not deny the miracle. But the movement, they resolved, had to be suppressed. Accordingly, they threatened the apostles severely and forbade them to witness of the Lord Jesus. But the apostles answered they would obey God rather than men, for it was from God they had received the mandate to preach Jesus Christ. It was through Jesus, they insisted, that God wanted to do His great work in the world. The Supreme Council threatened the disciples even more but could not punish them, for no punishable offense had been committed. In fact all the people glorified God by now. For forty years the man had been lame, and now he was healed. This was nothing short of a divine miracle. There's none so blind as those who will not see . . .

The answer from heaven. Upon their release Peter and John went directly to the circle of believers and reported everything the members of the Sanhedrin had said to them. They all joined in prayer. They confessed that God was the sovereign Lord who had made the heaven and the earth. In His love He had the right to everything He had made. And now, as Jesus had warned, hostile men again conspired against Him. It was as though Herod and Pilate again plotted against the Lord Jesus, in whom God's grace has come to us. All flesh was in the opposition. But as the Lord Himself had prophesied vigorous opposition they felt peaceful and assured. Nothing was beyond God's counsel. He would direct everything to serve the coming of His Kingdom. Therefore they did not first of all ask for protection but for boldness in witnessing, that it might please the Lord to strengthen their witness by performing many miraculous signs in the name of the Lord Jesus.

God answered their prayer, for at that moment the place where they were meeting was shaken. The world of Jews and Gentiles seemed so firm in its opposition to Christ but the Holy Spirit would shake the world's self-assuredness and lead it to find another certainty through faith in Christ. Moreover, the Spirit would one day shake the present earth and heaven and bring forth the new earth and the new heaven with the reign of Jesus Christ in eternal glory.

They were all filled anew with the power of the Holy Spirit, and they proclaimed the Word of God with boldness. The work of the Spirit could not be stopped.

27: A Holy Fellowship

Acts 4:32–5:11

It is wrong to suggest that in the Jerusalem church communism existed more or less in the form we know it today. Although no one claimed any possessions as his own but held everything in common, this does not imply dogmatic adherence to the principle of collective ownership. Whenever someone sold a house or a field, he gave the proceeds to the poor; that was a voluntary act according to this entire Scripture passage.

The Christian community in Jerusalem probably numbered a great many poor people, a conclusion that can also be drawn from *Acts* chapter 6. Previously these poor had been cared for by their own synagogues. Now suddenly their support fell to the new emerging community. For this reason the ordinary funds from the daily or weekly collections were not sufficient. Therefore, some of the richer brethren gave large gifts, which they obtained by selling a field or a house. Apparently a certain Barnabas had been the first person to do this, and he perhaps owes his surname to this. (His name was Joseph but the apostles had given him the surname Barnabas, which means "son of encouragement.") Barnabas and his fellow Christians were convinced that they possessed nothing solely for themselves. The community was based on the belief that they were one in Christ. Therefore, they should use all their possessions for their mutual benefit. As such there is always a certain service oriented economics in the Christian community. However, the individual still retains the right to dispose of what is his, although that right is qualified by communion in Christ.

Obviously, the punishment inflicted on Ananias and Sapphira is not meant as a warning against lying in general. Ananias and Sapphira lied to the Holy Spirit. They did not live out of the Spirit, who was bringing about a new community, but instead desecrated the work of the Spirit by their deceit. They profaned the real life the Spirit was creating, and that was the reason for their death. When we tell this story we must bring out the sanctity of the new life in communion with God.

143

Main thought: *The Holy Spirit creates a new holy fellowship.*

The revelation of the new fellowship. The congregation of five thousand which had come into being in Jerusalem through the preaching of the apostles formed a true unity. They were not only organized under the leadership of the apostles; they also felt love for one another and understood one another, because they shared the same sentiments. The love of the Lord Jesus which had come to them through the Holy Spirit and which had awakened this response of love in their hearts bound them together.

This bond manifested itself in their understanding that their possessions were not for themselves alone. By faith they knew they were one. Now they also understood their calling to live for one another. Not only their spiritual gifts but also their material possessions were to promote the fellowship they had with one another.

Why did they have such a strong awareness of their fellowship? It was because the apostles witnessed fervently to the resurrection of the Lord. And this preaching, in turn, exercised great power because the Holy Spirit blessed it. Thus they all shared in the new life of communion with God. They had arisen with the Lord Jesus to a new life in which they lived close to God as their Father. Since they were aware of sharing in His favor, they knew no fear. And it is always fear that makes us so self-centered.

There were many poor people in the congregation of Jerusalem. Formerly they had been cared for by the synagogues to which they belonged. However, their ties to those synagogues had been broken and now the congregation of believers would have to care for them. The daily and weekly collections and gifts which the apostles received for this purpose were inadequate. Therefore some of the richer brethren might sell a house or a field and give the proceeds to the apostles for distribution among the poor. This brought relief for the needs of the congregation. The Holy Spirit had worked this liberality in the hearts of those brethren. A certain Joseph was probably the man who started it. The apostles named him Barnabas, that is, son of encouragement. His act had greatly encouraged the apostles and the congregation. In that act they sensed the nearness of the Holy Spirit.

The fellowship in Jerusalem was the work of the Holy Spirit. Members loved one another for God's sake. They honored and served God, their Redeemer, by caring for one another. It was truly a holy fellowship, consecrated to God. Thus it was entirely different from any community that exists apart from faith. It was from God, through God and unto God, who is the Redeemer.

Sham. Did all of the people in the congregation see and experience it in that way? Apparently not. Even at that time persons who did not truly live out of faith joined the congregation. They were carried away by the movement the Holy Spirit had brought into being. Something of this power did indeed touch them, but they did not recognize it as a movement of the Holy Spirit. They saw in the power little more than human endeavor. They wanted to be a part of it for the benefit of self-fulfillment. Nor did they understand faith as a gift of God by which we see the miracle of God's grace in His Christ. They looked upon faith simply as an act of the human will.

There were two people, Ananias and his wife Sapphira, who viewed the movement this way. They wished to make their contribution to it because they noticed the honor Barnabas had received for his liberality and they wanted to be similarly honored. Thus these two people wanted to act by themselves and solely for themselves. They did not really know the Holy Spirit; faith had not freed them from their self-centeredness. They had not been liberated; thus they were not free from fear. Ananias and Sapphira therefore found it difficult to give to the apostles the entire proceeds of the field they sold. They decided to keep a portion for themselves. Still, they wanted all the credit and therefore agreed to tell the apostles their gift constituted the entire sale.

These persons lived very close to the work of the Spirit, physically at least, and were somehow swept up by it but never really knew the Spirit. They chose to dishonor the Spirit's glorious work by their selfishness and deception. They deceived the Spirit of the Lord Jesus Christ, who is present in the congregation. This deceit may seem somewhat extreme and yet anyone who joins the congregation while not living out of the Holy Spirit in principle commits similar fraud. Such a person will also take offense at the Holy Spirit, as did Ananias and Sapphira.

The discipline of the Holy Spirit. The apostle Peter, illumined by the Holy Spirit, perceived what had happened and confronted Ananias. He said, "Ananias, how is it satan has so filled your heart that you have lied to the Holy Spirit?" Peter perceived this was the work of satan who had fanned the flame of greed in Ananias' heart and thus wanted to destroy the Spirit's work. Peter wanted to make Ananias fully aware of the nature of his sin. "After all," Peter pointed out, "it was an act of your own free choice. You have given yourself into satan's hands; you have fought against the Holy Spirit."

The moment Ananias heard this, the judgment of the Holy Spirit struck him and he fell down dead. The Holy Spirit always guards His honor and that of the holy fellowship which He had established. This was a redemptive act of the Holy Spirit. He thereby redeemed His church from the corruption of sin. Great fear came upon all. The younger brethren of the congregation lifted Ananias up and buried him. In the meantime, his wife was not told. Through this judgment the Holy Spirit had spoken. Ananias was carried out as one who had been rejected.

About three hours later Sapphira came in. Peter asked her whether she had been a party to this deception. When it became obvious she was party to the same lie, the word of Peter struck her down too. The two had agreed to tempt the Spirit of the Lord. They had foolishly conspired to test the power of the Holy Spirit. She too was struck by the judgment of the Spirit. Immediately she fell dead at Peter's feet. The young brethren who had just returned from burying Ananias found her there and carried her out as well.

It was made clear to everyone that in this congregation there was a holy fellowship which had been established by the Holy Spirit. According to His covenant, God dwelt among His people whom He had begun to gather unto Himself, starting with Israel. The Lord repelled the sins of unbelief and contempt for His holiness. Thus He was redeeming His people.

28: Jerusalem Filled with His Name

Acts 5:12–6:7

Positioning the sick on beds in such a way that Peter's shadow would pass over them cannot have been a form of superstition. By His miracles the Holy Spirit does not promote superstition. Moreover, just before this passage we are told that none of the others dared to join these believers. There was a certain hesitancy concerning the holiness that existed in this community. They would not allow superstition to profane this aura of holiness. Faithful believers saw this passing of Peter's shadow over the sick as a sign that the power of Christ's grace would overshadow them.

The words of Gamaliel do not mean that he or the Sanhedrin had the slightest doubt that a person crucified was cursed of God. He did not believe this movement was from God. But he wondered whether the growth of this movement after the death of Jesus Christ was blessed by God. He pointed out how strange it was that the movements of Theudas and of Judas the Galilean had come to nothing, whereas this movement was spreading. It might, he reasoned, be the will of God to test the Jews. Gamaliel therefore advised against opposing the movement. Expansion, he surmised, was a sign that God was testing Israel. He wanted to scrutinize God's counsel in order to prepare a response that would be consistent with what he took God's counsel to be! By so doing he shrugged off his own responsibility. Gamaliel would have been more consistent if he had said, "This movement is accursed of God; let us crush it even though it may have been sent by God to test us." Gamaliel, however, was looking at God's guidance in history in the wrong fashion.

Main thought: *Through the Holy Spirit Jerusalem is filled with the name of Jesus Christ.*

147

The movement in Jerusalem. There was already a significant number of believers in Jerusalem and new members were being added daily to the community. This resulted in part from the power of the grace of Jesus Christ through the Holy Spirit, which was so richly revealed in the many acts of healing performed by the apostles. Furthermore, every day the gospel was publicly being proclaimed by the apostles in the Portico of Solomon, a covered portion of the temple's forecourt.

Yet no one dared to join the community solely on account of those acts of healing. The judgment that had come upon Ananias and Sapphira had made a deep impression. People sensed the presence of holiness in the fellowship and the believers were held in high esteem. Only when there was a true faith in the Lord Jesus did people seek to associate themselves with the community. And there were many who came to believe.

The acts of healing multiplied. The Holy Spirit revealed thereby that the power of grace to restore life had not departed even though the Lord was no longer seen on earth. There were so many sick people, some from the cities round about, that their relatives and friends simply put them down on their mats in such a way that Peter's shadow would pass over them. This was an expression of faith; they chose to see a sign that the power of grace would overshadow their sick. By its strength they would be healed. And indeed, all the sick and all who were possessed by the devil were healed. The mercy of God rested upon His people. He wanted to show how in His covenant He made life whole again. To that end He asked faith in the grace of the Lord Jesus. Even though in our time such miracles no longer happen, the grace of the Lord has not departed from His people and by faith we are to seek fellowship with them.

The opposition defeated. Of course the high priest and all his colleagues, especially the Sadducees who denied the resurrection of the dead, were well aware of what was going on. They were filled with anger. Clearly they had miscalculated. They had thought Jesus' death would bring the movement to an end, but now it was more prolific than before. In their fury they seized all the apostles and threw them in the public jail. Now their hostility showed itself in earnest, and persecution became more common. Before this only Peter and John had been arrested; now all the apostles were treated as criminals.

With such stern measures the enemies of the gospel intended to check its course and break the power of the movement in Jerusalem. However, the course of the gospel cannot be checked by men. God demonstrated this by sending an angel who, in the night, invisibly opened the doors of the jail and led the apostles out. The angel ordered them to preach the gospel of life, which is communion with God through Jesus Christ. Obedient to that command they were back at the temple the next day. This rescue was not so much for the sake of the apostles as to demonstrate that the gospel cannot be stopped. How often believers have given their lives in the struggle for the Christ! The power of the gospel was not to be checked in its operation; that was the reason for the apostles' deliverance. Nothing can hold up the course of the gospel. God is constantly opening up new avenues by way of the miraculous working of the Holy Spirit, making the hearts of men receptive.

That morning the Sanhedrin met officially. They sent for the apostles but learned to their dismay that the jail was empty. Incredibly, the guards had not noticed a thing! As they raked their brains for an explanation they learned that the apostles were teaching in the front court of the temple! Again they were confronted with the miraculous power of the Lord but even this did not make them listen to reason. When will the hostility of men be broken? Evidently not until the final day.

Appeal to the secret counsel of God. Avoiding violence the captain of the temple guard brought the apostles before the Supreme Council. They could not use force, for the people would have stoned them. Such was the people's respect for the Lord's community. All Jerusalem was involved with this movement; all the people were thinking about it. This had been the Lord's intention: the whole world had to be confronted with the gospel.

The Sanhedrin reproached the apostles for breaking the prohibition forbidding them to preach in the name of the Lord Jesus. They replied, "You have filled Jerusalem with your teaching." Had these rulers previously not sealed the Lord's tomb, presuming

Him dead? Yet now He lived on in His gospel and through the power of the Spirit. His name had not perished with Him; instead, it had filled the whole city. The proliferation of the gospel was a threat to their positions of authority. Moreover, they had sentenced Him to death and feared the apostles might be planning to avenge Him.

This turned out to be a tumultuous hearing. The members of the Sanhedrin were filled with fear and hatred. Nor were the apostles in a mood to capitulate; they rightly believed they had to base their position on the gospel. The gospel asks our total involvement; ultimately, conflict cannot be avoided. Peter and the apostles replied: "We must obey God rather than men. You killed Jesus by nailing Him on the cross." Thus they declared the Sanhedrin guilty before God. At the same time, however, they proclaimed the Word of grace, saying that God had raised Him up and exalted Him as Leader and Savior to give repentance and forgiveness of sins to Israel. "We are witnesses of the grace that is in Him; the Holy Spirit also witnesses in those who receive Him in faith. They have the wonderful peace and the joy which results from communion with God," they proclaimed.

When the members of the Sanhedrin heard the accusation and this preaching of grace they were furious. How could they be expected to subject themselves to the Christ! They deliberated, resolved to put the apostles to death. But Gamaliel, an astute, highly respected Pharisee, had the apostles wait outside. For the benefit of his colleagues he reviewed the case. A situation like this, he pointed out, had never occurred before. Ordinarily movements collapsed after the death of their leader. This movement, however, kept on going. That could very well be God's way of testing the Jews. If this was the case, he reasoned, they should not oppose it for fear of inviting God's wrath. With all his learning, Gamaliel was still a fool, for if this movement was blasphemous—and of that Gamaliel had no doubt—they should contest it with all their might, irrespective of whether God was using it to test the nation. But Gamaliel wanted to put himself in the place of God's counsel, thereby eliminating the Sanhedrin's own responsibility. That is often what arrogant men do. We have to decide, in accordance with the Word of God, what is good and what is evil, and what, consequently, we must do. Gamaliel turned these things around.

He wanted to analyze the secret counsel of God and disclaim any responsibility. But we cannot escape the judgment of God that easily. Any attempt to elevate oneself to the hidden counsel of God will be defeated by the gospel. The gospel brings the life of mankind to a point of decision-making. Man must choose between humble submission and open rebellion. Gamaliel's "third way" did not exist.

Joy in suffering for the gospel. For the time being the words of Gamaliel made an impression. The members of the Sanhedrin took his advice but also wanted to show the apostles they meant business. So they ordered them flogged. And, after they had ordered them again not to speak of the Lord Jesus, they let them go.

The apostles rejoiced that the Lord had counted them worthy to suffer for His name. In suffering they were one with the Lord Jesus. They lived in fellowship with Him all the more. And they did not cease to proclaim the gospel daily, publicly in the temple as well as privately in the homes of the believers. All Jerusalem had to hear the message of salvation.

Extension of the community. As a result of the expansion of the Christian community, the work of charity also increased. The apostles could no longer supervise the activity of the community. Some of the widows, particularly Jewish women who had returned to Jerusalem from abroad, came to be neglected. When complaints arose about this, the apostles suggested the community choose seven of the brethren, whom they would then charge with caring for the poor. It would have been wrong for the apostles to sacrifice preaching the Word in order to care for the poor.

The community did what the apostles asked. Seven reputable men, filled with the Holy Spirit were chosen. These were presented to the apostles, who installed them in the new office. These brethren would care for the poor in the name of the Lord Jesus Christ, to show thereby the mercy of our Lord in heaven. This is how it is still done in the church of Christ today. Life is thereby anointed with the Lord's mercy.

The number of believers continued to grow. A large number of priests became obedient to the faith. Besides practising the priestly office they came to exercise the office of all believers, dedicating all of life to the Lord.

Christ's Way
to the Gentiles

29: In Newness of the Spirit

Acts 6:8–8:4

The activity of Stephen set the stage for the preaching of the gospel among the Gentiles. Evidently he saw very clearly—and said so openly—that the gospel was not tied down to Israel, but would go forth to all nations. That is why the hostility of the Jewish leaders was directed especially against Stephen and he was accused of blaspheming the temple and the law. It is significant, in this connection, to note that Saul took pleasure in Stephen's death even though it was this same Saul who was later called to carry on Stephen's work. Luke shows us the work of the Spirit in this event.

The content of Stephen's speech seems to have little relevance to the charges brought against him. But it is evident that Stephen wished to convey how time after time God works new wonders. In the course of history the work of the Spirit was surprisingly new each time. This had been the case in the times of Abraham, Moses, David and Solomon. But the people had never been ready to accept this newness; they had clung to the past, to their "tradition," and had always rejected the innovative dimensions of God's revelation. Once, when they had received the tabernacle from God and Moses, they incorporated it in the worship of Moloch because they could not break with what had become part of their paganized tradition. Now they were so conditioned to formal temple worship in Jerusalem they did not understand that God does not dwell in temples made with hands. In essence their sin was resistance to the Holy Spirit.

Whether Stephen's speech was inspired in the same way as other writers of Holy Scripture, in other words, infallible, is a moot point. His speech was certainly not infallible. But we must focus on this speech as a thing of great significance, for the Holy Spirit had Luke reproduce it in this way. It is therefore still in doubt whether Stephen's reference to the grave Abraham is said to have bought from Hamor, the father of Shechem, should be regarded as an error. The reference can also be viewed as a summary of two different but related purchases: Abraham's and Jacob's. Joseph was buried in a different grave than Jacob (see Genesis 23; 49:29—50:13; Joshua 24:32). But Stephen ignores that difference and refers only to the patriarchs' burial in Canaan. Abraham had bought his burial plot from the Hittites but Joseph was later buried in the parcel Jacob had bought from Hamor. A speech made under the inspiration of the Spirit perhaps lacks the precision of a historian's detailed account.

Main thought: *The service of God in newness of the spirit is glorious.*

Stephen's conflict. Of all the deacons chosen by the congregation in Jerusalem Stephen soon stood out. The Holy Spirit had endowed him with special gifts, not only for the diaconate, but also for witnessing and doing many wonders. The Holy Spirit spoke and worked mightily through him. He also clearly saw what the Lord intended, how He was going to fulfill His promise that the gospel would go out to all the nations. The Gentiles would worship the God of Israel. But they would no longer have to do so in the temple in Jerusalem, for the meaning of that temple had been fulfilled in the Christ. We no longer look to the revelation of God in the temple, but to His revelation in Christ who is now in heaven and is the Savior of the world. God does not dwell in a shadowy temple anymore but in the hearts of His people by His Holy Spirit.

Stephen's speech was about all those things. He saw the glory of the dispensation of the New Testament which also made his own life glorious. Of course, in Jerusalem people resisted his message. They could not accept that Israel's special privilege was a thing of the past and that God was now extending His covenant to all the nations.

There were many synagogues in Jerusalem; in fact, every group had its own. People who had lived abroad spoke a foreign language and after they had returned to Jerusalem joined with others of similar background to form their own synagogue. Especially Jews who had come back from abroad offered strong opposition to Stephen. What was the point of returning to Jerusalem if it had lost its special meaning in the covenant of the Lord? However, they could not simply ignore the wisdom and the Spirit by which Stephen spoke.

Their hostility stirred up a commotion among the people and their leaders. They charged him with blasphemy against Moses and God. And when the atmosphere was sufficiently poisoned, they seized Stephen and brought him before the council. There were enough false witnesses on hand who would accuse him of blaspheming the temple and the law. They claimed to have heard Stephen say that Jesus would destroy the temple and set aside the law. But was it really blasphemy for him to say the promises given in the temple and the law had been fulfilled perfectly?

The council looked hard at Stephen and they saw his face shining like that of an angel. Stephen was being glorified, as it were, before their very eyes. His life had already been glorious because by faith he stood in the freedom of the Spirit. He saw more than others and he rejoiced in the Spirit's work. His face shone from that inner glory. Thus the life of the believers is glorified by faith. Stephen stood alone but the life of the whole community of believers is glorified just as his was.

The testimony of history. Asked if the accusations were true, Stephen gave them an answer. But like the apostles before him, he did not give a defense of his ministry; his answer was an attack on the Sanhedrin; it was both a testimony and a sermon. He showed how, throughout history, God in His grace repeatedly brought about something new and surprising. Yet how little the people had known the Lord or had trusted in Him.

Stephen recalled how God called Abraham and his kindred out of his land and promised them the land of Canaan. Abraham believed the Lord and accepted the promise, even though not an inch of ground in Canaan belonged to him yet. All the patriarchs believed this promise. They set great store by burial in Canaan even while their people lived as aliens in Egypt.

The people, however, often acted differently than the patriarchs. Although they groaned under the oppression in Egypt, they lacked the faith to expect deliverance from the hand of God. By a very special vision God called Moses to be their deliverer. But what was the people's attitude towards Moses from the very beginning? He was in the desert with the Angel of the Lord and took the Word of God to the people, but instead they stooped to idol worship at Sinai. The people did not see the glory of God's revelation.

In the desert God had given them the tabernacle (tent of witness). At David's request it was replaced with a temple by Solomon. The people usually did not see the glory of this revelation either. They enclosed God within the temple and thereby made God equal to men, while in reality heaven is His throne and earth His footstool. The temple symbolized a prophecy of His indwelling in the hearts of His people through His Spirit.* But the people were not inclined to see the temple this way. Such a symbol far exceeded their human imagination and expectation. Had they recognized the symbolism they would have become humble before God. But they didn't; thus they always resisted the work of the Holy Spirit, just as they were resisting it now.

Always the people had persecuted the prophets who pointed to the glory of God's revelation, a glory far surpassing all human standards. And now that the full glory had come to them in Jesus Christ they betrayed and murdered Him. They had thereby rejected the law in which the promise of the Righteous One, the Redeemer, had been given. And yet the law was so glorious. That was evident from the fact that it had been delivered by angels. Those angels revealed the majesty of God's grace.

Stephen's victorious death. When Stephen had finished speaking, his interrogators were enraged. How dared he accuse them of rejecting the law? But Stephen was not intimidated by their rage. Full of the Holy Spirit and gazing into heaven, he saw the glory of God and the Lord Jesus standing at the right hand of God. The glory of the grace of God, by which God accomplished great and new things, Stephen was now privileged to see. And he testified to what he saw.

Stephen's witness was a warning to them. God wished to reveal Himself to them through the glory written on Stephen's

---

*See Vol. I, pp. 310-17; Vol. II, pp. 202-211—TRANS.

face. But they would have none of it; they shouted loudly to drown him out and covered their ears. Thus they willfully rejected the grace of the Lord. They pounced on him and cast him out of the city with orders that he be stoned. They still maintained a semblance of justice because the witnesses had to throw the first stones.

While pelted by stones he prayed, "Lord Jesus, receive my spirit." He surrendered a life, lived in communion with God, into the hands of his Lord. After that he cried out with a loud voice for all to hear: "Lord, do not hold this sin against them." He had not become embittered against his enemies, for their enmity was really directed against the Lord and against His Spirit. He was moved with compassion for them and prayed for them. Stephen died a victorious and glorious death in accordance with the dispensation of the Spirit, whom he saw through faith. In life and death, it should be that way for the entire congregation of believers.

The line extended. Devout men carried Stephen to his grave and made great lamentation over him. From this fact alone it was already clear how Stephen's faith did not die with him. Furthermore, God was also at work preparing something equally wonderful. A certain Saul was present at Stephen's death. He was delighted for he despised Stephen's message. Confirmed Jew that he was, he assisted in the execution by "holding the coats" of those who stoned Stephen. In the meantime it was Saul whom God had chosen to carry on Stephen's message. Imagine the change of heart required of Saul! Another of God's great miracles! What could ever prevent His counsel from being carried out?

Immediately, with Saul still hostile to the Gospel, persecution broke out against the church in Jerusalem. Nobody dared to touch the apostles, but the other members were thrown into prison. Saul even dragged men and women out of their homes. Yet even this persecution served the Lord's purposes by spreading the gospel, for many fled from Jerusalem and proclaimed the Word of the Lord elsewhere in the land.

30: Victory over Magic

Acts 8:5-25

I have no wish to focus on the figure of Simon the magician. More importantly, Samaria became obedient to the Word of God and thus was delivered from magic.

Magic is man's attempt to subject divine powers to himself and to use them for his own purposes. There is no need to discuss the various means used to achieve that end but we should be aware of the forms of magic found within the Christian church. I mean not only the magical view of the sacraments in the Roman Catholic Church. Administering the Word or praying can well be made into a means of magic. And men who wish to manipulate God as, for example, in their legalistic righteousness, are also practising magic. Such is a rejection of the covenant in which a supreme God gives us His communion through His Holy Spirit, a communion that gives us life.

In verse 5 we read how Philip preached Christ to the Samaritans. Christ was the focal point of his preaching. Probably this short description of the content of his message was intentional. Christ is opposite to magic. The revelation of Jesus Christ does not encourage man to control divine powers but places man in subjection to the Word of grace and incorporates him into the Kingdom of grace. God has come down to us in Christ and thereby conquers us.

Main thought: *Samaria delivered from magic by the Word of the Spirit.*

The gospel of Christ and magic. Because of the persecution many had to flee Jerusalem. Among them was Philip who, like

160

Stephen, was a deacon. Philip traveled to the capital of Samaria whose people were of mixed Jewish and non-Jewish ancestry. These Samaritans often talked about the God of Israel who had revealed Himself to His people through Moses but they did not want to worship Him in the temple in Jerusalem. They had purposely set up their own form of worship in Samaria. Was Philip allowed to preach the gospel to these racially mixed people? He must have thought so; after all, he had Jesus' own example.

Samaria was under the spell of a certain magician called Simon who pretended to be a redeemer. He claimed he could open the way to God. He could mobilize divine powers and make them serve the redemption of man. He displayed his art in many forms of magic which always enchanted the people. They called him the great power of God, the promised Redeemer.

Through the person of Simon satan had the Samaritans in his power; he had the people spellbound. If a man could enlist divine powers, Samaritans believed, he had God in his power. And that meant the liberation of life! There were many such fanatics in those days but we also have them in our midst. If we could manipulate God and have Him do as we please, and if we could be supreme, we would be in total control. To accomplish that men often employ all available means, including prayer.

However, faith and the gospel are something else entirely. We do not rule over God; He rules over us in His grace. That was the message Philip brought to Samaria's capital. He told the Samaritans how God in His sovereign grace had come to us again in Jesus Christ. And he called for submission in faith to the Word of grace. Philip spoke by the Holy Spirit who in turn confirmed the Word through the signs and wonders Philip performed. The Word of grace wrestled with magic, as it does to this day all over the world. Shall we acknowledge God's supreme sovereignty over us or subordinate Him to our own machinations?

Submission in faith. Actually many in that city came to believe. For each person this required a complete turnabout, subordinating himself to God's grace. Who but the powerful Holy Spirit can bring about such a reversal? Our sins have blinded us to the extent that our own efforts at deliverance are doomed.

Not that the new believers, having submitted, suddenly felt chained to oppressive bonds. On the contrary, they rejoiced and the city was filled with happiness because they knew their deliverance had really come. Our freedom lies in communion with God which we obtain by faithfully submitting to His Word. The Samaritans now saw that their fascination with Simon had been a yoke. Following him brought no deliverance but bondage to sin and fear. As they were baptized they received the sign that the old man, the magic addict, had died and that the new man, the Christ follower, was alive.

Even Simon believed and was baptized. He abandoned his magic and submitted to Jesus Christ's reign of grace. At some point he was tempted to "purchase" extra power, possibly as a means of increasing his power. If faith does not make us totally submissive we are tempted to utilize the gifts of the Spirit for our own purposes. In any case, Simon was baptized and remained constantly in the company of Philip, amazed at the signs and great miracles Philip performed. Was his amazement, his faith in the Lord's grace genuine? Or did he merely ingratiate himself with the disciples in an effort to increase his influence?

The gift of the Holy Spirit. The apostles in Jerusalem heard that Samaria had accepted the Word of God. The apostles did not have the slightest objection that the gospel had been preached there. They remembered they had been in Samaria with the Lord Jesus more than once. They sent Peter and John, so the Samaritans might enjoy the fellowship of faith with the congregation in Jerusalem.

When Peter and John arrived in Samaria, they learned that many had come to believe and been baptized, but nothing was seen of the special gift of tongues which was repeatedly evident in Jerusalem. In that city the believers frequently prophesied or spoke in foreign tongues. This was a revelation of the powerful working of the Spirit in them which showed how an endowment of the Holy Spirit effected complete glorification of their lives. If Samaritans also received this gift of the Holy Spirit, they would be one in spirit with the Jerusalem congregation. It would prove that the Holy Spirit also worked through them. Therefore Peter and John prayed for the Samaritans to receive this gift and laid their hands on them. In so doing this they signified their solidarity with the whole community of believers and with the Head of the Church. When the Samaritans submitted the Holy Spirit also came upon them and they prophesied.

These special signs were only for that first period of struggle during which the church took root. They no longer occur. But the power of the Holy Spirit who produces faith and establishes communion with Jesus Christ and fellowship with His church is still with us today. That faith contains the promise and desire for the life's perfect glorification. In intimate communion with God through the Holy Spirit there is complete deliverance from witchcraft and superstition.

The judgment on the sorcerer. When Simon saw that through the laying on of the apostles' hands the Holy Spirit was given he offered to buy this power. He saw this act as a kind of magic, the secret of which could be sold. He had not recognized the sovereignty of God's grace. Simon seemed to think that the act of humble faith and submission to Christ on the part of the apostles was a variety of magic. Instinctively he saw the laying on of hands as a tool with which to seize divine powers. But what was really there he could not see.

Peter replied: "Your silver perish with you, because you thought you could obtain the gift of God with money!" Peter reproached him for lack of faith in the Word of God and pointed out that his heart was full of bitter premeditations. Simon tried to cheapen the grace of God into mere trickery. He would have to make a complete break, repent of his wickedness and turn to God's grace by faith. Peter urged him to pray for forgiveness.

Simon asked the apostles to pray for him, that judgment might not come upon him. Had he really been shaken by Peter's admonition he would have cried out to God. We are not told whether he was ever converted. But before we turn away from our self-sufficiency and ask God for His mercy the Spirit must often send us through the crucible.

After confirming Philip's preaching the apostles returned to Jerusalem. On their way home they preached the gospel in many Samaritan villages. Thus was Samaria opened up to the gospel. The Lord Jesus Christ had added Samaria to His reign of grace.

31: The Way to the Gentiles

Acts 8:26-40

With an incident such as this there is great danger that we tell the story of the government official's conversion by emphasizing the personal life of this important person and in the process lose sight of how Philip was led to this baptism by the Holy Spirit. Here the first Gentile was baptized. To get here the church was led along a surprising path. Faith in Jesus Christ flourishes without regard to race, nation or status. The covenant is open to all. It is the Holy Spirit who brings Jew and Gentile together in the covenant.

Main thought: *Through the work of the Holy Spirit Jew and Gentile meet each other in the covenant.*

Directed to the Gentiles. God had greatly blessed Philip's preaching in Samaria to a people of mixed ancestry. Yet various ties linked them to Israel. The Lord had to lead the church still further; bring it to the Gentiles. The church had to understand that salvation in the Lord is for all nations because God had opened up His covenant to all peoples. Salvation was no longer restricted to Israel; Israel no longer had any special privileges. But the church could not digest this thought right away. Only the Holy Spirit could bring the church to acceptance.

For that purpose the Lord again selected Philip. An angel of the Lord appeared to Him and said, "Rise and go southward on the road that goes down from Jerusalem to Gaza, which is a desert road.'' Evidently Philip had already learned that to be in the service of the Lord requires unquestioning obedience. Thus Philip rose and went to the Gaza road.

When he had reached it he saw a chariot coming. Obviously it belonged to an important official. The man in the chariot was a man from the south, the minister of finance at the court of the queen of Ethiopia. He was reading out loud from a scroll he was holding up in front of him. The Holy Spirit spoke in Philip's heart, telling him to join the man on his chariot. It was for reasons of meeting the Gentile that the Lord sent Philip out here. It must have seemed strange to Philip but he had learned to obey. He would presently see the great work of the Spirit who was transmitting faith from Israel to the Gentiles. Then he would be truly amazed. The Spirit's work in the world is full of surprises. The whole world is summoned to obedience of faith in Jesus Christ. And while the Spirit calls in His own way, at His own time, we must stand ready to obey His summons.

Come from the ends of the earth. How did the official happen to be on this particular road? He had come from Ethiopia to worship in Jerusalem, apparently on a leave of absence granted by his queen. The urge in him must have been strong. He had somehow heard of the God of Israel and he longed for the knowledge of His name.

Thus he had arrived in Jerusalem. No matter how wonderful to be where the true God was worshiped, his stay in Jerusalem must have been a disappointment. He had not been incorporated into Israel and thus was outside the covenant. He was only permitted to come into the Court of the Gentiles and was restricted to worshiping from afar. His heart must have longed for a more intimate communion with God. He had come from the end of the known world but his visit had not brought him any closer spiritually.

Puzzled he had started for home. However, he had with him one of the sacred books of Israel and, unwilling to postpone examining it, he started reading on the journey back.

This too was the work of the Holy Spirit. It was He who made the man restless and brought him to Jerusalem. It was He who directed him to examine the Scriptures. The Holy Spirit wanted to bring him near who was afar, to have him share in the communion with God in His covenant. Always we are amazed at where the Holy Spirit goes to find people in order to bring them to the Lord's fellowship.

Proclaiming the gospel. When Philip approached the chariot, he heard the official reading the fifty-third chapter of the prophet Isaiah about the humiliation and exaltation of the Lord Jesus. That must have moved Philip deeply. Here was a Gentile reading about the suffering and condemnation of the Lord Jesus! Philip interrupted to ask if he understood what he was reading. The official replied that he could not because there was no one to explain it. He invited Philip to explain the Word to him. Evidently he had paid attention to the words he had read for he asked who was meant in the chapter.

What a splendid opportunity Philip had to proclaim the gospel! Knowing it was the Holy Spirit who had given him this opportunity, he witnessed about Jesus, starting with this chapter. He also knew it was God's intention to have the gospel preached to the Gentiles. As he explained the good news to the man, Philip must have seen more and more clearly that only the covenant and faith in Jesus is important. God laid down no restrictions for race or nation. And how much the evangelist had to tell that foreigner who understood and drank in the words of the Scripture. Faith rose up in him to full clarity.

Here Philip was faced with the miraculous activity of the Spirit. The Spirit had brought them together and opened the Gentile's heart in faith to the Word of the Lord.

Oneness in the covenant. As they went along the road and talked together they came to a pool of water. Apparently Philip had told him that all who believed were baptized as a sign of the new life in communion with God through His covenant. This had made an impression on the government official. If only he too might belong to this new fellowship; accordingly, when he saw the water he asked, "See, here is water; what is to prevent me from being baptized?'' If we believe in the Lord we long for the sign of our incorporation into the covenant.

Philip faced a tremendous decision. Was he permitted to baptize a Gentile? According to the Word of God the only requirement for baptism was faith in Jesus. Moreover, he knew that the Holy Spirit had opened the official's heart. Without hesitating he made his decision: ''If you believe with all your heart, you may be baptized.'' Instantly Philip saw that the covenant had been opened up to the Gentiles. In reply, the government official confessed his faith: ''I believe that Jesus Christ is the Son of God.'' In Jesus Christ the full love of God has come to us and that love embraces all nations.

They went down into the water and the official was baptized. It was a sign that the self-sufficiency of the Gentile had died; within him had risen faith in Jesus Christ. That must have been a very special moment for Philip as well. Jew and Gentile were one in the covenant through faith in Jesus Christ. All obstacles had been overcome. How the angels must have rejoiced and glorified God!

Suddenly the Spirit of the Lord took Philip away. Had the beautiful unity been broken? The minister knew the answer to that; he did not go back to Jerusalem to look for Philip, but went on his way rejoicing. He knew that the oneness in the faith would be preserved even though they did not see each other. The Holy Spirit would continue to tend to His own work. That too is an insight and trust that arouses amazement. Is there anything the Holy Spirit cannot do? For that matter, is there anything we cannot do provided our hearts have been opened by faith? The official must have spread the good news of the gospel in Ethiopia. Later Ethiopian Christians tied in with the world church and a flourishing national church developed.

Philip was next seen at Azotus on the coast. He preached uninterruptedly. He proclaimed the gospel in all the towns until he came to Caesarea, where he stayed a long time. Thus the message of salvation was spread abroad and the church took root everywhere.

32: Called to Be a Bearer of the Word

Acts 9:1-30

To put the heading "The Conversion of Saul" above this section would suggest a description of Saul's personal conversion. However, as the Christ said to Ananias, Saul was called to carry the name of the Lord before the Gentiles. He was the Lord's chosen instrument. As such, he was elected. Election, however, is not limited to eternal blessedness, but includes election to a present calling. It was this way for Saul and for all of God's elect. Like Saul, every individual believer has been called to carry the Word of God to the world. That must not make us overlook what was special in Saul's calling. It was his special task to carry the gospel before the Gentiles; he was to be a pioneer for the gospel in the Gentile world. Saul, above all others, proclaimed unequivocally that the covenant of the Lord had been opened up to the Gentiles.

In verse 7 we read that although the men accompanying Saul heard the voice, they saw no one. In chapter 22:9 it says that although they saw the light, they did not hear the voice. Probably this must be understood to mean that while they saw a light and heard a sound they did not see the figure of Christ or understand the words.

Verse 23 reads "When many days had passed" which refers to Saul's stay in Damascus. Very likely we must place his stay in Arabia in this period of time. From there he returned to Damascus (see Galatians 1:17). The visit in Jerusalem was very brief, only fourteen days (Galatians 1:18, 19). After that he stayed in Tarsus for about ten years.

Main thought: *The calling of the Spirit to be a bearer of the Word of God.*

Hostility to the gospel. Saul's persecution of the community of believers in Jerusalem continued. When the gospel was being proclaimed everywhere and everywhere disciples were being won, Saul requested letters of recommendation from the high priest to the synagogues in Damascus. Damascus, of course, lay outside the borders of Palestine but the high priest had sufficient authority over the synagogues of the Jews there that they would obligate them to assist Saul in his persecution of believers. Saul wanted to drag the believers in Damascus to Jerusalem to be judged.

No matter what the cost, Saul intended to arrest the gospel in its course. Why was he so hostile to the gospel? He was a gifted man, who had been educated in the manner of the Pharisees in the school of Gamaliel, a member of the strictest sect of the Pharisees. What's more, he was full of burning zeal for the sect and wanted to earn his salvation by his own works. His whole life had been possessed by that thought. And now the gospel proposed the totally opposite message that salvation, the redemption of our life, is a gift of God's grace. Saul couldn't tolerate that message, for it denied everything he believed.

And yet the Lord Jesus had great plans for this Saul. He was to carry the gospel to the Gentiles and lead the church in confessing that the covenant of the Lord had been opened up to the Gentiles. Saul would certainly not have been our choice but the Lord's calling can turn a person completely around. And was the Lord not already making him restless? Was his rage against the gospel not an attempt to silence the inner restlessness and emptiness of his Pharisaical way of life? Jesus later had to warn him that by persecuting believers he was simply hurting himself. He had been called long ago; his continued resistance was self-destructive. He had been present at the death of Stephen; he had read the Scriptures; he had heard of the Lord Jesus. Yet he did not want to submit and instead raged on. What would Christ have to do to turn him around? How would he be broken and become an instrument in the Lord's hand?

Encounter with Christ. When Saul and his party came near Damascus, suddenly a light from heaven shone around them all. Saul fell to the ground and heard a voice saying to him, "Saul,

Saul, why do you persecute me?'' Evidently he also saw some kind of figure in the light, for he said, "Who are you, Lord?" To which the Lord replied, "I am Jesus, whom you are persecuting. It is hard for you to kick against the pricks" (compare Acts 26:14). The glorious grace of the Lord shone around him. Later he recalled that the light was brighter than the sun. The sun, after all, owes its light to the grace of the Lord. That grace far surpasses the light of the sun in glory. However, to Saul the splendor of God's grace was horrifying because he was hostile to that grace. The Lord appeared and revealed Himself to Saul and at the same time revealed Saul to himself as the Lord's persecutor. This struck Saul down.

Trembling and amazed, he asked what the Lord wanted him to do (compare Acts 22:10). Then the Lord only instructed him to go to Damascus, where he would be told what to do. When he got up he was blinded; the men who were with him had to lead him by the hand. The others had seen some light but no figure; they had heard a sound but not understood the words. Only Saul had been struck and blinded because he was raging against the Lord even while the Lord was seeking him.

In Damascus he was totally blind for three days. During that time he neither ate nor drank. He was completely crushed and could think of nothing but the enmity between the Lord and himself. The Lord was against him and he was against the Lord. In his blindness he discovered himself. He realized that in fact he had been blind all along, blind in his opposition to Christ and his persecution of Christians. During those three days he prayed for deliverance. How could he be reconciled with the Lord? Was the Lord's rough treatment of him evidence that the Lord sought to save him, not destroy him? Slowly Saul must have learned what grace meant. At this time he had not the slightest idea what kind of calling the Lord had in mind for him. First he had to learn what it meant to live by grace alone; otherwise he would remain unsuited for the gospel.

His eyes illumined. On the third day the Lord appeared in a vision to Ananias, a disciple in Damascus. When the Lord called him he answered, "Here I am, Lord." That suggested he was wholly prepared to listen and to serve. Whether this was entirely true we shall see. The Lord told him to go to the street called "Straight" and inquire at the house of a man named Judas about Saul of Tarsus. The Lord told Ananias that this Saul had seen a vision in which a man called Ananias laid his hands on him, restoring his sight. Having heard of Saul, Ananias promptly had some objections. Ananias was prepared to be obedient up to a point. He still had to get used to the Lord's wonders. Patiently the Lord explained to him what He wanted of Saul. He had chosen Saul to be an instrument to carry His name to Gentiles and kings and the sons of Israel. Saul would have to suffer much for the name of the Lord. The Lord gave Ananias a glimpse into His counsel and a look at Saul's future life. Through Saul the Lord would fulfill His promise that the Gentiles would come to know of Him.

After that Ananias went obediently. He found Saul and laid his hands on him, explaining the Lord had sent him so that he might regain his sight and be filled with the Holy Spirit. The shells fell from Saul's eyes and he was healed. This healing reminded him of his blindness in former days but it also told him the Lord had removed his blindness, that is, his guilt. Addressed as a brother in the Lord Saul believed the Lord had sought him, believed there was grace and forgiveness for his sins. He was baptized signifying the washing away of his sins and his ingrafting into the church of the Lord. Saul had become a new man; he could hear the Lord's calling. Now he recovered and returned to life, risen from his sins and self-righteousness.

The time of testing. After his conversion Saul remained in Damascus for a while. Immediately he proceeded to proclaim in the synagogues that Jesus is the Son of God, that in Him the fullness of God's love has appeared to us.

This caused great dismay in the synagogues, because the Jews were well aware of the purpose of Saul's visit to Damascus! As he preached, God's grace in Jesus Christ became clearer and clearer and he proved to the Jews from the Scriptures that Jesus was the promised Messiah.

He stayed for some time. In the meanwhile he also made a trip to Arabia. Upon his return he started preaching again but found the Jews' animosity had grown to the point of planning to kill him. Day and night they guarded the gates to prevent him from leaving the city. But one night the disciples lowered him down from the city wall in a basket and he escaped. It was ironic that he should be subjected to the same hostility he formerly inflicted on others. His preaching was made ineffective by their hate; he could not change their hearts. Damascus was a sore trial for Saul. However, it must have made him understand God's electing grace all the more.

From Damascus he went to Jerusalem. There he wanted to join the disciples but they did not trust him. He had his past against him. However, Barnabas had heard what happened on the road to Damascus and how Saul had preached Jesus Christ in the synagogues there. He therefore recommended him to the apostles who then accepted him. In Jerusalem he also spoke boldly in the name of the Lord Jesus. He preached mainly to Greek-speaking Jews (Hellenists) because he also came from abroad. As in Damascus, Jerusalem also plotted to kill him. So the brethren sent him away, accompanying him as far as Caesarea.

From Caesarea he went to his home town, Tarsus, in Asia Minor where he withdrew for at least ten years. There the Lord taught him many things in order to prepare him for his future calling. This was the time of his testing, his sanctification and maturing. The Lord had determined all this for him beforehand so that He might be able to use Saul in His service to carry the Word to the Gentiles. Thus the Lord leads all those who believe in Him in preparation for His service.

33: Everlasting Life

Acts 9:31-43

When the widows showed Peter the coats and garments Dorcas had made, they did so not as a boastful display of her good works. Dorcas' sewing for charity was simply a work of the Holy Spirit. In Joppa people were dismayed that this work of the Spirit had been discontinued. With the raising of Dorcas it could now be continued. This revealed that the work of the Spirit could not be destroyed; life that is of the Spirit is everlasting. The gates of hell—that is, of the realm of the dead—will not prevail against the community of believers. The life of the Christian community will not be delivered up to futility and oblivion in the realm of the dead. Dorcas' life of charity conquers death and will one day be restored to eternal splendor because it is of the Spirit.

This is the real work of charity: to be prepared to sacrifice one's life for Christ's sake. Such indeed is the life lived out of the Spirit of Christ.

The healing of Aeneas, bedridden for eight years, also shows that our lives may not be spent in emptiness.

These miracles were performed by Peter, the one who had confessed Jesus as the Christ, the Son of God, after which confession Christ gave the promise that the gates of hell would not prevail against His church. The church which holds to this confession is invincible.

Main thought: *By His Spirit Christ grants everlasting life.*

The healing of the paralytic. After Saul's conversion persecution of the believers stopped. Meanwhile, churches had been established throughout Judea, Galilee and Samaria. These churches continued to grow. Internally, they were strengthened in

173

the faith. The believers lived in the fear of the Lord; they bowed before His Word and before His gracious counsel, and thus were comforted by the Holy Spirit.

Peter visited all those churches, including the one in Lydda. Between Peter and these believers there was always the fellowship of faith. They rejoiced in the life that had been given them in communion with the Lord Jesus Christ through the Holy Spirit.

In Lydda Peter encountered a person who had been bedridden for eight years, a man named Aeneas. This man was condemned to an inactive life. From all appearances he led a futile existence. But there can be much fruit in the life of a person who has to endure years of suffering if only he bows in faith before the Lord. It could be that way with Aeneas too. However, he was unable to take an active part in common social intercourse. So here the powerful life of the Spirit encountered the impotence that sin had brought into his life. Peter and the congregation of believers evidently were aware of this conflict.

In the Lord Jesus Christ God's full love has come to us, a love that restores life. Peter therefore said in simple trust: "Aeneas, Jesus Christ heals you; rise and make your bed." At once Aeneas stood up. He too saw by faith that the Lord Jesus had come to give us life. In his restored life he would serve the Lord. This healing was a revelation of the powerful life granted to us by the Holy Spirit.

Such miracles no longer take place. Sometimes we may have to suffer our whole life long. But even then we must hold fast to God's revelation that the Lord Jesus came to give us life in all its fullness. Then we believe in life, even when in some respects we suffer under the power of death. Life has still won the victory.

Many residents of Lydda and surrounding area saw Aeneas after he had been healed. Many were confronted with the power of life as given by the Spirit. As a result many turned to the Lord.

The raising of Tabitha. Near Lydda was the town of Joppa, where a certain woman named Tabitha, or Dorcas, lived. This woman, a believer, did a great deal for the needy. All her life she offered herself up for others, though not in the sense that she lost her own life in the process. To save our lives means to surrender them to the Lord and, for His sake, to our fellow-men.

Just at this time Dorcas became ill and died. They did not bury her right away but laid her in an upper room. No one could imagine that an end had come to this blessed life. In Dorcas they had seen the fruit of a life lived out of the Spirit. All the saints rejoiced in such a life. It simply could not be true that it had been cut off. Their faith struggled within them, the same faith by which they had seen Dorcas' life as the fruit of the Spirit.

Then they heard that Peter was in Lydda. They had probably also heard of the healing of Aeneas. The Word that Peter preached had the power of healing. Was it not possible He could bring Dorcas back to life? In any case, Peter had to be informed of her death. They could not simply resign themselves to being conquered by death without making an attempt to fight back. So they sent two men to Lydda to ask Peter to come as soon as possible.

Immediately Peter went back with them. They took him to the upper room where Dorcas lay. The distraught women showed him the coats and garments Dorcas had made for them, the fruit of a life lived out of the Spirit. Could this now be over forever?

Peter understood this could not be the end. The life-giving Word protested within him against death. The life of the Spirit is not just temporary and fleeting but eternal. Peter dismissed them, then knelt down and prayed. Turning to the body, he said, "Tabitha, arise!" She opened her eyes and sat up. Then he led her back to the believers in Joppa. Many witnessed the power of the Word of life and became converted.

All who see in faith are further strengthened by faith. If we live with the Lord and give ourselves to Him and our fellow-man this life is not just for a time, soon to pass into oblivion. Life in the Spirit is victorious over death. It originates with God and one day will be restored to glory. Thus we do not live in vain, but we know the purpose of our life, namely, to bear everlasting fruit for God. That fruit may not be identical to that of Dorcas but each life requires sacrifice. In giving our life for the Lord's sake it is preserved for ever.

34: The Cleansing of the Gentiles

Acts 10 and 11

The minister of finance of Candace, queen of Ethiopia, was only a single convert; here we read (11:1) that the Gentiles in general received the Word of God. Peter required a vision from heaven before he felt free to baptize Gentiles. Moreover, the Holy Spirit first came upon the hearers of the gospel before they were baptized. Usually the order was the other way around. Peter needed this sign before he felt free to baptize the converted Gentiles. He learned that God is no respecter of persons. He had not adopted Israel as His people because they were better than every other people. He now extended His covenant to include all nations. Anyone who feared Him and did what was right—that is, who in faith put his hope in Him and lived before His face—was acceptable to Him. It was to people who recognized the Lord's original covenant with Israel that the preaching of the gospel was directed. Through that proclamation they would come to the freedom of the Spirit. Such freedom made it unnecessary for them to be incorporated into Israel by circumcision. It was entirely possible for Jewish believers to enjoy fellowship with Gentiles in the Spirit through faith in Jesus Christ. That the church began to realize this meant an enormous transition in those days. When Peter later broke off communion with Gentile believers in Antioch (Galatians 2:11-21) it represented a sinful step backwards, especially when seen in the light of this passage.

Main thought: *Through the Holy Spirit all nations are cleansed in the covenant.*

The hour of remembrance with God. After Peter performed the miracle in Joppa, he stayed in the home of a certain Simon, a leather craftsman. While there something peculiar happened in Caesarea, a coastal town about 45 kilometers away. A company of Roman soldiers, consisting of Roman citizens, was quartered there. The centurion in charge, a man named Cornelius, together with his household, feared the God of Israel. He had not been incorporated into Israel but he worshiped the Lord, prayed daily and gave liberally to the people of the Lord. Through his association with the Jews he had heard of the Lord and his heart had been won over.

However, that was like serving the Lord from a distance, for he did not belong to the covenant. This must have been difficult for him and no doubt he sought prayerfully to know the Lord's will. Then God provided a solution for his difficulties in a way that far exceeded any of Cornelius' expectations.

One day, about mid-afternoon, an angel of the Lord appeared to him in a vision and called him by his name. When he asked what the angel wanted of him, the angel replied that the Lord was mindful of his prayers and alms and was providing a way out of his difficulties. In His grace the Lord addressed Himself to Cornelius' life, the life of a Gentile. What happened to Cornelius was the Lord's work. Now was the time to bring that work to its full glory. God was going to adopt the Gentiles into His covenant. Cornelius was to send messages to Simon Peter in Joppa, who would tell him what he should do.

When the angel had left, Cornelius called two servants and a soldier, who also feared the Lord. He told them about the vision he had seen and sent them off to Joppa. Eagerly he must have awaited Peter's arrival. God's good pleasure was directed to the Gentiles for Christ's sake.

Peter's vision. At noon the next day when the messengers of Cornelius were approaching Joppa, Peter was up on the housetop praying. It was mealtime and he was becoming hungry. While his food was being prepared, he too had a vision. He saw the heavens opened and a big linen sheet held up at the four corners coming down to earth. In it were all the four-footed animals of the earth, the wild and creeping animals, and birds of the air. A voice said to him, "Rise, Peter, kill and eat!" That vision and command were well suited to his hunger. Yet he would not eat because the animals he saw were unclean. Consequently, he answered the Lord that he had never yet eaten anything unclean.

In the Old Testament the Lord had made a distinction between clean and unclean animals; actually all animals had become unclean through sin. Those animals the Lord had sanctioned through His covenant to Israel all had to be cleansed. The same was true of mankind. All were unclean; only His people Israel had He wished to sanctify in His covenant. But from now on He intended to cleanse all nations. Therefore a second revelation came to Peter, saying he was not to call unclean what God had made clean. Then the vision disappeared. It was repeated twice more to prevent Peter from concluding the vision was merely a delusion. He was now confronted with the revelation of the tremendous fact that God had cleansed the Gentiles in His covenant.

God shows no partiality. While Peter reflected on this vision, the messengers from Cornelius came to his house and asked for him. The Holy Spirit told him to go with them. When they had conveyed their message, he received them in his house. The following day he went with them, accompanied by some of the brethren from Joppa.

The next day at about the time he was expecting Peter, Cornelius called his family and closest friends together. When Peter arrived, Cornelius came to meet him and fell down at his feet and worshipped him. That was still a mistake, a pagan idea. He thought that the divine power was embodied in Peter. But Peter raised him up and told him he was just an ordinary man whose only task it was to bring the Word of God to Cornelius. As he talked Peter went inside and found many persons gathered there.

Peter then first addressed those people. "You know," he said, "that a Jew may never enter a Gentile's house without becoming defiled." And yet he was doing just that. However, he was not doing it because he had been persuaded by man but by God Himself. God had shown him that he should not consider any man unclean. God's dispensation had now changed, he explained. He had come freely and asked why they had sent for him.

For his part, Cornelius told of the vision and the angel's words. Obedient to that word, they had sent for Peter. They were gathered in the sight of God to listen to the Word of God which Peter was going to bring to them.

Peter now saw how the Lord had prepared the course His gospel was to take in the world. And how he rejoiced! Through the proclamation of the gospel the Lord intended to turn not only to Israel but also to the Gentiles. Now he saw very clearly how Israel was no better than any other nation; God had not chosen Israel because of some special endowment in Israelites. God wished to give the life of faith to all nations and to that end awakened a hunger in them for the gospel. Henceforth the Lord's people would be gathered from all nations. And everyone who looked to Him in faith and who lived as in His presence was acceptable to Him.

Peter told them all this, combining it with the preaching of the gospel of Jesus Christ. All knew about Christ's sojourn on earth, how He had been sent by God and anointed with the Holy Spirit, and how He had ministered among the people, healing and redeeming them. Although He had been delivered up to the death of the cross, God had yet raised Him from the dead. All the apostles were witnesses of this, for He had appeared to them and they had eaten and drunk with Him after His resurrection. They had been commissioned to bear witness of Him, for one day He would come again to judge the living and the dead, according to whether they had accepted the gospel of His death and resurrection. So it had been prophesied of Him in the Old Testament that everyone who believed in Him would receive forgiveness of sins through His name.

Obedient to the One who sent him, Peter showed no partiality either but proclaimed the gospel to the Gentiles just as he did to the Jews. The wall separating Jews from Gentiles had been broken down as a result of the work of the Lord Jesus. There was forgiveness of sins for everyone who believed.

The inclusion of the Gentiles in the covenant. While Peter was still speaking, the Holy Spirit came upon his hearers and they began to speak in foreign tongues to magnify God. The Holy

Spirit opened their hearts in faith to the gospel and made them share in the special gifts He granted in those days. Thus the Spirit ingrafted them into the church of the Lord. The life-giving stream of the Spirit spilled over into the life of these Gentiles.

The men who had come with Peter were amazed at what had happened. No one had expected this. And yet they witnessed the union of Jew and Gentile in the Spirit before their very eyes. At this point Peter said that baptism could not be refused and at his command they were baptized. Thus they received the seal of their incorporation into the church of the Lord and into His covenant. For the believing Jews as well as for these Gentile believers this was a tremendous moment. Undoubtedly they talked about it a great deal during the days that Peter, at their request, stayed on in Caesarea.

In today's world too the Holy Spirit wishes to remove all opposition and bridge all chasms. Through faith in the Lord Jesus Christ all people may now be one.

Giving an account to the mother-congregation in Jerusalem. The apostles and the brethren in Judea heard that the Gentiles also had come to believe in the Word of God. Not everybody liked this idea. They didn't all understand the way of the Holy Spirit yet. When Peter returned to Jerusalem, some criticized him for seeking fellowship with Gentiles. He had eaten with them and thus had set aside all the laws regarding ceremonial purity. Peter had also given up the Old Testament concept that Israel had been set apart from other nations. That change was still too great an obstacle for them. They were not yet aware how God's grace had cleansed the nations and accepted them into His covenant.

Peter explained how it all had happened. Afterwards, they perceived the work of the Spirit and glorified God because He had also given conversion of life to the Gentiles. None other than the Holy Spirit convinced them of this.

The first community of believers among the Gentiles. The Spirit's dynamic did not stop here. The Holy Spirit had other goals as well. The believers who had been scattered abroad as a result of

Saul's persecution had moved far beyond the borders of Palestine. Wherever they went they proclaimed the gospel only to Jews living abroad. Some believers, originally from Cyprus and Cyrene, came to Antioch. They also proclaimed the gospel to the Gentiles. The Lord greatly blessed their preaching, so that many Gentiles believed and were converted.

When this news also reached the church in Jerusalem Barnabas was sent to Antioch to see what had happened. There he saw the grace of God and rejoiced, exhorting them all to remain close to the Lord in faith. Moreover he preached the gospel in Antioch himself, and as a result a large crowd believed in the Lord.

This was no longer merely a group of believers; a true congregation of believers, many of them Gentiles, had been born. Barnabas looked for someone who, with him, could take charge of this church. He thought of Saul, whom he had introduced to the apostles in Jerusalem. Barnabas felt he was the right person, so he went to Tarsus to bring Saul to Antioch. One whole year they taught in the Antioch church and the community of believers grew. Those outside this church also saw very well that this was not just a group or sect of Jews with peculiar ideas of their own, but that a distinct movement was forming. They began to call them "Christians." The name was an honor to the believers for they shared fully in the anointing of Christ.

Contact grew increasingly close between the church in Jerusalem and the one in Antioch. Some prophets came down from Jerusalem to instruct the Antioch believers. One of them, a certain Agabus, prophesied that a great famine was going to come over the entire world. Under the emperor Claudius (A.D. 41-54) this prophecy was fulfilled. Through these prophets the Jerusalem church shared its spiritual gift with the church in Antioch; for its part, the Antioch church sent money, by way of Saul and Barnabas, to support the brethren in Judea, who had become rather poor. This personal contact further strengthened the ties between the two churches.

35: The Victory of the Word of Grace

Acts 12:1-24

James and Peter were persecuted as bearers of the Word of God. After James was killed, Peter was delivered from prison. The impression could not be left that the course of the Word of God might somehow be frustrated. Hence Peter's deliverance.

Yet this deliverance also had great significance for Peter's personal life. He had to put himself again at the service of the gospel, though in a different way. He was forced to flee from Jerusalem. James "the just," the Lord's brother, now took over the leadership from the apostles in the church at Jerusalem. Peter gradually retreated into the background and Saul took his place. For Peter this was the beginning of that special road Christ had prophesied for him (John 21:18, 19).

Main thought: *The Word of grace conquers and reigns supreme.*

Oppression because of the dominion of the flesh. When Saul persecuted the church, the common believers were threatened though the apostles were left alone because the people held them in such high esteem. As a matter of fact, many people held the whole community of believers in high esteem. Some changes occurred after a congregation of Gentiles had been established at Antioch. The gospel was also being preached to the Gentiles, followed by fellowship between Jew and Gentile. Especially the latter was not to some people's liking.

182

This shift of mood, the growing displeasure, among the people was exploited by a man who had long been waiting for such an opportunity. He was King Herod Agrippa I.* His life had taken a strange course. Once, in Rome, he had been deprived of all his rights by Emperor Tiberius and had been near despair. Suddenly, however, he had been elevated to the throne of his grandfather, Herod the Great. In his youth he had been very frivolous, but once he was on the throne he kept the Jewish law as much as he could in order to win support from the Jews.

This opportunistic ruler understood very well that the Word of God called for quite a different rule, namely, the sovereign rule of Jesus Christ. Though not necessarily hostile to earthly rulers, Christ's rule demanded obedience even from them. Of course, to Herod that was unacceptable. Hence, he only saw in Jesus Christ's reign of grace a threat to his own rule.

Now, supported by a shift in popular opinion, he took action. Some who belonged to the church were imprisoned and put to death. He even ventured to seize James, the brother of John. He had him taken prisoner and killed.

The government's "power of the sword" was clearly abused in order to arrest the growth of the gospel. Herod's indiscriminate execution of James was to stop the Word of grace and discredit Jesus Christ. It must have been quite a struggle for James to surrender himself to death for the sake of the gospel, but he gained the victory in that struggle. He must have been troubled especially by the question whether the cause of the gospel would suffer loss as a result. The church too must have been concerned about this question.

James' trial was a test-case for Herod. How would the people and their leaders view the results? He saw that the people approved. As long as the cause of the Kingdom of God appeared to champion Jewish national interests the people still had respect for it. But now that Christ's rule was expanding to all nations and Israel was beginning to love its privileged position, hostility began

---

*This Herod Agrippa had been sent to Rome by his grandfather, Herod the Great, to be educated. He grew up in the imperial court with the young Claudius and was an intimate friend of the emperors Caligula and Claudius. He showed himself a zealous champion of the Jews and bitterly persecuted the nascent Christian movement—TRANS.

to rear its ugly head. Herod and the other leaders, together with all the people, allied against Jesus Christ's reign of grace. The leaders all felt threatened because they sought their own gain rather than Christ's Kingdom.

Assured of the people's approval, Herod proceeded to imprison Peter, the disciple who until now had been most in the foreground. This, Herod thought, would be the decisive blow. However, it was just before the Feast of Passover and the trial had to be put off until after the feast. The church was greatly upset and even Peter in prison must have questioned the will of the Lord. Would he also be killed? The church was greatly attached to Peter and would mourn his death. But what would happen to the gospel and the cause of the Kingdom if Peter were to die? He must have pondered the same question himself. During the days Peter was in prison, the church continually prayed to God on his behalf.

The expectation of the flesh put to shame. The night before the trial a chained Peter was sleeping between two soldiers, while watchmen in front of the door guarded the prison. Suddenly an angel of the Lord stood in the jail and all at once it was wondrously light throughout the prison. The angel woke Peter and as he got up the chains fell off his hands. Peter got dressed, put on his sandals and followed him. Throughout he must have wondered whether he was dreaming.

They passed both guards and left through the iron gate at the entrance to the prison. They went on together for one more street whereupon the angel suddenly disappeared. Outside Peter came to himself at last and realized that his deliverance was real. Herod's evil machinations would be put to shame by God's own hand.

This was undoubtedly a great relief for Peter but he was probably happier to realize that it was impossible to halt the progress of the gospel or to bind the Word of God. That will never be possible, no matter what men and governments undertake against the sovereign Word of grace and the church of the Lord. Nothing can stop the gospel, not even sinful things in our hearts, if the Lord wants His Word to be victorious. This is such a great comfort for all times!

The Spirit's guidance. Peter presumed most of the community of believers would be gathered in the house of Mary, the mother of John Mark. He decided to go there. When he knocked on the door of the gateway the maid who answered recognized Peter's voice. From pure joy she failed to open the gate but instead ran inside to tell the assembled believers that Peter was outside. They told her she was hallucinating but when she insisted it was true, they concluded it was Peter's angel, come to announce his death. Little did they understand the power of the Lord, though they had prayed for Peter's deliverance incessantly. That is how little we are attuned to the Lord's work and the victory of His Word!

Peter continued to knock until they finally let him in. They looked at him in amazement. We stand in awe at God's wonders although at such times He is very close to us. At a sign from Peter they became silent and he explained how the Lord's angel had led him out of prison. Great was their happiness, because they saw that the dynamic of the gospel could not be stopped.

They also rejoiced because they were together again. However a shadow fell over their joy, for the present persecution made it impossible for Peter to remain in Jerusalem. At that time, however, James, the Lord's brother, had begun to assume leadership in the Jerusalem church. They would tell him and all the brethren of Peter's deliverance, that they might also be assured that the course of the gospel could not be stopped. Then Peter said goodbye and left town.

Peter's deliverance brought a great turnabout in his life. He was free again to serve His Lord in preaching the gospel. But he would no longer hold the most important position in Jerusalem; henceforth he would wander from place to place. To spread the gospel over the whole world, someone else, Saul, would be pre-eminent. Peter now dropped into the background. This was a difficult lesson for him even though the Lord Jesus had foretold this to him. It was a contributing factor in his sanctification; his life ended in a martyr's death, through which he glorified God.

Judgment of the Word of grace upon the enemy. The next day there was a great commotion among the soldiers because Peter had disappeared. No one had seen anything. Herod instituted a search for Peter but could not find him. The guards were judicially interrogated but they were unable to shed any light on the matter. Yet Herod held them responsible and had them put to death. He was unwilling to acknowledge the miraculous working of God, or bow before the hand of God. Frustrated by his defeat, Herod took vengeance on innocent men.

From Jerusalem, Herod travelled to Caesarea, where he rested. He was contemplating a war against Tyre and Sidon, cities that would never be able to hold out in a conflict with Herod because Palestine was their granary. Their officials, therefore, approached Blastus, Herod's chamberlain, to beg Herod for peace. This only boosted Herod's pride, however. One day Herod, dressed in royal robes, addressed the people, making such an impression on them that they shouted, "The voice of God and not of a man!"

The bearer of governmental authority was deified, as has so often happened. The king took that honor as his due. Thus he came all the more into conflict with the Kingship of Jesus Christ, who alone is God. The Word of the Kingdom of grace, which he resisted, would fall upon him. An angel of the Lord struck Herod and he was eaten by worms and died. By contrast, the Word spread abroad more and more and the number of confessors of the Christ multiplied. We know that the victory belongs to Him, and His Word reigns supreme.

Christ
and the Gentiles

36: The Door of Faith Opened to the Gentiles

Acts 12:25–14:28

An important remark is made in chapter 14, verse 27, about the fruits of the first missionary journey, namely, that God had opened the door of faith to the Gentiles. This is the first time the phrase "door of faith" is found. The Gentiles now enter the Kingdom of God through faith, and no longer by way of circumcision. Faith is the absolute surrender of oneself to the grace of God. In surrendering ourselves we lose everything upon which we had built our lives. Faith is the narrow gate through which we can take nothing with us. Thus faith is in contrast with every other form of confidence in the world. It stands opposed to the magic of Elymas (13:6, 8), to the self-righteousness of the Jews at (Pisidian) Antioch (13:45, 46, 50) and to the idolatry of the Gentiles at Lystra (14:11-18).

Main thought: *By God's Spirit and Word the door of faith is opened to the Gentiles.*

Sent out by the Holy Spirit. After Barnabas and Saul had brought to Jerusalem the money collected in Antioch for their

189

brothers in Judea, they returned to Antioch. From Jerusalem they took with them John Mark, the son of Mary (Barnabas' sister; see Colossians 4:10).

In Antioch lived several prophets and teachers, among them Barnabas and Saul. The believers had a strong desire to understand the Lord's will regarding the Gentiles. They sensed that their own community was just the beginning of the non-Jewish church. The entire Gentile world would have to be brought into subjection to the reign of Jesus Christ. They waited and prayed for the revelation of the Lord's will. They also fasted; these believers wanted to overcome all their own desires in order to be open to the revelation of the Lord's will.

Truly the Lord answered their prayers. The Holy Spirit prompted these prophets to set Barnabas and Saul apart to preach the gospel to the Gentiles. Again they fasted and prayed, that together with Barnabas and Saul they might submit completely to the Lord's will for the Gentile world. Then they placed their hands on these two servants of God not just as a sign that Barnabas and Saul would be doing their work in fellowship with the prophets and the entire community of believers in Antioch, but also as a sign of the commission of the Holy Spirit. By faith these two had to be obedient to the Spirit's calling and attend to nothing else. In that spirit they went on their way. They took John Mark along on the journey as their assistant.

The gospel and magic. From the Syrian coast they crossed to the island of Cyprus. In Salamis they proclaimed the Word of God in the synagogues of the Jews. The message had to be brought to the Jews first. The opportunities for speaking in their synagogues were readily available. God would open the way to the heathen. They traveled through the whole island until they came to Paphos.

Paphos was the seat of the governor Sergius Paulus, a wise man. He was influenced by a Jew who claimed to be a prophet and who practiced magic. It was a disgrace that a Jew was leading the Gentiles astray in this way. The Word of God had been entrusted to the Jews for the edification of the Gentiles. The Jews also knew the covenant of the Lord, in which they were privileged to live in righteousness through faith in the Lord. Instead, Elymas seduced the governor with lies. He did not preach faithful subjection to the Lord's grace in His covenant; instead he sought to gain control over the divine powers through magic. This was the exact opposite of the righteousness of life in the covenant.

The governor had heard of the work being done by Barnabas and Saul. He summoned them to his court, very eager to hear the Word of God. But Elymas opposed Saul and Barnabas and tried to dissuade the governor from accepting the Christian faith. Saul, who in the Greek world was called Paul, was full of the Holy Spirit and of the wrath of the Spirit. He saw right through Elymas, the enemy of Christ. He looked Elymas straight in the eye and called him a child of the devil, full of deceit and an enemy of everything that is right. In the name of the Lord he caused Elymas to be temporarily blind. The Word of grace, which Paul was privileged to bring, had power over this magician and subdued him. Helpless, he had to be led by others, quite opposite from trying to control divine powers!

Sergius Paulus was overwhelmed by the gospel and submitted to it in faith. The gospel's manifestation of power in the blinding of Elymas was also a contributing factor.

The gospel and self-righteousness. From Paphos on the island of Cyprus they crossed over to Pamphylia, a district of Asia Minor. There John Mark left them to return to Jerusalem. Did he shrink from the difficulties of the journey? Or was he not inspired with missionary zeal, doubting whether the gospel could unconditionally be preached to the Gentiles? Did he too perhaps still feel a certain Jewish jealousy towards the Gentiles? Whatever the case may be, Paul deeply resented John Mark's turning back.

Passing through the countryside they came to another Antioch, a city in Pisidia and a Roman colony. Among the colonists were many Jews who occupied an important place in the city. They belonged to the city's leading families. Because of that the God of Israel was not unknown in Pisidian Antioch. Many Gentiles wanted to serve Israel's God, and therefore associated with the Jews in one way or another. Yet life in the town was not liberated by all this. How could it be otherwise? The Jews themselves were not liberated by faith in the grace of God. Because they thought they had to earn their own righteousness, they lived a life of bondage, a poor example to the Gentiles.

On the sabbath Paul and Barnabas entered the synagogue. After reading from the Law and the Prophets the rulers of the synagogue asked them if they had a word to say to the people. Paul stood up, and after silencing the crowd he spoke to them. He wanted to show that Israel was entitled to nothing; Israel could not, and need not, earn anything for themselves because God had first bestowed His grace upon His people. To illustrate this he gave them a brief overview of their history. Out of free grace God had chosen the patriarchs. By the mighty power of His grace He had delivered the people from Egypt. Although for forty years Israel had sinned against Him in the desert, He had eliminated seven hostile nations and given Israel the land of Canaan as an inheritance. He had guided the people through judges and the prophet Samuel. When they asked for a king, He gave them Saul. And when that first king led the people astray, He put David in his place—David, the man after God's own heart. The entire guidance of His people had been a manifestation of grace.

Then Paul went from King David directly to the Christ. From David's seed God had raised the Savior Jesus, just as He had promised David long ago. John the Baptist had pointed Him out and spoken of His glory. Israel, however, had not received Him but instead delivered Him up to death on the cross. Should not God abandon His people for this rejection? Yet in spite of this God wanted to show His people grace in this Jesus; for God had raised Him from the dead, a deed many persons had witnessed. And now in His name forgiveness of sins was proclaimed. Had it not been prophesied in the Scriptures that the Redeemer would be God's Son and He would indeed die, but that in the grave He would not see corruption but be raised from the dead. It had also been prophesied that everyone who believed in Him would receive forgiveness of sins. Paul warned them against hardening their hearts against this preaching. Judgment would come upon them, a warning also prophesied in the Scriptures.

Many of the Jews and their Gentile associates believed. Paul and Barnabas urged them to hold fast to the grace of God and not seek any other foundation for their lives.

The news of this preaching spread through the whole city. There was, as a matter of fact, a great deal of contact between Jews and Gentiles in this city. The Gentiles requested that during the next sabbath the same message be delivered. On that day almost the whole city gathered to hear Paul and Barnabas preach the Word of God. Again the proud nationalistic Jews rose up in protest against this gospel message. They spoke abusively against these two men. But Paul and Barnabas replied that in accordance with the promise of the Old Testament they had addressed the Word of God to Jews first (see 13:46); now that the Jews rejected the gospel and did not consider themselves worthy of eternal life, Paul and Barnabas were turning to the Gentiles. Throughout they fulfilled the Word of the Lord which prophesied that the Jews would be made a light for the Gentiles. The Gentiles were glad to hear this; they heard and saw that God wanted to show them His grace. All of the Gentiles ordained to eternal life became believers. They regarded this privilege to hear the call of the gospel as evidence of God's electing grace.

From Antioch the Word of the Lord spread through the whole region. This filled many Jews with still greater anger. They stirred up the women of high social standing, who were associated with the Jews and the leading men of the city, in order to persecute Paul and Barnabas and expel them from their country. In return, these two believers shook the dust from their feet in protest against their enemies, symbolizing that the Jews' judgment would be on their own heads. The messengers of the gospel continued on. The believers in Antioch and the surrounding region were not dismayed because of this, but instead were filled with joy and the Holy Spirit. The Spirit guided them further in understanding God's Word and made them live in the joy of faith.

The gospel and idolatry. From Antioch Paul and Barnabas journeyed to Iconium in the district of Galatia. There too they preached the gospel in the synagogue and both Jews and Gentiles listened to them. For a long time they proclaimed the Word of God there with great boldness. The Lord confirmed the Word of His grace by miraculous signs, causing many persons to believe. But dissension also arose here. A disturbance broke out and the enemies of the gospel plotted to stone Paul and Barnabas. The two men saw that it was best to leave the city. But the Spirit of the Word of God remained.

Traveling on Paul and Barnabas came to Lystra, a city in that part of Galatia called Lycaonia. Here the Jewish element was not as strong; the population was predominantly Gentile. Here they hoped to work in peace.

Lystra worshiped Jupiter and Mercury, Greek and Roman gods. The gods of the Greeks and Romans were deified human powers. The worship of human powers is a form of idolatry. They had to make those gods favorably disposed towards them by bringing sacrifices. In contrast, the apostles preached the living God who had shown His favor in Jesus Christ, whom man accepts through faith.

One day Paul was addressing a crowd of people among whom was a man who had been a cripple from birth. His heart was opened to the gospel and he saw that the grace of God had come to redeem life. Would God's grace be able to heal him of his crippled condition? Paul sensed what was going on in this man and saw he had faith necessary for healing. Paul called out in a loud voice for all to hear: "Stand up on your feet!" At that, the man jumped up and began to walk. It was a marvellous demonstration that grace sets life free!

The healing made a deep impression on the inhabitants of Lystra but it turned out to be a wrong impression. It had not shown them the grace of the Kingdom, received only in faith. On the contrary, they saw the healing as a result of the power in Paul and Barnabas. They saw faith as a human power. And in their heathen way they deified this human power. They thought the gods had come down to them. Barnabas they called Jupiter (Zeus), and Paul they called Mercury (Hermes), because he was the speaker. (Mercury was the messenger or spokesman of the ancient deities.) Their paganism had not been broken. They even wanted to offer sacrifices to these "gods" to gain their favor.

Saddened, the apostles rent their clothes and rushed into the crowd, shouting: "We have just been preaching to you that you must reject idols you have made for yourselves and turn to the living God, who made heaven and earth and sea and everything in them. You do not have to make Him favorably disposed by your sacrifices, for He has come in Jesus Christ to bestow His favor upon us. Indeed, in times past He allowed heathen nations to go their own way because they rejected and forgot His covenant. Yet even then He showed you His kindness. That was a witness against your sins. But now He has overlooked your guilty ignorance and wants to reveal His full favor to you.''

The apostles had difficulty keeping the crowd from sacrificing to them. But then their mood changed. They wanted to worship human power, not subject themselves in faith to the grace of God which had appeared. Some Jews came from Antioch and Iconium and stirred up the people. As a result, Paul was stoned and dragged out of the city. They thought he was dead but as it turned out he was still alive. After the believers had gathered around him he got up and went back into the city. The next day he and Barnabas left for Derbe. God had protected Paul because he was to carry the gospel still farther. Lystra seemed to reject the gospel, but even in this place Christ had established His reign, for there were some who believed.

The organization of the communities of faith. After proclaiming the gospel in Derbe they returned home. On the way back they visited the places where they had been. They looked after the organization of the communities of believers by appointing elders in every place. The members approved the appointments by raising their hands. Everywhere the office was to be regarded as giving direction to the community, and thus the communities were molded into unity. Barnabas and Paul also prayed with the congregations and exhorted them to abide in the faith.

From Asia Minor they returned again to Antioch, from which they had set out. There they reported all the great things God had done through them and how He had opened the door of faith for the Gentiles. They stayed there a long time with the disciples. The first thrust had been made into the Gentile world (heathendom) and walls of separation and opposition had fallen down.

37: Freedom of Faith

Acts 15:1-34

Some Judaizing agitators from Judea had come to Antioch, arguing for a continuation of Pharisaic practices in the Christian Church. In matters of worship Pharisaism is characterized by seeking of one's own righteousness; in political affairs it tends towards nationalism. Both meritoriousness and nationalism were continued in Judaism. It demanded strict adherence to the law of Moses, without which one could not be saved. Paul later opposed this renewal of the preaching of meritoriousness, especially in his Epistle to the Galatians. When these Judaizing agitators demanded that Gentile believers be circumcised and thus be incorporated into Israel, they demonstrated their nationalistic character. In contrast, Paul fought especially for justification by faith alone, apart from the works of the law, and for the ecumenical character of the church.

A man could keep strictly to the law of Moses himself without imposing its demands on believers among the Gentiles. That is what James, the brother of the Lord, did; he owes his surname "the Just" to this fact. This did not obscure the gospel, for keeping the law evidently was not regarded as necessary for salvation. For James, observing the Mosaic law was a decision each believer made within the perimeters of Christian freedom. That was the conclusion Paul also reached in his Epistle to the Romans. In that epistle he writes in an entirely different way than in his Epistle to the Galatians, because in Rome this Judaizing tendency was not present.

The decision of the apostolic council in Jerusalem, recorded in this chapter, provided a threefold norm: Gentile believers were to abstain from idolatry, sexual immorality and consuming blood in any form. Keeping the first two requirements would demonstrate the complete

196

break with paganism for idolatry and sexual immorality were the two main sins of heathendom. Abstention from idolatry included not taking part in the banquets in idol-temples, a requirement that later caused a difference of opinion in the community of believers at Corinth. Sexual immorality was often excused among the Gentiles but in that respect too the gospel was unambiguous. As to the third requirement, James states (in verse 21) the reason for the prohibition. In every city there were still synagogues or places where the law of Moses was preached. There was no need to break the continuity with the past in this regard; it would be too great a shock for the Jews and proselytes (Gentiles who had already come to faith in the true God by keeping the law of Moses) if in the Christian community it was permitted to consume blood, regardless how it had been prepared. This prohibition was only temporary and should be distinguished from the prohibition of drinking uncooked blood, a prohibition given in the Noachic covenant and valid for all times.

But the main point about the Jerusalem decision is that the apostles based their three decisions on the acknowledgement that the covenant of the Lord had now been extended to all nations.

Main thought: *Through the Holy Spirit the freedom of faith has been upheld.*

Laying snares for freedom. In the period after the first missionary journey some brethren from Judea came to Antioch. These men spoke up in the congregation, saying that if a person was not incorporated into Israel and did not keep the law of Moses, he could not be saved. This meant all Gentile believers would have to be circumcised. These brethren believed the Lord's covenant was and remained for Israel alone. They did not see that the Lord now wanted to extend His covenant to all the nations. Worse, they wanted to force again upon the church the idea that man has to earn his salvation by keeping the law.

These brethren did not have a commission from the Christian community or from the apostles and elders in Jerusalem. However, they were so bold in their actions that they confused the congregation in Antioch. Paul and Barnabas in particular opposed these zealots. To settle the matter Paul and Barnabas, with certain others, were sent to Jerusalem to consult with the apostles and elders.

Fortunately, the Lord has not kept His salvation restricted to the borders of Israel. What happened on the day of Pentecost promised something else. Neither is our salvation dependent on our merit. By faith in the Lord Jesus Christ we may serve God in freedom.

Deliberations at the apostolic council. Paul and Barnabas and those who went with them traveled through Phoenicia and Samaria, telling all the Christian communities what God had done among the Gentiles. Everywhere their message was met with great joy. No one thought of demanding that Gentiles be incorporated into Israel.

When they had arrived in Jerusalem they reported to the apostles and elders how greatly God had blessed the preaching of the gospel among the Gentiles. Then they explained the controversy that had arisen in Antioch. A meeting was called in the presence of the brethren of the congregation in Jerusalem to deal with the matter.

At that meeting a great dispute arose concerning this question until Peter stood up and spoke to the assembly. He reminded them how God had instructed him to preach the Word of God to the Gentiles and how God had given them His Holy Spirit. The Gentiles were no longer unclean, but cleansed by faith in the Christ. If God had ordained it thus, men were not to test the Spirit of the Lord in the Gentile believers by laying on them a burden which they would not be able to carry. God did not require it and neither could man. Under such a burden the life of the Spirit would need much greater power to reveal itself. Men should not tempt God to such a revelation of power. Even the Jews had never been able to keep the law of Moses. That law had always convinced them of sin in order to lead them to Christ. Now that He had come they were freed from the law in the Old Testament sense. "Along with the Gentile believers," Peter said, "we want to be saved only by faith in the Lord Jesus Christ."

The whole assembly was greatly impressed by Peter's words but were not yet wholly convinced. Then Barnabas and Paul testified of the miraculous signs and wonders God had achieved through them among the Gentiles.

When they were finished, James, brother of the Lord, stood

up. James kept the law of Moses to the letter and was therefore called "the Just." In this controversy the opinion of such a man had great authority. He agreed with what Peter had said and showed from the Old Testament how God had already foretold in His covenant that He would turn to all the nations. He therefore proposed that they only require the Gentile believers to make a complete break with paganism. Furthermore, they should abstain from blood in any form. Though this command no longer applied *literally* to the New Testament churches, it had been so deeply ingrained in the Jews and those Gentiles who came regularly into the synagogues that it would have been too much of a shock if the consumption of cooked blood were to be permitted in the Christian communities.

The decision. James' proposal received general approval; along those lines the decision was made. Thus the confession that the covenant of the Lord had crossed the boundaries of Israel was upheld. A life by faith could bring us all to a service of God in freedom.

The members agreed to send a written statement of their decision to Antioch with Paul and Barnabas who would be accompanied by Judas Barsabbas and Silas, leaders of the Jerusalem congregation. The written communication declared it was agreeable to the Holy Spirit and to the Jerusalem leaders not to burden the Gentile believers with anything beyond the necessary requirements. Thus they were convinced of the Spirit's special guidance in taking this decision. The Holy Spirit Himself had safeguarded the freedom of a life by faith. When the decision was announced in the congregation in Antioch, the people were all happy for the encouragement. In the church, life in freedom had triumphed through the Spirit.

Judas and Silas, both prophets, remained for a while in Antioch, teaching and exhorting the congregation there. Then Judas returned to Jerusalem, but Silas preferred to stay in Antioch. Apparently he was attracted by the prospect of preaching the gospel among the Gentiles.

38: Overlooking the Times of Their Ignorance

Acts 15:35–18:22

With the second missionary journey of Paul the gospel arrived in Europe. Here we have another of the transitions in the work of the Spirit. Anyone who takes the Lord's covenant into account, and thus the nations with their histories, will never say it is only important that here and there some individual persons come to believe or that a congregation has been established somewhere. We cannot suggest it is inconsequential where these things happen. God's revelation is along covenantal lines; accordingly, it brings the nations and their development into the light. Now the continent of Europe was to be conquered by and opened up to the gospel. What happened at Philippi makes that particularly clear.

In Athens Paul wrestled with the religious thought of those days. It started with the altar to the unknown god. Within natural man or his works there are no points of contact for divine grace. Whatever remnants of the image of God in the form of knowledge of God remained in man only led him to flee from God. When the Holy Spirit changes the heart, those remnants become points of contact for grace.

For their own security the Athenians had dedicated an altar to the unknown god. That attempt to secure themselves against the wrath of a possibly unknown god had nothing to do with true godliness. Nevertheless, Paul began with this starting point in the hope they might listen, and the Word might convince them of their guilt, illustrating how the true God was unknown to them.

We must not look upon Paul's speech at Mars' hill as a failure. If we read it wrongly, we can easily conclude that Paul devoted the larger part of his speech to what is called general revelation and the common knowledge of God, with only a few unrelated remarks about Christ ap-

200

pended. This alleged weakness has sometimes been explained as a spiritual collapse on Paul's part. He is said to have made the mistake of building on the existing knowledge of God without placing the gospel foursquare in opposition to the lies of the pagan world. We should remember, however, that Paul's spirit was incensed as he saw the idolatry practised in Athens. That suggests something other than a spiritual breakdown and compromise!

To consider his speech in the above light therefore is totally wrong. Paul says that God overlooked the times of ignorance (compare Romans 3:25). Those were the times of guilt through ignorance. The whole human race possessed the knowledge of God and of His Kingdom, His special revelation through His Word and the revelation of His covenant. However, the nations willfully rejected the bond of the covenant. The Athenians did indeed serve the unknown god, but they did so in their own way.

The true God is not served by human hands, as though He needed anything. He is only served in submission by faith, which receives everything from Him. Thus God is served only in His covenant, which was there in the beginning when mankind was still one. Afterwards God caused mankind to break up into nations, so that, holding fast to the Word of His covenant, they might seek and find Him in all things throughout the earth. That searching for Him would certainly not mean looking for something alien, for we live and move in Him, are encompassed by Him who in His covenant had gone out to the world with His favor. Furthermore, He originally created us in a relationship of dependence upon Him. Men did not, however, seek after and find the true God in all His works, but instead made their own representations of God and of His service. They forgot the covenant of the Lord. Now God has overlooked the guilt of that ignorance and has commanded all men everywhere to repent. Whoever among the nations of the world does not subject himself to the Lord's covenant will be judged by Christ whom God has appointed for that purpose and to whom God has given the victory over death.

Main thought: *God sends out His gospel to all the nations, having overlooked the times of their guilt through ignorance.*

Led by the Holy Spirit. For a while Paul and Barnabas stayed in Antioch, teaching in the congregation. Then Paul told Barnabas he would like to pay another visit to all the congregations that had been established. The Holy Spirit was making Paul restless; the gospel had to be carried on. Barnabas agreed with his plan, but wanted to take his cousin, John Mark, with them (Colossians 4:10). Evidently Barnabas hoped his cousin's heart would be fully won for this mission work. However, Paul definitely refused to take him because John Mark had faltered and turned back on the first missionary journey. Such a person, in Paul's judgment, was not fit for the work which, on this second journey, surely would demand no fewer sacrifices. The dispute resulted in bitterness. No agreement could be reached so the two parted ways. Barnabas took John Mark with him and sailed away to Cyprus, his home town (Acts 4:36). Paul chose Silas as his traveling companion. No matter how much these men were led by the Holy Spirit, sin was still present in their lives. Difference of insight should not result in division. Yet the separation of Paul and Barnabas was also used by the Holy Spirit to advance the progress of the gospel.

Paul traveled overland through Syria and Cilicia, strengthening all the churches, until he came to Derbe and Lystra. There he found a disciple named Timothy, the son of a Greek father and a Jewish woman who was a believer. Timothy was highly praised by the brethren in Lystra and Iconium. Apparently Paul was much impressed by this young man. He invited him to help serve the cause of the gospel. Later there was a very special tie between Paul and Timothy as Paul came to regard him as his son (I Timothy 1:2; II Timothy 1:2; 2:1). However, Timothy was not circumcised. This bothered the Jews because he had a Jewish mother. In those days this really was a sign of negligence. To prevent the Jews from holding this against him Paul took Timothy and circumcised him. Paul received from the Lord a faithful helper in Timothy.

Everywhere the churches were strengthened in faith and grew in number. Paul and his associates informed the various congregations of the decisions reached by the apostles and elders at the conference in Jerusalem to make sure the earlier Antioch problems did not become cause for unrest in the churches.

Paul also tried to extend his service to other areas but the Holy Spirit prevented it. He could only go west but was also prevented from working there by the Holy Spirit. Just how Paul was prevented is not known. In any case, he was coaxed to the northwest until he came to Troas on the coast.

Opposite Troas lay the continent of Europe. What reason did

the Holy Spirit have for steering them to the coast? Was it the Spirit's intention that the gospel be expanded to Europe? On the one hand, Paul must have longed for that; on the other, he probably dreaded it. Europe was unknown, a mysterious fortress. Without the Spirit's special instruction Paul could not risk going to Europe.

Yet God wanted to bring peace to Europe to dispel the gloom. God would overlook its sins and shine His light into the darkness. Paul received God's instruction through a vision of a man of Macedonia standing on the other side of the water, calling out, "Come over to Macedonia and help us!" The Holy Spirit had gone before Paul and awakened Europe. That is how Paul interpreted the vision. He could now proceed confidently since the Spirit of the Lord had opened the gates of that mysterious fortress.

The first door opened. Upon receiving the vision they crossed over to Macedonia and soon came to Philippi, Macedonia's leading city and a Roman colony. In contrast to Antioch, however, very few Jews were living there; there wasn't even a synagogue. Those few Jews who lived in Philippi met every sabbath just outside the city along the river. How would this purely pagan city where Jewry was not a significant factor be opened up to the gospel? Paul and his companions must have pondered that question extensively.

On the sabbath they met some women by the river. Paul brought the gospel to them. Among them was a Greek woman who knew and served the God of Israel. This was Lydia, a rich woman, a dealer in purple cloth. The Holy Spirit opened her heart and she believed the Word.

When Lydia and her household had been baptized, she placed herself and her house at the service of the gospel. She urged Paul and his companions to stay at her house. When Paul hesitated, she asked Paul whether he doubted the genuineness of her conversion. Thus Lydia's home became a center for the believers who were added to the church of God. The first door, the first heart, and the first house in Europe had been opened for the gospel. Was this not an encouraging sign to Paul that this apparently inaccessible fortress would one day fall? Thus the seeds of the gospel message fell in soil already prepared by the Lord.

The power of the gospel. For yet some time Paul and his companions stayed on in Philippi. Each day they gathered outside the city for prayer with the believers. Several times they were followed by a slave girl who had a spirit by which she predicted the future. Supernatural, satanic powers let her see the future and her owners earned a great deal of money from her fortune telling. As she followed Paul she would cry out, "These men are servants of the most high God, who proclaim to you the way of salvation." Her words were both true and false. She spoke of a bliss, a felicity, as only pagans would understand it. Paul did not wish to be put on a par with such preachers of bliss. The gospel is squarely opposed to any human understanding of salvation. That opposition had to become clear; the gospel had to make an attack on this pagan world. Because she had thus followed Paul and his companions for many days, the attention of the city was fixed on them. But then, in the name of Jesus Christ, Paul posed the antithesis by ordering the spirit to come out of her. The spirit immediately obeyed. The Word of the Kingdom of grace is stronger than any power in the pagan world, and has authority even over the devils.

But now the conflict also had entered that city. The slave girl's owners counted their losses and dragged Paul and Silas into the marketplace before the two Roman magistrates who presided over the administration of the city. An accusation was easy to find: these Jews were trying to make the people accept customs alien to Rome. This induced a hostile mood. Silas and Paul's garments were torn off them and at the orders of the magistrates they were beaten with rods by Roman lictors, men who carried rods for this purpose while attending the magistrates (compare II Corinthians 11:25).

Both Paul and Silas possessed Roman citizenship. They could thus have appealed to protect themselves from being beaten. However, both felt they could not protest under these circumstances and leave the impression they were unprepared to suffer for the gospel. The victory of the gospel in Philippi had to come by way of their suffering.

And come it did! They were promptly thrown into a closely guarded prison. The jailer threw them into the innermost cell and locked their feet in stocks. These Gentiles bound the bearers of the gospel, thinking the government could thus bind the gospel itself.

However, at night Paul and Silas prayed and sang songs of praise to God and the other prisoners listened. They sang of the gospel's power that conquers the heathen world. They rejoiced in God's grace and its certain victory.

Suddenly there was a great earthquake which shook the foundations of the prison, forced open the doors and unlocked the prisoners' chains. Obviously a miracle had taken place as God had intervened; it was a display of the power of His grace which cannot be bound by the power of any man. Would the Lord in some similar way not move all of Europe and shake its very foundations? And would the power of grace not conquer Europe? That is what Paul and Silas must have seen in that earthquake. And one day God will shake heaven and earth as He ushers in the glory of His Kingdom.

The jailer woke up and, realizing what had happened, wanted to commit suicide because he thought some prisoners had escaped. Paul stopped him, explained all were present. Unable to see in the dark the jailer called for light. Seeing all the prisoners accounted for, including Paul and Silas, he fell down trembling. Then he asked them what he should do to be saved. Evidently Silas and Paul's behavior had made a deep impression on him. Possibly he was reminded of what the slave girl had said. He knew they had been unfairly imprisoned. He saw this earthquake as the response of the true God, whom Paul and Silas served.

As a pagan he still asked what things he had to do to be saved or blessed. The answer was totally different from what he had expected. Paul and Silas said: "Believe in the Lord Jesus Christ and you will be saved, you and your household." Then they proclaimed the Word of the Lord to him and to all who were in his house. That awakened faith in him, and he treated them differently. He washed their wounds. He and his whole family were baptized. Then he prepared them a meal, rejoicing that he and his family had found God. Now the jailer honored his prisoners at his own table. Thus the gospel would be honored throughout Europe.

In the morning a message arrived from the two magistrates ordering Silas and Paul's release. Possibly those magistrates also saw the earthquake as a demonstration of power on the part of the God whom Paul and Silas preached. The magistrates also had become afraid. The jailer would gladly have complied with the order but not so Paul. Now he openly declared they were Roman citizens and demanded that the magistrates themselves escort them out of prison in honor. The gesture was not for Paul's benefit but rather for the honor of the gospel, implying official recognition of the righteousness of the gospel. In this way the gospel was received into the city.

After the magistrates had complied with Paul's demand, they asked Paul and Silas to leave the city for fear of possible riots. The apostles first went to Lydia's house, consoled the brethren and left town. As centuries ago Jericho was the first to fall to God's people, Philippi was the first European city to be conquered by the gospel.

The revelation of the Lord at Thessalonica and at Berea. From Philippi Paul and his companions traveled to Thessalonica. There was a Jewish synagogue in this city, and thus he could first direct himself to the Jews again. For three sabbaths he proclaimed Christ to them. Some Jews believed, as did many of the Greeks attending the synagogue, and many of the leading women as well.

However, unbelieving Jews instigated a riot by hiring some scoundrels from the marketplace. They rushed to Jason's house where Paul and Silas were staying. Even the city authorities became involved. The Jews accused the apostles of preparing a rebellion against the emperor, because they preached that Jesus was King. Admittedly, the Kingdom of Jesus stood over against the power of the emperor but if the emperor should subject himself to Christ he would be blessed by Christ's sovereign rule. But the Jews charged Paul preached revolution against the emperor. Jason put himself up as security and paid bail for Paul and Silas. Nevertheless, the brethren found it advisable that they leave town. But the Spirit of the Lord remained behind; the sovereign reign of Christ had been established.

The same thing happened in Berea, their next stop. Again, many Jews received the Word with great eagerness and examined the Scriptures daily to see whether things had thus been prophesied of the Messiah. Many believed as did many prominent Greek women and men. But the hostile Jews from Thessalonica came over and stirred up a commotion at Berea as well. The brethren urged Paul to leave but Silas and Timothy stayed on. In Berea Christ had also established His throne.

The revelation of the power of the resurrection. Some of the brethren from Berea accompanied Paul as far as Athens. After Paul had asked them to send Silas and Timothy as soon as possible, they left Paul in Athens.

As Paul walked through the city, he was struck by the number of idols. Everywhere were temples and pagan gods; the entire life of the city was saturated with idolatry, as the people tried to obtain success and happiness. Absent, however, was a confession that guilt and death had been conquered and that there was resurrection unto eternal life. Man sought temporal happiness, convinced that life would terminate in the realm of the dead. Pagan cults and pagan philosophy, centered in Athens, had not come to any other conclusion. But Paul did not avoid Athens. He knew the gospel would also have to make an impact on this center of pagan learning, and the Christ could also be victorious here. Upon seeing all this idolatry Paul was incensed. How clearly the truth of God testified against these lies! How he would like to proclaim that truth here!

But how? Where to start? In the synagogue he reasoned from the Scriptures with the Jews and those God-fearing Greeks who attended the services. But that did not bring him in touch with life in the city. Therefore he spoke in the marketplace every day with any who would listen. Gradually, this began to attract attention. Some philosophers started to argue with him, advocating a way of living that should lead to a life of happiness. For the time being Paul was still looked down upon. They called him an idle babbler and a proclaimer of strange gods. They saw in Jesus and in the power of the resurrection strange deities. For people who are captivated by their own ideas the gospel is absurd and contemptible.

Still, their curiosity had been aroused. So they brought Paul to the company of scholars on the Areopagus to give him the opportunity to declare himself in their midst. He was brought before the great of the earth, the intellectual elite! But what were these men in the light of the gospel? They neither knew nor wanted the truth. Therefore they continually had to look for something new to keep the world's attention. However, all was falsehood.

Paul began by saying that he had noticed how very religious the city was. He had even found an altar to an unknown god. This God, whom they wanted to serve in their own way, he would proclaim to them. This is the God who has made heaven and earth. He is far above all the idols and does not dwell in temples built by men's hands. He is not dependent on men but is sufficient unto Himself. We cannot give Him anything that would put Him under any obligation to us. On the contrary, we receive everything from Him and are under obligation to Him for everything. Through all He gives us He wishes to reveal His grace. Once, when mankind was still one, this God was known to all men, for God has made the whole human race from one man. When He caused mankind to break up into nations, He determined the history of each people and the exact places where they should live. He wanted them to preserve the knowledge of His name and to observe His greatness in everything in creation.

It should have been easy for man for all men live and move and have their very being in Him. His hand carries us every day. Moreover, originally He had placed us in a relation of dependence to Him. The Greeks should have understood that for some of their own poets had believed themselves to be God's offspring. However, all nations forgot Him and started serving idols of gold, silver or stone which are said to dwell in temples. Yet that certainly is in conflict with how man was originally created. But although the nations have wantonly forsaken God, He does not wish to remember their guilt, and now He is making Himself known to man again. He proclaims to men everywhere that they should turn back to Him in faith. His grace is for everyone who believes. Only then will there be deliverance from guilt and death. If, however, men will not believe, they will one day be judged by Christ whom God has given authority for judgment, the Christ whom God has already raised from the dead. He has won the victory over death for us.

When Paul came to the resurrection of the dead they had heard enough. Some began to sneer while others politely excused themselves by saying they would hear him on this subject some other time. What could Christ's miraculous victory over death possibly mean to people who lived solely by their own thoughts and insights? They lacked any sense of God's grace; they were not convinced of their guilt or of the judgment that awaited them in death.

Thus Paul left them. Had his preaching been in vain? No, for some believed the gospel. Among them was Dionysius, one of the intellectuals, and a member of the Areopagus; another was a woman by the name of Damaris. In Athens too the gospel had obtained a place. The Word of God had locked horns with unbelieving science and would never give up.

The light of Christ in the darkness of the times. From Athens Paul went to Corinth, an entirely different kind of city. Corinth was a major trade center, a place of great wealth, but also of offensive godlessness and immorality. What could the gospel possibly do in such a city?

Determined to stay, Paul watched for the Lord's guidance. He stayed with a Jewish couple, Aquila and Priscilla who, together with all the rest of the Jews, had been driven out of Rome by Emperor Claudius. Paul joined them because they, like him, were tentmakers. Every sabbath he spoke in the synagogue to both Jews and Greeks. Here Silas and Timothy joined him again. Their arrival greatly encouraged Paul and, impelled by the Spirit, he testified to the Jews that Jesus was the Messiah.

The opposition, however, became stronger so Paul broke with the synagogue. The Jews' judgment would be on their own heads, Paul warned. As a sign he was breaking off all relations with them, Paul shook out his clothes. From now on he would go to the Gentiles. Next door to the synagogue, in the home of a God-fearing Greek named Justus, Paul found a place where he could proclaim the gospel. His preaching was not without fruit. Crispus, the head of the synagogue, and many other Corinthians believed and were baptized.

Yet in this city Paul wrestled with the power of godlessness and immorality. Would the light of the gospel break through? One night Paul saw a vision in which the Lord encouraged him to continue. The Lord assured Paul there were many potential believers in Corinth. Even in this sinful city God had His elect, though still bound by the fetters of sin. In the good pleasure of His grace God exercises His sovereign sway over man and saves whom He will.

Paul remained in Corinth a year and a half. Finally conflict arose. The Jews rose up against him and took him to court before Gallio, the Roman governor. They accused him of sins against Jewish law. The governor refused to become involved in such a dispute and had them ejected from the court. Apparently the Jews were not overly popular in Corinth and an uproar could only make matters worse. In the end the Greeks beat up Sosthenes, the synagogue ruler, right in front of the court. Gallio did not let that bother him either; he kept out of it. Thus the Jews were not successful in opposing Paul and the gospel continued its course in Corinth.

Hope set on Ephesus. Paul stayed on in Corinth for many more days. Then he left, intending to return to Antioch. Priscilla and Aquila, in whose home he had stayed, sailed with him. Evidently Paul thought of going to Ephesus hoping Aquila and Priscilla would go to live there so that Paul could stay with them. This would help settle Aquila who had wandered from place to place since his exile from Rome.

According to their plans they first stopped off at Ephesus, where Aquila and Priscilla remained. Paul spoke in the synagogue and for once there was no opposition; the people wanted to hear what he had to say. When he told them he had plans to travel on, they asked him to stay. But he promised only to return. Ephesus offered him hope! Would the whole synagogue there be won for the Christ? Paul had set his hope on Ephesus, because that city had many access roads to the hinterland of Asia Minor, thus opening the whole area to the gospel.

However, Paul wanted to keep the upcoming feast, probably the Passover feast, in Jerusalem. He had not yet cut the tie with the people of the former covenant. Moreover, he wanted to see the church in Jerusalem. After he had been there a while, he went to Antioch, his home. He knew now that Europe had been opened up to the gospel. God would carry it from there.

39: The Way of the Lord

Acts 18:23—20:38

More than once in this section we come across the expression "the way of the Lord" or simply "the way." This is not so much the way of God to us or our way to God, but it is the way the Lord has opened up before us in life, the way in which we may walk with Him, the way in which we may have communion with Him in the fellowship of His covenant. As Israel traveled through the wilderness with the Lord going before them, so we travel the way of the Lord.

The disciples of John the Baptist who were only familiar with his baptism did not know that way sufficiently. These disciples of John should not be equated with the earlier disciples of John the Baptist. John had always pointed away from himself; the baptism of John had been adopted by Christ. So if, after his death, people maintained John's baptism in order to honor him, they were not really honoring him as the herald of Christ. Worse yet, they were opposed to John's being eclipsed by Christ. Thus, the baptism exercised by these followers of John was not really a Christian baptism. It is through the Holy Spirit that man walks in the way and has full communion with the Lord. Through that same Spirit the fullness of life is opened up to us. We cannot remain aloof, as did John's disciples because our concern is for the sanctification of all of life. Thus Paul's concern was for all of Israel and the entire world including Rome! That we repeatedly run across the expression "the way of the Lord" in this passage is connected with the fact that Paul at this time was engaged in a struggle for the whole synagogue at Ephesus; he longed for Rome in these days (19:31). Only when it was no longer possible did Paul separate the church in Ephesus from the synagogue.

211

Main thought: *The revelation of the way of the Lord in the world.*

The way of the Lord and Apollos. Paul did not have rest at Antioch for very long. He thought of his promise to the Jews in Ephesus and his heart longed to take up his work there. That city was so full of promise. Therefore he soon went on another journey.

In the meantime Aquila and Priscilla had not sat still in Ephesus. A Jew named Apollos had come to the city. He was a native of Alexandria which had a large Jewish colony engaged in Old Testament studies. In fact, Apollos proved to be very well versed in the Scriptures. He had also heard and believed the gospel of the Lord Jesus Christ. He also knew of the baptism of John the Baptist. What he did not know was that the baptism of John the Baptist had been adopted by the Lord Jesus and that the significance of John's baptism had only been fully realized in the outpouring of the Holy Spirit. He knew nothing of the outpouring of the Spirit and of the special gifts which had accompanied it. He did not understand that now Christ, by His Holy Spirit, intended to establish His sovereign reign among all the nations. He knew only of a salvation for Israel, just as John had only been instructed to baptize Israel. Of the whole meaning of Pentecost he had never heard.

This Apollos was an eloquent speaker and very enthusiastic in spirit. When he arrived in Ephesus, he began to speak in the synagogue about the Lord Jesus without knowing anything of Paul. Aquila and Priscilla, who still attended the services in the synagogue at Ephesus because it had not yet made a decision for or against the Christ, heard him speak. What a powerful witness this Apollos was for the Lord Jesus! But what a gap there still was in his knowledge! So these two took him home with them and told him everything they had learned from Paul. Wide vistas were opened up for him. He saw that not only was there communion between God and Israel and a walking together of the Lord with that people on the way through life, but the covenant of the Lord was now for all nations. He now saw not only John's baptism, but how that baptism had been completely fullfilled in the baptism with the Holy Spirit. Thus, from being a teacher in the synagogue, Apollos became the pupil of simple believers like Aquila and Priscilla.

However, Apollos' role did not end there. He was planning to go to Greece. Aquila and Priscilla and those at Ephesus who had already made a definite choice for the Lord Jesus informed him that in Greece the believers had been forced to break with the synagogue. There he would run into the hatred of the Jews. They therefore urged him to remain faithful to the gospel. They also gave him a letter of introduction to the believers there. After he arrived in Greece, Apollos conducted a powerful ministry. He earnestly refuted the Jews in public debate, proving from the Scriptures that Jesus was the Messiah. As a result of his work many came to believe. Apollos had come to understand the meaning of Pentecost and the way of the Lord with all the nations.

The way of the Lord and the baptism of John. After Apollos had left Ephesus, Paul arrived there. The first persons he came in contact with were some believers who held the same position Apollos had earlier maintained. Perhaps they had even been influenced by Apollos. They knew nothing of the baptism with the Holy Spirit.

Paul did not like halfway measures. He knew they were ignorant of the call which, since the day of Pentecost, went out to all nations. They still held to the Jewish national position. He therefore asked them point-blank whether they had received the Holy Spirit when they had come to belief. At once their ignorance came to light when they replied, "We have never even heard that there is a Holy Spirit." The entire revelation of the Holy Spirit, who on Pentecost had come to dwell in His church, as well as those gifts of the Holy Spirit, by which He proved that the partition separating Israel from the nations had been removed—all this was totally unknown to them.

Astonished, Paul asked them into what they had then been baptized. Did baptism, as the sign of the ingrafting into the church, not bring with it the participation in the gift of the Holy Spirit? Their answer to Paul was: "We were baptized into John's baptism." Then Paul explained to them that John's baptism had been the baptism of repentance, the sign and seal of the conversion to the grace of the Lord, which had appeared fully in the Lord Jesus Christ and as a result of which the Holy Spirit had been poured out. The baptism of John had been adopted by Christ and had been made into a baptism for all nations. If people still wanted to hold on to the baptism of John, as in the Jewish national tradition, it meant the baptism was not genuine. These people in Ephesus had no knowledge of all the things that had happened on and after Pentecost. Those who had thus instructed them were probably persons who opposed the course of the gospel among the nations, and used the name of John the Baptist for their own purposes.

These persons, about twelve in number, were convinced by Paul of the truth and were baptized into the name of the Lord Jesus. When Paul had laid his hands on them, the Holy Spirit came upon them and they spoke in foreign tongues and prophesied. Then they saw the salvation of the Lord for all peoples and understood something of the depth and breadth of the grace of God.

The way of the Lord and the synagogue at Ephesus. After this episode Paul entered the synagogue. For three months he debated with the Ephesian Jews, proclaiming the Kingdom of God in Jesus Christ. He knew the Lord's concern for Israel and thus also for the synagogue at Ephesus. All people had to be liberated by the Holy Spirit from a life of bondage under the law. This is why he struggled with them, hoping to win the whole synagogue.

But here too it turned out differently as some disobeyed the calling of the Lord. Before the assembled congregation they spoke evil of the way of the Lord; they were loathe to share salvation with other nations. For that reason the Ephesus synagogue split. Paul took the believers with him and left. Similar separation will take place everywhere because everywhere there are unbelievers. One day the Lord Jesus Christ Himself will separate the believers from the unbelievers.

Paul met with the believers in the school of a certain Tyrannus. Each day, for two years, he proclaimed the gospel to both Jews and Greeks. As he had hoped, the gospel radiated from

Ephesus throughout the entire area of Asia Minor. The whole world had to know that Christ is King.

The way of the Lord and the church at Ephesus. God performed many miracles in Ephesus by the hands of Paul. It became unmistakably clear that the grace of the Lord means the redemption, the healing, of all of life. The Lord was so very near with the power of His grace that when handkerchiefs and aprons that had touched Paul's body were brought to the sick and the possessed, they were healed. This may have seemed to some onlookers as magic but was very different. Carrying items of clothes touched by Paul to the sick was seen as a sign of communion with Paul or, rather, with the Word of grace he preached. By faith they had to accept that Word.

Still there remained a danger this would be looked upon as magic, especially in a city so full of heathen magic until something happened that showed the immense difference between magic and faith in the Lord Jesus Christ. In Ephesus lived a Jewish high priest named Sceva, whose seven sons practiced magic. Here we are faced with the same abomination as in the case of Elymas: the Jews, who on account of the truth were supposed to be a light for the nations and were to preach subjection to the Word of God, were making the darkness even worse by their lies. With their magical arts, they pretended to be able to subject divine forces to their own control. These men saw and heard about the miracles being done by Paul. They looked on this as a magical power and wanted to imitate Paul. Once, when they encountered a possessed person, they said, "We adjure you by the Jesus whom Paul preaches . . . ." In other words, they wanted to use the name of the Lord Jesus as a magical formula. However, the evil spirit answered them, "Jesus I know, and Paul I know; but who are you?" Before the power of the Lord and of the Word that Paul preached, satan trembled, but what power did these exorcists of devils think they had over him? The man who was possessed leaped on them with such fearsome power that they had to flee out of the house wounded, their clothes tattered. Everybody in Ephesus, both Jews and Greeks, heard about it. Fear fell on all and the name of the Lord Jesus was magnified. They had clearly seen the difference between magic and belief in Him.

The incident made such a deep impression that many who had performed magic believed and confessed their sins. They brought all their magic books together and burned them publicly, making a clean break with their sin. The value of those books was no less than 50,000 drachmas, indicating how widespread the practise and influence of magic was. Now the Word of the Lord gained the victory; it grew and prevailed. In the way of the Lord the people were liberated from magic.

The way of the Lord and the people at Ephesus. Paul had now been in Ephesus for two years and three months. The Lord had richly blessed the preaching of the gospel in the city. Paul started thinking about going through Macedonia to visit the Greek churches and then return to Jerusalem. And he had still other plans: he wanted to go to Rome. He longed to bring the gospel into the world's capital, for his concern was not just to collect little groups of believers here and there, but to have the whole world and all nations acknowledge Christ as King. He sent two of his helpers ahead to Macedonia but he himself stayed in Ephesus for a while longer.

During that time there was a riot in Ephesus. In the city stood an image of the goddess Artemis (Diana), which was said to have fallen from heaven. In fact, there was also a famous temple of Artemis there. A certain Demetrius, a manufacturer of miniature silver temples, supplied his products to many storekeepers who kept up a profitable trade in these items. Because the gospel was gaining such great influence, Demetrius saw his trade in these icons threatened and accordingly stirred up everybody who had an interest in this business. First he appealed to their own interest; the prospect of financial loss frightened them. Then he gave a religious tint to his action: the worship of Artemis might fall into disuse. But because idolatry serves its own interests there was a great commotion. The people ran into the streets, shouting, "Great is Artemis of the Ephesians." The whole city turned out and together they rushed into the theatre, dragging with them Gaius and Aristarchus, Macedonians who were Paul's traveling companions.

When Paul heard what was going on, he wanted to go there.

The cause of Christ was at stake. However, the believers wouldn't let him go; apparently they feared that Paul would be torn to pieces by the mob. Besides, Paul received a warning from several prominent persons in this part of Asia Minor that under no circumstance should he show himself in the theatre. We can see how many prominent citizens were among the followers of Christ.

Meanwhile the shouting outside continued and many joined in without really knowing what the excitement was all about. Unbelieving Jews feared they would also be implicated, for Christians originally were regarded as a Jewish sect. These unbelieving Jews therefore wanted it to be very clear they had nothing to do with those Christians. They appointed a certain Alexander to explain the Jewish position to the crowd. But he couldn't silence the crowd, for when they noticed he was a Jew, their hostility really erupted. For two solid hours they kept shouting, "Great is Artemis of the Ephesians."

What would this come to? Who was there to mollify the mob? Fortunately the town clerk appeared and settled the irate mob. This man knew how to control the people. He assured them that no one could doubt the honor of the goddess Artemis and that Ephesus enjoyed preferential status since Artemis' image had been found in the city. There was no need to riot as no one had slandered the goddess or robbed the temple. Besides, he concluded, any charge should go through the courts. He warned them that news of this unrest could reach Rome, giving Ephesus a bad name. His speech silenced the uproar and the people went back to their homes. Still, the hostility to the way of the Lord had now come out into the open. Not the entire city was won for the gospel. Here too a split was in evidence.

Victory over death. Paul then left Ephesus, traveling through Macedonia to Greece until he came to Corinth again, where he stayed for three months. He intended to sail straight from Corinth to Syria because his plan to go to Rome was urging him on more and more. But first he wanted to celebrate Pentecost in Jerusalem and hand over the collections he had received from the various churches for the impoverished Jerusalem church. The Jews, however, had devised a plot against his life. They were planning to kill him either as he boarded ship or on the sea voyage itself, so Paul had to go back through Macedonia after all. Believers from various regions accompanied him. There was a strong bond of faith with this preacher of the gospel.

During the Passover Feast he was in Philippi. From there he crossed to Troas, where he stayed for seven days, for there too a church had been established. On the first day of the week—already celebrated as the day of Christ's resurrection—the congregation came together to celebrate the Lord's Supper. This supper was celebrated at the end of a love-meal (the Agapé), which was held at the conclusion of the service. But first Paul addressed the meeting, speaking for a very long time. He explained that this could very well be the last time he would speak to the churches in Asia Minor. In fact, time after time on this return to Jerusalem the Holy Spirit revealed to him by the prophets that fetters and imprisonment awaited him in Jerusalem. What was going to happen to him? Would he have to suffer death already for the sake of the gospel? And what would come of his desire to bring the Word to Rome? In Troas something happened that greatly strengthened him during those days. He spoke until midnight. The church was gathered in a room on the third floor of a house. The room was full and many candles had been lighted so that it became very warm. A young man named Eutychus was sitting on the window sill in an effort to escape the heat. Even then he fell asleep and fell out of the window, dead. However, Paul went downstairs, covered the young man, embraced him and declared that life had returned to him. Here Paul put his own life on the line for the life of that young man and the Lord heard his prayer. There was power in the Word of the Lord to overcome death. That must have greatly strengthened Paul. Whatever was going to happen in the future he too would overcome death. They went back upstairs and celebrated the Lord's Supper together. Afterwards, Paul talked until daybreak. Together with Eutychus, Paul came downstairs, both men redeemed from death. One day they would have to die but death could not harm them.

Paul sent his companions ahead by ship to Assos while he walked the forty kilometers along the coast. Evidently he wanted to be alone. He had so much to work out in his mind. Then they sailed together from Assos.

Compelled by the Holy Spirit. Sailing along the coast, Paul also passed Ephesus where he had so many close ties. He could not stop in for then he would not be able to be in Jerusalem in time for Pentecost. But simply to sail past that place would also not be right. Would he ever see Ephesus again? In the end Paul summoned the elders of the Ephesian church to come to the beach at Miletus. There he talked to them. They knew about his work at Ephesus and in Asia Minor, and of all the tribulations he had suffered for the sake of the gospel. Now he was on his way to Jerusalem, knowing that he probably faced imprisonment. Nevertheless, he simply had to go because the Holy Spirit was leading him there; Paul was prepared to die for the gospel. One more time he wanted to exhort them to be faithful in their supervision over the congregation, as he himself had been faithful to the full scope of the gospel. Tempters would come into the congregation, Paul predicted. He urged the elders to be reminded how, in complete submission to the gospel, Paul had not sought his own well-being but had worked to provide for his own needs and had supported the poor.

When he had thus spoken he prayed with them, kneeling down on the beach. The farewell was emotional and sorrowful because he said that possibly they might never see him again. Compelled by the Holy Spirit and governed by the Word of God, Paul finally departed. Paul, to be sure, had a special calling for the gospel, but we too are subject to the Word of God and must serve that Word in everything we do.

Christ's
Worldwide Reign

40: Imitator of the Christ

Acts 21:1-23:35

Paul's action here seems very calculated. Along with others he took a Nazarite vow; he appealed to his Roman citizenship to avoid a flogging; and he threw the matter of faith in the resurrection of the dead, as the main bone of contention, into the midst of the Pharisees and Sadducees in the Council (Sanhedrin). However, we must bear in mind that Paul, compelled by the Spirit, was prepared to suffer imprisonment and even death for the gospel. He did not allow himself, however much they begged him, to be held back from his trip to Jerusalem. Why was Paul so anxious to meet the brethren in Jerusalem and to celebrate the Feast of Pentecost with them? It was not because of a division between the Jerusalem church and the Gentile churches. In his letters Paul gloried in the great mystery which in previous centuries had been hidden, namely, that Christ removed the hostility between Jew and Gentile. The Christ made the two into one body. For this oneness Paul was prepared to offer himself as a sacrifice. In that respect Paul was an imitator of the Christ.

The fact that Paul and four others took a temporary Nazarite vow was not in conflict with his attitude towards the ceremonial or his letter to the Galatians. Paul squarely opposed attempts to impose the ceremonial law on the Gentiles and to consider it necessary for salvation. It would be a denial of Christ's all-sufficiency. But Jewish believers could observe the law themselves as long as they did not obligate Gentiles to it. That was also Paul's position in his letter to the Romans. Thus, as a Jewish believer, he could follow one of the precepts of the law provided such observance did not disturb the unity between Jewish and Gentile believers. This is why he resisted Peter at Antioch when Peter broke the fellowship at the table with the Gentile believers. Paul took this vow at Jerusalem in order to promote the unity between Jewish and Gentile believers.

Paul was not dishonest in promoting discord in the Sanhedrin by raising the resurrection issue. Indeed, the issue for him was the resurrection of the dead in connection with the resurrection of Christ. On this point the Pharisees held literally to the Scriptures. The fact that faith in the resurrection meant something else for Paul than for the Pharisees was the fault of the Pharisees, not Paul's. Faith, as Paul understood it, was faith according to the Scriptures.

Main thought: *By faith we are imitators of Christ.*

Prepared for imprisonment and death. After Paul and his party had said farewell to the Ephesian elders on the beach at Miletus, they boarded ship. Everything went well on this journey. Long before Pentecost they arrived at Tyre, where the ship had to unload its cargo. During the seven day stopover Paul stayed with believers. To these believers the Holy Spirit revealed that Paul would soon be imprisoned. They begged him not to go. The temptation to disobey the Spirit became stronger and stronger. However, he remained faithful. At the end of Paul's stay the people sent him off with prayers.

There was another stopover of several days at Caesarea where Paul stayed in the house of Philip the evangelist with whom he became acquainted earlier. This man had four daughters with prophetic gifts. While Paul and his companions were there a prophet named Agabus came down from Judea. Prompted by the Holy Spirit, this man symbolically took Paul's belt and bound his own hands and feet with it. He then prophesied that Paul would thus be bound at Jerusalem and handed over to the Gentiles. That made a deep impression not only on the believers at Caesarea but also on Paul's traveling companions. Together they begged him not to go to Jerusalem. Paul reproached them for trying to weaken his resolve. He declared he was ready not only to be imprisoned but also to die in Jerusalem for the name of the Lord.

What was it that compelled Paul to go to Jerusalem and why would he make any sacrifice to get there? It was imperative for the bond between the Gentile churches and the Jewish church at Jerusalem to remain intact to avoid estrangement between Jewish and Gentile believers. Christ had given His life to make Jewish and

Gentile believers one people. Paul's life had been a constant struggle to establish that union and he felt compelled to sacrifice even
his life for it. In this way he was to be an imitator of the Lord
Jesus. We too must be willing to give our lives to serve in the work
for which the Christ came to earth.

When Paul would not let himself be dissuaded, his friends
resigned themselves to his decision, saying, "The will of the Lord
be done." Thus they went to Jerusalem. Some of the brethren
from Caesarea also went along to introduce Paul to a certain
Mnason of Cyprus, an elderly disciple with whom Paul would be
staying. As Mnason had lived among the Gentiles he understood
Paul's work more readily than the brethren who had never been
outside Jerusalem.

The vow. The brethren in Jerusalem received Paul joyfully.
The next day there was a meeting at the home of James, the
brother of the Lord, who had the leadership in the church. All the
elders were present. One by one, Paul related the things God had
done among the Gentiles. When they heard it, their hearts
overflowed with thanksgiving and they glorified God.

However, there was one difficulty. Thousands of Jews in
Jerusalem and in Judea had come to faith. They all kept strictly to
the law of Moses. James did that too, earning him the title "the
Just." However, now the story was circulated that Paul advised
Jews throughout the world not to circumcise their children or keep
the ceremonial law. The story was inaccurate because Paul only
preached that keeping the law was not necessary for salvation and
therefore the Gentiles should not be obliged to keep it. He had
declared this most emphatically so that the issue of the law of
Moses might not drive a wedge between Jewish and Gentile
believers and destroy the unity of faith. However, Paul had no objection to Jewish believers keeping the law for themselves. As
such, keeping the law was a symbol of what Christ meant to them.
Observing the law could only confirm them in their faith in Christ.

However, this slander had to be nipped in the bud. The
brethren suggested that Paul join brothers who had taken a
Nazarite vow. These men had vowed to let their hair grow as a sign
of devotion to the Lord and to eat nothing produced from the

grapevine as a sign that they wanted to be moved only by the Holy Spirit. If Paul would take the vow with them and, moreover, agree to pay the expenses of the purification and of the sacrifices at the end of the week for all five, he would demonstrate his high regard for the Nazariteship and thus for the law of Moses. This would not make it appear that observing the law of Moses was essential for salvation because earlier the Gentiles had been informed that nothing would be required of them except to abstain from idolatry, immorality and consumption of blood.

Paul accepted their advice, anxious to promote unity between Jewish and Gentile believers. He gladly took the vow in order to remove all misunderstanding and to contradict the slander. He had a high regard for the Nazarite vow because the true fulfillment of that vow was only possible through faith in Christ, who had devoted Himself to God and who had allowed Himself to be led only by the Holy Spirit. The work of Christ was also a fulfillment of the Nazariteship. In that faith Jews and Gentiles should be one.

Bonds for Christ's sake. In accordance with their agreement, Paul took the vow. He went with the four other brethren into the temple to inform the priest when the days of their purification would be completed and to remain there until the sacrifices had been offered for them.

Towards the end of the week Paul was recognized in the temple by several Jews from Asia Minor. They seized him and called out for help. They complained that Paul taught men to reject the law and the temple worship. In addition, they charged he had brought Greeks into the front court of the temple, a place reserved for Jews, and thus had profaned the temple. Apparently they had previously seen him in Jerusalem accompanied by a Greek from Ephesus and assumed he had brought the Greek into the temple.

Their outcry aroused the whole city and the people assembled at the temple. They dragged Paul out of the temple, intending to kill him. At once the doors of the temple were shut for all disorder was forbidden in that holy place. Suddenly the commander of the garrison with his troops appeared in the streets. He had already been tipped off about the riot and feared a popular uprising. He decided to intervene immediately. When the people saw him they stopped beating Paul. He took custody of Paul, bound him with two chains and asked the people what he had done. He learned nothing for the mob started shouting incoherently. Accordingly, he had Paul brought to the barracks but because the enraged mob wanted to do away with Paul, he had to be carried by the soldiers for his own protection.

Just before going into the barracks, Paul asked permission, in Greek, to speak to the people. That shook the commander for he thought Paul was the same Egyptian who only recently had caused an uprising in Jerusalem. When Paul had told him he was a Jew born in Tarsus, the commander gave him permission to speak to the people. Bound now, he proceeded to witness of Christ before the people of Jerusalem.

An apostle by the will of God. (See II Corinthians 1:1, Ephesians 1:1, Colossians 1:1, II Timothy 1:1.) When Paul, standing on the stairs, motioned with his hand, the crowd became silent, even more so when he addressed them in Hebrew, which was not the common language in Palestine. (That was Aramaic.) He wanted to point out he had not appointed himself to proclaim the gospel, but that the Lord had called him to this task. He did nothing but follow obediently.

To get his point across he told them of his former allegiance to the Pharisees and his education in the school of Gamaliel according to the strictest views. He had even persecuted believers at Jerusalem and obtained letters of recommendation from the former high priest to the elders of the synagogues in Damascus to stamp out faith in the Lord Jesus Christ. He then told them what had happened on the way to Damascus and subsequently. The Lord had conquered him, that he might know Christ as the fulfillment of the law and thereby testify of Him to all men. Thus he had been baptized.

Later in Jerusalem he had seen the Lord Jesus in a vision. The Lord had ordered him to leave Jerusalem quickly because the people would not accept his testimony there. He had been against leaving and had tried to assure the Lord that the people would surely accept his testimony since he had previously persecuted the church. But despite his protests the Lord had sent him to the Gentiles.

Paul wanted to prove that it was not for lack of love for his people that he went to the Gentiles. He informed the crowd that the Lord had predicted they would not listen to him and repent.

However, those words struck the wrong chord. The crowd would not let him finish; they discarded their garments in disgust, threw dust in the air and shouted, "Rid the earth of him! He's not fit to live!" But the prophetic Word of the Lord was fulfilled through their unbelief.

The trial before the Sanhedrin. As a result of the people's mania Paul remained in bonds. It was through suffering that he would have to follow his Lord. The incident ending the way it did, did not leave the military commander much wiser. He ordered Paul questioned and flogged. When a centurion was about to execute this order, Paul asked whether it was lawful to flog a Roman citizen. The centurion relayed this information to his superior who was shocked by the news. He had not known that Paul was a Roman citizen though he knew Paul had been born in Tarsus. Roman citizenship was a privilege granted to all the citizens of Tarsus. In fact, Paul was technically superior to the military commander who had purchased his citizenship. The flogging was called off; the commander was even worried because he had kept a Roman in chains.

This time it was appropriate for Paul to appeal to his Roman citizenship. The Lord Jesus Christ had abolished the enmity between the nations, thus also between Jews and Romans. It was unnecessary for a believer to refuse the privileges of his Roman citizenship, for everything in the world was sanctified by Christ. He restored the community of the nations.

The next day the commander called a session of the Sanhedrin. This in itself was a humiliation for the Supreme Council. He then brought Paul into the meeting after having removed his bonds. In a certain sense Paul stood before the Council as a free man. The commander wanted to hear both sides of the story so that he finally might understand why the Jews were against him.

Without ceremony or introductory flatteries Paul began to address the Supreme Council. He called them "My brothers" and said that he had always acted with a good conscience before God.

This made the high priest so angry—he was already agitated owing to the humiliation inflicted on the Council—that he ordered Paul struck. Against this injustice Paul protested angrily: "God shall strike you, you whitewashed wall. You pretend to judge me according to the law, yet you violate the law by striking me." Paul did not know the order had come from the high priest. When he was made aware of this fact he apologized, reminded of the words of Scripture: "You shall not curse the ruler of your people" (Exodus 22:28). He was justified in opposing injustice, as the Lord Jesus also had done when struck, but the authority of government was to be honored.

With the Council in this mood it was impossible to have an orderly trial. Paul would not even be given an opportunity to witness of Christ. Therefore, because he wished to show how the nation was divided against itself as a result of the revelation of Scripture, he said he was on trial for the hope of the resurrection of the dead. The Pharisees believed in the resurrection while the Sadducees rejected it. Even concerning God's revelation there was no agreement among Council members. And in Paul's trial the issue was indeed the blessed resurrection of the believers, which, after all, is the fruit of Christ's resurrection. Was there really a victory over death and a restoration of life in communion with God?

Paul's identification of the issue caused serious discord in the Council. The Pharisees said they found no fault in him, conceding it was entirely possible that a spirit or angel had spoken to Paul. But the Sadducees wanted Paul's hide. The dispute became so violent that the commander feared they would tear each other to pieces; he quickly had Paul removed from the meeting.

The next night the Lord revealed Himself to Paul. He stood by him and said, "Take courage, Paul, for as you have testified about Me at Jerusalem, so you must bear witness also at Rome." What a comfort that must have been for Paul! Although his speech to the people had been interrupted and his address to the Council cut short, Paul had attempted to witness of Jesus. There had been a witness made to His name and Jerusalem was now in turmoil because of the gospel. For Paul it meant he could now go to Rome even though he didn't know how yet.

Rescued from death. The following day some of the Jews vowed they would neither eat nor drink until they had killed Paul. More than forty persons were involved in the plot and they arranged with the Supreme Council to ask the commander to bring Paul down to their meeting. On the way down he would be killed.

News of this conspiracy leaked out. A nephew of Paul warned him and the commander. The commander secretly sent Paul out of Jerusalem, escorted by almost five hundred troops. Paul was taken to Caesarea, the seat of the Roman governor Felix. The commander, Claudius Lysias, explained in a letter to Felix his reasons for sending Paul to him.

That the plot leaked out was the Lord's doing; in this way Paul was rescued from death. Paul's mandate to proclaim the gospel had not yet come to an end.

41: Standing before Kings and Governors

Acts 24-26

Christ had foretold to Paul that he would stand before kings and governors (see Acts 9:15, and compare Mark 13:9). This prophecy was fulfilled in the account Paul had to give before Felix, Festus and Agrippa. His speeches each time were thus not only an account of his personal conduct, but a witness to the gospel.

The witnessing was different on each of the three occasions, depending on the person to whom Paul is speaking. Felix was the arbitrary despot, the man who offended the rights of the Jews. To him Paul spoke of the coming judgment. Festus made a great deal of the fact that Romans were not accustomed to handing someone over to death simply as a favor to third parties. Paul declared to Festus that he was not unwilling to die if deserved; the gospel, Paul explained, does not scorn the justice of the state but rather upholds it. Agrippa knew of God's revelation in His Word, especially from his father, Herod Agrippa I. Paul launched a direct assault on Agrippa by drawing his attention to that revelation.

Main thought: *The witness to Jesus Christ also goes out to kings and governors.*

Testimony regarding the coming judgment. When Paul arrived in Caesarea, he was kept in custody in Herod's judgment hall on the orders of the governor Felix. Five days later the high priest Ananias and several members of the Supreme Council arrived to present their accusations against Paul to the governor. Their legal counsel was a certain Tertullus.

231

This Tertullus understood the art of flattery, for he began by praising the governor and thanking him for all he had done for the Jews. Cunning it was because Felix was hated passionately by the Jews for his discrimination against Jews. Tertullus thereupon listed the grievances: a) Paul was said to be an agitator among all the Jews throughout the world; b) he was a ringleader of the fanatical sect of the Nazarenes; and c) he had profaned the temple. They would have judged him by their own law, Tertullus added, if Lysias had not removed him from their custody. Felix could question the persons who had witnessed Paul's crimes to corroborate the charges. Needless to say, all the members of the Supreme Council confirmed their lawyer's charges.

The presentation of the accusations was extremely crafty. Nothing aroused fear in a Roman more quickly than the rumor of sedition. Furthermore, Felix now had an excuse for his arbitrary and despotic treatment of Jews: he could blame the Nazarenes. Furthermore, the Romans sanctioned the religious cults of their subject peoples and profanation of any temple was a punishable offense. Tertullus tried to conceal the fact there were no unbiased witnesses to the alleged profanation of the temple by presenting the Council members as "witnesses."

In his defense Paul refrained from flattery. He did observe that Felix had been governor of the Jews for many years and was thus familiar with their customs. This made it all the easier for Paul to make his defense. Only twelve days had passed since Paul had come to Jerusalem; thus there had not been much opportunity to stir up a crowd. For that matter, no one had even seen him talk to the people. He admitted belonging to the sect Tertullus had called the Nazarenes. However, this was not a dissenting sect; its members served the God of their fathers according to His Word. Paul had an opportunity to say what God had revealed in His Word and he said it in such a way that it would have to affect Felix, whose conscience was disturbed by his prejudice.

Paul spoke of the resurrection of the dead, both just and unjust, thereby pointing to the judgment that one day will face all men. He said he strove to keep a clear conscience before God and before men. By this he did not mean he was without sin, but he was prepared to confess his sins before God and to men. He stood in freedom because he knew he had peace with God. Probably

Felix was deeply offended, especially when told how government should relate to God!

Paul then went on to speak of his own affairs. He had come to Jerusalem to hand over the offerings collected from all over the world. Furthermore, he had brought sacrifices in the temple. Some Jews from Asia Minor had rashly accused him of profaning the temple, but were unable to prove it. Those accusers should step forward but didn't. By rights, the Supreme Council could not bring any charge against Paul either, since he had only spoken to them about the resurrection.

None of this helped Felix. Moreover, Paul's words about the resurrection of the dead worried him, probably because the Council was split on the issue. So he postponed the matter until Claudius Lysias could come down from Jerusalem. In the meantime Felix alleviated the conditions of Paul's imprisonment; all his friends were allowed to visit him and care for his needs. Thus Paul maintained contact with the congregation of the Lord.

Yet Felix continued to be disturbed. He was married to Drusilla, a Jewess, who shared his sinful life. When he was in Caesarea with his wife, he had Paul brought before him again while Drusilla was present. As a Jewess she should be better able to form an opinion on the matter. Again Paul spoke of faith in Christ through which we have peace with God and an untroubled conscience. But he also spoke of a life of justice and self-control, which is the fruit of faith. On this occasion too he pointed to the judgment to come.

Troubled by his inability to resolve the problems Felix postponed the matter again. At the same time he hoped that Paul would offer a sum of money for his release. He therefore took up the matter again and again. How many times was he exposed to the gospel? But it was of no use; Felix continued in his life of sin. Two years later he was recalled to Rome. The Jews had a great many complaints against him. To keep them at least reasonably disposed towards him, Felix left Paul in prison. Thus the bearer of the gospel suffered at the hands of the governor's malice. In this respect Paul shared in the sufferings of his Lord.*

---

*See Philippians 3:10 and compare Vol. III p. 156-161.

Testimony regarding justice. When Festus, the successor to Felix, arrived in Jerusalem, the high priest and his colleagues confronted him with their charges against Paul. They asked him, as a favor, to have Paul come to Jerusalem for they were planning to ambush and kill him along the way. Haughtily, Festus replied that Romans were not accustomed to handing someone over as a favor to be killed; the Romans acted strictly according to the law.

Festus remained in Jerusalem no longer than ten days. When he reached Caesarea, he had Paul brought before him. Also present were his accusers from Jerusalem. Before Festus, who had made such a point of Roman justice, Paul maintained that he had done nothing against the law of the Jews, against the temple or against Caesar.

Now justice was not always so strictly maintained by the Romans, and favor sometimes also played a role. This became evident when Festus suggested the case be settled in Jerusalem. He was evidently planning to humor the Jews. If need be, he would even sacrifice Paul, for he must have noticed how the Jews hated Paul.

Then Paul showed, by appealing to the emperor, that the gospel did not fear justice in the world. He wished to be tried before the highest court in the empire. The gospel and justice in the world are not in contrast to each other. The government too has the power to administer justice while remaining subject to Jesus Christ, the King of kings. Each government has the duty to protect the confession of God's name and the church of the Lord. No longer might government act as though the gospel of Jesus Christ was none of its concern. The entire world, state and government included, would become involved with the Christ. That is why God has directed events in such a way that Paul had to go to Rome.

Resolutely, Paul declared that the gospel does not protect injustice. If he had committed a crime he would pay the price, even death. In fact, the gospel teaches man to assume full responsibility for his actions, a far greater sense of accountability than had ever been present in the consciousness of any Roman. The gospel put a Roman's sense of justice to shame. But then Paul also demanded justice be done to him; he would not be handed over to the Sanhedrin because the governor refused to accept responsibility.

After conferring with his council Festus decided to comply with Paul's appeal. Paul would make his defense before the emperor. He would go to Rome as a prisoner, different certainly from what he had imagined. But whatever the circumstances he would be permitted to carry the gospel into the emperor's palace. Throughout he offered his life as a sacrifice to his Lord.

Testimony regarding the Word of God. When some days had passed King Agrippa, ruler over several provinces in the north, came to visit Festus and to welcome him. Agrippa was accompanied by his sister Bernice. Agrippa was a son of Herod Agrippa I, who had been king of the entire country. Agrippa had his children instructed in the law of the Jews as much as possible, but those children had not learned to bow before the Word of the Lord. On the contrary, they surrendered all the more to sin.

During this visit Festus told the king about Paul's case. Then Agrippa expressed a wish to hear Paul himself. This would take place the next day. Because both Agrippa and Bernice appreciated a display of great splendor, they convened a meeting full of pomp. Festus indicated he would like to have King Agrippa advise him regarding Paul, a man he was sending on to the emperor.

Paul expressed his delight at being privileged to defend himself before Agrippa, knowing the king was especially familiar with everything that went on among the Jews. He then explained his education as a Pharisee and reiterated that his trial was about faith in the resurrection of the dead. What was really at stake was the resurrection of Jesus Christ, the fruits of which could be seen in His own people. In that faith Paul did not deviate from the line of the Pharisees. Was the resurrection of the dead an impossibility for Agrippa and his family? Agrippa knew the law and the prophets regarding the resurrection.

Paul then told Agrippa of his own fanatical opposition to the gospel and how the Lord had called him to proclaim the gospel to Jews and Gentiles. Through that proclamation all nations had to be converted from darkness to the light and from the power of satan to God. All would receive forgiveness of sins and an inheritance among those who are sanctified by faith in Christ. Paul spoke deliberately of darkness, the power of satan and about the light of the gospel, knowing Agrippa lived in sin. Since his conversion, Paul had been obedient to the Lord's calling and he now testified to Agrippa of the light, the way. And yet Paul said nothing to contradict the law and the prophets for there it was written that Christ would have to suffer and rise from the dead, following which He would become a light for all nations.

When Paul referred to the Old Testament, Festus shouted, "Paul, you are out of your mind; your great learning is driving you insane." Festus understood nothing of the Scriptures.

Paul answered he spoke the truth, as Agrippa well knew because all the things relating to Jesus were common knowledge. Then Paul went on the offensive: "King Agrippa, do you believe the prophets?" He added, "I know that you believe them." King Agrippa knew certain things had been foretold by the prophets. Unfortunately this did not mean he surrendered in faith to what the prophets had said. He did not. Accordingly, his knowledge witnessed against his conscience. That is why Paul attacked him on this point. But Agrippa dismissed Paul by sneering, "Do you think that in such a short time you can persuade me to be a Christian?" Paul almost passionately responded, "Whether short or long, I would God that not only you but also all who are listening to me today may become what I am, except for these chains." He was praying they all might see the light of the gospel and thus be delivered from the bonds of sin.

Now the king had heard enough. With Bernice and the others he rose, bringing the hearing to an end. The gospel had left him unaffected. Nevertheless, the testimony had also gone out to this king; Christ had maintained His rightful claim to the subjection of kings. Privately Festus and Agrippa agreed that Paul had done nothing to deserve death, and that he could have been set free if he had not appealed to Caesar. The attitude of the authorities was still that the gospel was of no concern to them.

42: Christ's Global Reign

Acts 27 and 28

Particularly in this narrative Paul emerges as the bearer of the Word of God. Just as formerly the life of Elijah was very intimately connected with the Word of God,* so was Paul's. Thus we have to tell the children not only of Paul's deliverances but of the gospel and of Christ, who reveals His universal reign.

In this passage the gospel penetrates to Rome, the world's center. The gospel is not something to hide in a secret place on earth; it must govern the life of all nations.

Main thought: *Christ puts His claim on the center of the world.*

In God's way. Because he had appealed to the emperor, Paul had to be transported to Rome. Together with some other prisoners he was placed under the supervision of a certain Julius, a centurion of the imperial troops. They all boarded a ship and set off for Rome.

It had been Paul's desire to bring the gospel to the capital of the world-empire. The gospel had to have a place in the center of the world; all earthly authority would have to be made subject to the sovereign rule of Jesus Christ. But in chains? How different from what Paul had dreamed! His hope had been to preach the

---

*See Vol. II, especially pp. 257ff and 290—Trans.

Word in freedom. Would he still have an opportunity to preach the Word? But Paul went in God's way. Paul had to be willing to surrender to the Lord's will; in this way he was being sanctified and also equipped for the proper service of the gospel. No one dictates terms to the gospel; instead, the gospel rules over us and equips our lives for service.

On that difficult journey to Rome God's consolations were not lacking. When they arrived in Sidon, Julius allowed Paul to see his friends. Paul at least enjoyed a certain measure of freedom. Was this prophetic of the opportunities he would have in Rome to bring the word? Moreover Aristarchus, a Macedonian from Thessalonica and an old friend of Paul, was permitted to travel with him. (See Acts 19:29; 20:4 and compare Colossians 4:10 and Philemon 24, from which it is clear that Aristarchus remained with Paul during his [first] Roman imprisonment.)

Having left Sidon by ship, they sailed under protection of the island of Cyprus along the coast of Syria and Asia Minor, because they were up against strong headwinds. It was as if they were being hindered in their journey. Would Paul, that is, would the gospel ever reach Rome? Sometimes everything in the world appears to frustrate the spread of the gospel. At Myra in Lycia, in the western part of the south coast of Asia Minor, the centurion transferred them to a large ship sailing from Alexandria to Italy.

Under the protection of the Word of God. From Myra they sailed south and then further along the south coast of Crete. They made very slow progress because of headwinds. Finally they dropped anchor in a place called Fair Havens on the island of Crete. Meanwhile, because of the constant headwinds, the favorable season for sailing had passed. Winter with its storms was approaching. They debated passing the winter in Fair Havens. Although there was a fairly secure roadstead or anchorage, there was no harbor. Then Paul stepped forward as the bearer of the Word of God. Because he had surrendered to the service of his Lord, the Lord showed him what would happen on the voyage. The ship and the lives of all men aboard, Paul warned, would be in danger. However, the centurion put more faith in the captain and the first mate than in Paul. It was decided to look for a better harbor on the island of Crete to spend the winter. Of course, the centurion and his prisoners went along. How could the centurion possibly have had faith in the Word of God? What had he ever heard of it? Still, he should have trusted Paul rather than anyone else, even experienced seamen. But when do we surrender ourselves completely to the Word of God?

At first the captain and the first mate seemed to be proven right. With a gentle south wind they sailed along the south coast of Crete, close to shore. But that did not last very long. Soon a tempestuous wind called the northeaster swept down from the island, driving the ship completely off course. The second day they were already in such danger that they threw the cargo overboard. The third day they even cast the ship's tackle overboard. To make matters worse there was no sun or stars for days, making it impossible to determine their position. There was no time to eat, for at any moment they could perish. The sails had all been lowered; they were abandoned to sea and wind.

At this point Paul stood up and reproached them for not having heeded his advice. But he also urged them to keep up their courage, for an angel of God had revealed to him that he would reach Rome safely. He would see his wish fulfilled: to be allowed to witness of Jesus Christ before Caesar. That was the answer to the prayer he had offered during the storm. For the sake of the gospel Paul had wrestled for the safety of the ship. The angel had revealed to him that, although the ship would be lost, all persons on board would be spared. God had put the lives of all crew members and passengers into Paul's hands; their deliverance was the answer to Paul's prayer. They would all realize that it is safe to be under the protection of the Word of the Lord. While that does not mean we will be spared from every temporal distress, our lives will not be in vain; we shall be saved forever. Paul predicted they would run aground on some island.

On the fourteenth night of drifting in the Adriatic Sea, the sailors sensed they were approaching land. They took soundings, which confirmed their suspicions. Fearing they might crash against the rocks, they dropped four anchors from the ship's stern and waited for daylight. Some sailors secretly planned to escape from the ship with the lifeboat on the pretext they were also going to lower the bow anchors. Paul saw through their scheme and alerted the centurion. If the sailors did not stay on board, Paul warned, no one would survive. The entire crew had to place itself under the protection of the Word of the Lord. By now Paul had so much influence that the soldiers believed him. The soldiers cut the ropes of the boat and let it drift out to sea. They were now forced to surrender to the Word of the Lord. That most certainly did not mean all those men on that ship had true faith; in fact, most were probably highly superstitious, but at this point they had no choice.

Towards daybreak Paul urged them all to eat. He renewed the promise that not one of them would perish. Paul took bread, gave public thanks to God and ate. His words and example gave them courage, and they too began to eat. All told there were 276 persons on board. When they had eaten they threw the grain into the sea in order to lighten the ship. In a certain sense, that was also an act of faith. They had confidence in Paul's word that they would no longer need the grain.

At daybreak they saw unfamiliar land. The crew spotted a bay with a sandy beach, an ideal place to run the ship aground. The rudders, which had been secured long ago, were now let down into the sea again. They hoisted the foresail, cut loose the anchors and made for shore. But their misfortunes had still not come to an end: the ship struck a sandbar. The bow was high and dry and all rushed forward, abandoning the stern which was broken to pieces by the pounding surf. The soldiers then became edgy; the prisoners might just try to escape, for which the soldiers would have to pay with their lives. To avoid that they wanted to kill all the prisoners. However, the centurion wanted to spare Paul's life and ordered his soldiers back. He ordered those who could swim to make for land. The others grabbed planks and other pieces of the ship and floated ashore. Everyone reached land safely. The Word of the Lord preserved them; for God's promise is sure.

Appointed as a sign. The island was Malta and the islanders showed them unusual kindness. They built a bonfire and cared for the shipwrecked as best they could. Paul helped gather firewood. As he was about to throw a bundle of sticks on the fire, a viper clung to his hand. The inhabitants of the island saw the venomous snake hanging from the prisoner's hand. It was obvious to the islanders that divine vengeance was pursuing Paul: although he had escaped from the shipwreck, he was now going to die from the bite of a poisonous viper. They expected his hand to swell and waited for Paul to drop. And, indeed, Paul's life was very much in danger. However, he was the bearer of the Word of the Lord and his mission was still to proclaim that Word in Rome. Therefore he was safe under the protection of the Word of the Lord. His life was spared by yet another miracle of God. When the natives saw that nothing happened to him, they changed their minds and declared him a god. Paul decided they could not remain living in superstition; they had to hear the Word of God. The Lord clearly provided the opportunity.

Near the place where they had landed was an estate belonging to Publius, the chief official of the island. For three days he showed them kind hospitality. It happened that his father lay sick with fever and dysentery. Paul visited him and, after prayer, laid his hands on the sick man and healed him. Then the others who had diseases came and were cured. What a wonderful disclosure of the power for salvation there is in Christ and in the Word of His grace! Paul would not have wanted to miss this opportunity to preach the Word on Malta. Thus the grace of the Lord was revealed and the Kingdom of God came also to Malta.

Proclaiming the Word in Rome. They remained on the island for three months. Then they boarded a ship from Alexandria with the figurehead of the twin gods Castor and Pollux, which had spent the winter on the island. Now the voyage went smoothly. At Syracuse they stayed three days, and then they traveled on over Rhegium to Puteoli where they found some brethren. At their invitation they stayed with them for seven days. As a result of all that had happened the centurion must have developed a great respect for Paul and he rewarded him with all possible freedom.

Meanwhile, the brethren in Rome had heard that Paul was coming. Through commerce and trade the gospel had penetrated to the Jews in Italy and many had become disciples. When Paul arrived in the vicinity of Rome the brethren came out to meet him. This meeting made a deep impression on Paul. He had reached the goal of his journey and, indeed, the goal of his life. He would be privileged to carry the gospel to this place. What a swift course the gospel had taken through the world! And now he was standing on the threshold of the capital, not alone but in the company of fellow believers. He thanked God for this meeting and took courage.

When he arrived in Rome, Paul was treated with great distinction. The other prisoners were handed over to an army officer but Paul was allowed to live in a house of his own and to receive whomever he wished. Under house arrest he was guarded by a single soldier. This too the Lord had ordained so that he would have opportunity to proclaim the gospel.

Paul immediately made use of this freedom. While there were indeed some believers in Rome, the gospel had not yet been preached to all Jews attending the synagogue. Yet this had to happen. However, as Paul could not go to the synagogue, he invited all the Jewish leaders to come to him. He told them of his imprisonment and his treatment by the Romans. He denied having violated the law of Moses but he had been falsely accused and compelled to appeal to Caesar. However, he explained, he had not come to Rome to accuse his people. Rather, he wished to talk with them about the hope of Israel for which he had been made a prisoner.

The Jews were a bit hesitant. They had heard nothing about Paul's case either by letter or by oral report. What they did know was that this sect of which Paul evidently was an advocate was rejected in synagogues all over the world. They would, however, still like to learn what Paul thought. Undoubtedly they knew there were already some of these believers in Rome as well.

One day many of the Jews came to see Paul. From morning until evening he spoke to them of the Kingdom of God and showed from the Scriptures that Jesus is the Christ. Some believed the gospel but others did not. Paul warned the unbelievers that already the prophets (Isaiah 6:9, 10) had predicted that the people of the old covenant would disobey and harden their hearts. First the message was to go to them, but afterwards it would go to the Gentiles. The Gentiles would hear and put Israel to shame. In the end there was no agreement. The effort had been made in Rome to bring all Israel to faith, but here again only some of the people came to believe.

Paul stayed in his rented house for two whole years. To many people, Jews and Gentiles alike, he proclaimed the gospel. Without any hindrance he brought the message of the Kingdom of God. Christ had laid His claim on the center of the world. Now the gospel could go forth more easily unto the ends of the earth. All the world had to be won for Christ. All peoples and governments would have to serve Him.

Consummation

43: The Victory of the Kingdom

Matthew 24 and 25

The history of God's covenant has been dealt with up to Paul's mission to Rome, but the story is not complete without telling of the completion of all things. This consummation is not history yet but will one day belong to the history of "this age." Therefore, the history of this present age until the consummation is part of the history of the covenant.

Main thought: *One day the Kingdom of grace will be victorious.*

The disappearance of the Kingdom from view. One day when the Lord Jesus was leaving the temple with His disciples, they pointed out to Him the beauty of the temple buildings. How horrible his prediction must have sounded in their ears: "I tell you the truth, not one stone here will be left on another; every one will be thrown down." That made a deep impression on the disciples. As soon as they were seated on the Mount of Olives opposite Jerusalem, they asked Him when that would happen. They understood such destruction would come on account of Him because Jewry, which was proud of its temple, had rejected Him. With the glorious coming of His Kingdom the temple would be destroyed. That coming would mean the end of the age. They asked Him what signs would precede His coming and when they might expect it.

The disciples had seen many things correctly. They longed to have the Kingdom come in its glory and desired to know the signs. They also saw correctly how this Kingdom would result in the disintegration of unbelieving Jewry and its temple. Nor was it entirely wrong for them to think that this breakup would usher in the end of the age. Only they were unable to grasp the length of time between the destruction of the temple and the end of the age.

We can see this more clearly than the disciples, though we should not divorce the destruction of Jerusalem from the end of the age. The Jewish world was to disintegrate because it had not bowed before the Lord's Kingdom of grace. Similarly, the world would be destroyed because it would become disobedient to His gospel. First, however, the gospel would be preached in the entire world as a testimony to all nations. But following the world's disobedience the destruction would come. Thus the downfall of Jerusalem would foreshadow the end of the present world. One day the Lord would come for judgment. Of all these things He began to tell His disciples.

Certainly not all people in the world would believe in the Kingdom. On the contrary, false prophets would proclaim themselves redeemers of the world and would lead many astray. Men would look for salvation everywhere except in Christ's Kingdom of grace.

Neither would the spirit of that Kingdom take hold of the world. The nations would be divided against one another. The world would be filled with wars and rumors of wars. People would not understand the righteousness of the Kingdom.

As a result, the blessing of the Kingdom would disappear from the earth. The Kingdom was to subject the world and all of life to man and man in turn would submit to God in obedience of faith. That was biblical peace. But in rejecting the Kingdom man would live in terror because of earthquakes and epidemics.

All this, however, would only signal the beginning of suffering. An avowed foe would emerge to challenge the believers. The church would be persecuted. Many of its members would lapse and even betray each other. The apostates would join the ranks of false prophets who would bring their own gospel.

Because faith would be purged from the life of the world, wickedness would multiply and life would steadily become more godless. Almost no one would be able to escape those influences. The believers would have a serious struggle on their hands.

What would be left of the revelation of the Kingdom in the world? It would be increasingly difficult to believe in the Lord Jesus as the King of grace. How difficult already in our time! But he who endures to the end will be saved.

The great tribulation. Believers have the calling to work everywhere in life for all of life has to be subjected to Christ and the righteousness of His Kingdom must rule everywhere. However, eventually life will be so completely saturated with sin that believers can no longer participate meaningfully in life and will have to withdraw from it. This will be terrible because people's lives will become impossible. Young lives in particular will be greatly affected.

This too Jesus wanted to foretell so that believers might be prepared. He predicted how it would go towards the end of the age by comparing the behavior of believers at the time of Jerusalem's destruction.

The Jews would rise up against the Romans and try to shake the yoke from their necks. But when Roman legions invaded Canaan, once sacred ground, the Jews were not to take up the sword in defense of their national honor, for then the judgment of God would come. They should flee, Jesus said, across the Jordan River to the mountains. It would be painful, Jesus predicted, and what would the future hold for their children? Still, it was inevitable. They could only pray that their flight would not have to take place under the most difficult circumstances.

This is also how it would be towards the end of the age. Through the multiplication of wickedness life would be oppressive. This oppression caused by sin would choke life. Particularly for believers, existence would become impossible and their children would have no future. But because God loves His own, He will shorten those days; things will happen at a faster pace than anyone would have thought possible.

Escape from this ordeal, however, will be impossible. During those days people will say strange things. They'll say that here or there the Christ has appeared. But those who belong to Christ should not believe these rumors, for when He comes He will be revealed to everyone at the same time, just as lightning is visible to all. The judgment concerns all and therefore will come upon all.

The crisis will be terrible if even the Lord Jesus is unable to speak of any relief. The world will remain in this oppression, without relief until He appears.

The judgment that comes upon us all. Immediately after this great tribulation judgment will come. Heaven and earth will be shaken. Sun, moon and stars will be darkened. The whole world will be terrified when it sees the glory of the Son of man. Then He will gather His elect out of the world.

The elect are called to pay attention to the signs. When in the spring the trees come out we know summer is near. Similarly, believers will be able to determine from the signs in history that the coming of the Kingdom is at hand. That coming will be sooner than we expect. No more new dispensations will be coming; the church here on earth, living under the present dispensation of grace, will remain until the coming of Christ in His Kingdom. We are to remember these words of the Lord Jesus for they will surely be fulfilled.

In general, people in the world will not be alert to the end-time. It will be much the same as in the days of Noah when people lived only for themselves and were suddenly swamped by the flood. Men will be busy with their work as usual, believers as well as unbelievers, until suddenly the great sifting will take place separating those who lived for the Lord from those who put themselves first. Two men will be working in the field; the one will be taken away by judgment while the other will be spared. Two women will be grinding at the same mill; one will be judged, the other spared.

The entire world should live in high expectation of that end! No one knows the day and the hour, not even the angels in heaven. The coming of judgment will be sudden as a thief in the night. Unfortunately, few will be looking for it except, Jesus warned, the believers. They better be on guard so as not to be unpleasantly surprised!

The Lord Jesus reinforced His warnings with examples. A

master appoints one of his servants to administer his household during his absence. A responsible servant need not worry if his master returns unexpectedly. He is always prepared for it. But if he neglects his duties or cheats his master, the master will most certainly punish him. Similarly, if we live in obedience to the Lord we will always be ready for His return.

The test. Then the Lord Jesus portrayed the judgment itself. He received authority to judge from the Father. Christ will separate the believers from the unbelievers much as a shepherd separates sheep from goats when returning to the pen at night.

Placing the believers at His right hand He will say to them: "Come, you blessed of my Father, inherit the Kingdom prepared for you from the foundation of the world." He will usher them into the glory of His Kingdom saying, "I was hungry and you gave me food; I was thirsty and you gave me drink." On earth they lived only for the Lord Jesus.

They will not understand what He says, not knowing what they have done for the Lord. They certainly cannot boast of their own deeds. Then the Lord will say to them: "As you did it to one of the least of these my brethren, you did it to me." For Christ's sake they gave themselves in love and in so doing showed that they understood what the Kingdom is all about. They did not earn anything by doing it but when they saw how Christ gave Himself so completely in His Kingdom, they gave themselves too. That was a response to His love and it made for an entirely different attitude towards life than is otherwise found in the world.

The unbelievers on His left hand will hear His reproach that they did nothing for Him. And when asked how they might have done something, Jesus will reply that they showed no love for His sake towards others. They gave nothing and loved no one except themselves because they rejected His gifts and His love.

The unbelievers will plunge into eternal misery. They will harden themselves forever in their rebellion against God and in their rejection of His love. Forever the wrath of God will burn against them. The believers, who have known the righteousness of the Kingdom, will enjoy God's communion forever.

44: The Victory over Satan

Revelation 12

Together with the above-mentioned portion of Scripture we shall consider what is said in Revelation 20 about the judgment upon satan. Of course, we cannot here discuss the millennial difficulties raised by the first few verses of chapter 20.

Main thought: *Christ will conquer satan.*

The woman and the dragon. The apostle John outlived all the other apostles. After the death of Paul he provided the leadership for the congregation at Ephesus for a long time. From there he sent out his message to the other congregations. For the sake of the gospel, however, he was seized and exiled to the island of Patmos off the west coast of Asia Minor. During the part of his life he spent there John was not idle, for Christ revealed much to him of "what must soon take place." He was shown the things that are occurring now and that will occur up to the return of the Lord Jesus. It has now already been a matter of many centuries although the Lord said to John that it would soon take place. Things are happening quickly; the Lord is hastening to the end of the age and the glory of His Kingdom. Because there is so much that must take place, however, it still takes centuries.

The Lord revealed these things to John in visions. Although he received these visions while awake they still resemble our

252

dreams. In our sleep we see strange things and sometimes one image flows into the other in a very confusing way. So too John's visions were strange and there were unusual transitions. One by one, however, they formed a revelation of the Lord.

One day John saw a great and wondrous sign in the sky. There was a woman to whom God had granted all the glory and all the light that He had created, for she was clothed with the sun. She was standing on the moon and on her head was a crown of twelve stars.

While John stared at the sign, another one appeared in the sky: an enormous red dragon with seven heads and ten horns. On his heads he had seven crowns. With his tail this serpent or dragon controlled one-third of the stars in the sky and flung them down to earth. The dragon was decidedly hostile to the woman.

What was the Lord's revelation in that vision? Obviously there was enmity between the dragon and the woman, an enmity that governed the world's history. From everything John saw in his vision it is clear that the woman represented God's people while the serpent represented satan. Satan is the implacable foe of God's people and this hostility runs through all of history. The people of the Lord know His communion and through that communion they are glorified. Hence, all the light surrounded the woman. But satan's only purpose is to destroy that communion, break the bond between God and His people and rob that woman of her glory! Satan wanted nothing but to obscure the honor of God's grace and interfere with the work of Jesus Christ, for it was Christ who brought communion between God and His people.

The child. The vision showed that the dragon's anger was especially directed against Christ for the child represents the Lord Jesus, born out of the people of God. He was not only Mary's treasure, but the treasure of His people as a whole. Without Christ, the dragon knew, the people would not survive.

The dragon, maddened by rage against that little child, wanted to devour him. After all, this child was to rule over all the nations. The judgment of the Lord Jesus upon the nations would be a judgment in righteousness; He would condemn those who had rejected the communion with God. However, satan did not want to acknowledge Christ's right over all the nations; he would have them groan under his own yoke and live in godlessness and unrighteousness.

We know how satan persecuted Jesus when He was on earth. Because of satan's promptings in the hearts of the Jewish elders and Judas, Jesus was indeed put to death on the cross but God raised Him up and took Him to Himself in heaven. John also saw this in the vision; the child was lifted up to God and to His throne.

War in heaven. There was more to the vision. John saw angels appear under the archangel Michael. Opposite them the dragon and his angels took their stand. In the beginning of the vision the tail of the dragon controlled one-third of the stars, that is, one-third of the angels. They fell with him and, like him, became devils.

Between these two forces a violent war broke out in heaven. What was this war supposed to mean? Angels serve Christ in maintaining the communion between God and His people through His Spirit; devils have no other intention than to break up this communion. Hence war between the two forces is unavoidable.

Satan and his forces could not hold their own against Michael and his angels, to whom Christ in His sovereign grace granted the greater strength. The victory went to those who fought for Christ. It will never be possible to break the communion between God and His people; satan shall never enter heaven. In heaven and in the heavenly sovereignty of Christ which the Father has granted Him that communion is secure.

Satan then wanted to bring charges against the people of God and thus break the communion. However, as Christ made atonement for the sins of His people with His blood God is eternally with that people. And if God is for them, who shall be against them? Therefore Michael and his angels had superlative power against satan's army, who were ejected from heaven forever.

Shouts of joy and exultation rose up in heaven because of this victory. Angels rejoiced at the salvation of God's people, because in that salvation the grace of God was glorified, and they were privileged to be engaged in its service. The Kingdom of grace had now been established for all eternity.

This victory had not come about without God's people. They too had fought in faith, holding on to their communion with God. They looked to the atonement of their sins through the blood of the Lamb. They had witnessed of Christ on earth, would even have sacrificed their lives for that testimony. Truly there was war in heaven and on earth—angels and men took part in that conflict—but the real victor was Christ.

Continuing warfare on earth. This victory did not mean the struggle on earth had now ended, for John saw something else happen. Heaven was now definitely closed to satan but he and his fallen angels were hurled down to earth. There they would continue to exercise their influence to break up the communion between God and His people. What would become of the church on earth and of the whole human race if satan could still make his influence felt there? At the same time the angels sang their song of praise about the victory, they also warned: "Woe to you who inhabit the earth and the sea; for the devil has come down to you; he is filled with fury, because he knows that his time is short."

John saw that the woman was given two wings, as of a great eagle, with which she fled into the wilderness beyond the serpent's reach. What John saw reminds us of what once happened with Israel. When the people of the Lord were in imminent danger of perishing in Egypt, the Lord led them out into the wilderness beyond the reach of Pharaoh. It was, to be sure, still a wilderness into which the people were brought, a place full of dangers, but they were led there safely because the Lord had provided that place for His people. Thus the woman was saved from the power of the evil one; the real life of the people, their communion with God, satan can never break up. The church is outside the range and reach of the serpent. Yet in this life the church is still as it were in the wilderness, in a place full of dangers. It is a comfort to her to know that God has provided this place for her, for then He will also protect her.

The dragon made one more effort to destroy the woman. He poured water like a river out of his mouth to sweep her away with the flood. But the earth opened up and swallowed the river. The life of the church will never come within satan's power. Because of his failure satan's fury was aroused all the more, and he would do all he could to harm the believers on earth.

Judgment. Even though he will never be able to get the church within his power, satan nevertheless fights for dominion over all peoples out of which the church is gathered. Thus he fights against the Christ, for those people have been given to Christ so He might reign over them and claim their lives by His Word and Spirit, thereby gathering His church to Himself.

At His ascension Christ ascended to His throne, His position of honor and His place of power and authority. At that moment began the reign of grace of the exalted Mediator over all peoples. From that moment on His Word is being proclaimed among all nations. Was it not also for this reason that He poured out His Spirit? By His Spirit and Word He would influence the life of the nations everywhere on earth in order that He might be acknowledged as King. He had commissioned His disciples to make disciples of all nations and to baptize them in the name of the triune God.

Conquering the nations by His Spirit and Word Christ is everywhere thwarted by satan, because satan previously had the nations in his power. But he cannot stop the gospel in its course, and nation upon nation bows before the authority of Christ. That does not mean all individual persons in those nations come to faith and conversion of life. It also does not mean that sin is entirely conquered among those nations. But it does mean that among those peoples the church is no longer persecuted; on the contrary, it finds recognition, and those nations thereby acknowledge the kingship of Jesus Christ.

However, this state of affairs will not continue to the end of the world. Satan will recapture the nations again from Christ; then at the end it will appear as if satan is winning the struggle after all. The nations that have not stood in the center of world history will rise up. Their spirit will influence the world. Satan will then have things his way again. At this point the last great persecution of the church will take place. Just as Jerusalem was once besieged by surrounding heathen nations, the people of God will be encompassed by the enmity of the nations. Life for the believers will be made impossible. It will look as if the church is going to perish in that persecution.

But then fire will come down from heaven and consume the enemies of the church. That is how John saw it in a later vision (Revelation 20:9b): the devil was thrown into the lake of fire. God's wrath will be kindled against him forever. Then satan's kingdom will be finished for good.

After that John saw a great white throne on which Christ was seated, whose glory tolerated nothing unsanctified. From His glory came a renewal of heaven and earth. All the dead were raised and judged by Him according to whether they had responded to Him and His love in faith. After that judgment death and the realm of the dead (Hades) were conquered. In the new earth there would no longer be any power of death. All who had not confessed Christ, whose names were not written in the book of life, would be thrown into the lake of fire. In the new earth only true life will be known, that is, life in communion with God, which nothing shall ever disturb.

45: The Victory over the Beast

Revelation 19:11-21

In this section we shall also make use of what is revealed to us in II Thessalonians 2, Revelation 12 and other parts of Revelation. We proceed from the idea that we have to think of the antichrist as a particular person, mainly because of such expressions as "the man of lawlessness (sin)" and "the son of destruction" (II Thessalonians 2:3). If the antichrist is going to be the world's tyrant, then "the restrainer" in II Thessalonians 2 probably refers to the government whose authority still finds sufficient recognition. For the tyrant can only come to power when the world has been brought to a state of disintegration by revolution and anarchy. However, as long as the authority of government finds sufficient acknowledgment this disintegration is restrained.

Main thought: *The One called Faithful and True shall conquer the beast out of the sea.*

The antichrist. When John was on Patmos the Lord showed him visions in order to reveal to him and to us what would happen in the end-time. One day he was standing at the seashore. Before him John saw the rolling waves. Suddenly the waters parted and a frightening monster emerged from the sea. That monster had seven heads and ten horns. On each horn was a kingly crown. The whole appearance of the beast made the impression on John that it had come to blaspheme God; the beast had a burning hatred for the Lord.

While John looked on terror-stricken he saw that one of the

258

beast's heads was mortally wounded and yet miraculously healed. Apparently satan's power kept that beast alive.

Gradually the image in the vision changed, as images so often do in our dreams. The beast came to have something human about it and it made its appearance in the world of men. Everybody on earth began to idolize the beast and invited it to be their leader. The world could not resist it because it acted with satanic power.

That beast constantly blasphemed the Lord. It therefore turned in fury against all who loved the Lord and believers were oppressed and persecuted.

That could happen all over the world for the beast was given authority over all the nations. The whole world recognized its authority and revered the beast instead of God. Only those were excluded who belonged to the Lord, whose names were written in the book of life. These have been purchased by the blood of the Lamb and because they are His possession He preserves them by faith in Him.

The beast John saw is the antichrist, the archenemy of the Christ. The spirit of the antichrist, the spirit of enmity against Christ, has been in the world for a long time already. But one day the antichrist himself will come. All the nations will be subjected to his authority and he will bring all men together in warfare against Christ. Satan will give him such power.

The false prophet. This antichrist is going to have an ally. The Lord showed John that as well, for a second vision followed upon the first. His eyes were now no longer directed out to the sea, but towards the land. All at once the earth split open and John saw another beast emerge, this one with quite a different form. Everything connected with the beast from the sea spoke of power and force and dominion. That was not the case with the beast from the earth. It had two horns like a lamb and spoke as a serpent hisses. This beast would not rule by force but would subtly deceive the minds of men.

However, it would ally itself with the beast from the sea. Together they would lead the world. This second beast would function as a false prophet. It would get people to revere and worship the beast from the sea and to make an image of it.

This false prophet will perform great and miraculous signs on earth. Because he is in the service of the beast from the sea satan will give him that power.

He especially will set up and organize the battle of the human race against the church of the Lord. All persons who participate in the worship of the antichrist will bear his external mark. And everyone who does not go along will be excluded from society. That will be the moment of truth for believers. Only faith and grateful love for the Lord Jesus will cause them to remain faithful. The Lord will give them the strength to remain true.

Babylon the Great. The world will be organized by the antichrist and the false prophet according to their own insight. They will be guided not by the Spirit of Christ, but by the spirit of satan, the spirit of hostility toward the living God. Christ came to have us live in communion with God; the antichrist brings a life without God and of hostility toward God.

Only in communion with God through the Lord Jesus Christ can our selfishness be overcome and put to death. Out of that communion there rises in us a new life of love for God and for one another. Then we can offer our lives up as a sacrifice, as the Lord did.

The antichrist and the false prophet, however, want something completely different. Without God mankind will seek itself. At first every individual supposedly must offer himself up for the glory of mankind as a whole, but man can do that only under the delusion of that pretended glory. In the final analysis all men will seek themselves and in so doing will recognize no laws or restraints. Then iniquity on earth will be multiplied and man will make life hell for himself and the other.

Such a world Scriptures calls "Babylon the Great." Scripture reminds us of the old Babylonian world-empire of which the magnificent Babylon was the capital. In its day that empire also sought only its own glory and therefore perished in godlessness and iniquity. Similar conditions will emerge under the guidance of the antichrist. It will be Babylon revisited if everyone thinks only of himself and tramples on everybody else. Selfishness will be man's only guide. Even natural love—the love of parents for their children and of children for their parents, the love of brothers and sisters and, further, all natural ties—will weaken and vanish. Men will be like wolves tearing their fellow men to pieces. Such is life when the antichrist incites man to abandon God. Isn't it much like that already?

People will exploit each other. The so-called great, the rich and the prominent, will capitalize on this trend at the expense of their fellow man.

This enemy of Christ can rightly be called the antichrist, for in everything he is Christ's counterfeit. Christ came to redeem and heal our life. He especially sought out the poor and the oppressed, the crushed and the sick! His love by which He offered Himself up for our human race was balm for our many wounds. By contrast, the antichrist inflicts countless wounds on our life. It is good to know his dominion will not be without end!

The coming of the One called Faithful and True. It is not possible for Babylon the Great to last. One day she will fall and all who have profited from her will mourn. Mankind will be appalled at her collapse, particularly those who have benefited from her ruthless injustice. They will rightly feel that the end of the world has come. After this destruction there will come no repeat for the antichrist will himself be conquered and condemned. Christ will see to that when He returns.

John was also permitted to see the antichrist vanquished. For that he did not look out to the sea or over the land; instead his eyes were drawn to heaven. He saw heaven opened and riding forth a white horse whose rider was called Faithful and True. He came to judge and make war.

The rider was Jesus Christ. His eyes were aflame and He wore many crowns on His head. No one can ever fully know His name for He is God and He came to us in the fullness of divine love. Who will ever understand that fullness?

Yet He does bear a name by which we may know Him. He is called the Word of God, for He speaks God's love to us and brings us God's communion through faith in Him. However, as the Word of God He also brings the separation between believers and unbelievers. Besides bringing God's love He also judges those who reject God's love. Consequently, the robe that John saw Him wear was sprinkled with blood.

The armies of heaven, dressed in fine linen, white and clean, followed Him on white horses. The angels had ministered to Him when He came to bring the communion with God; now they would also be His servants at the judgment.

John saw the following name written on His robe and on His thigh: "King of kings and Lord of lords." Precisely because He brought us God's communion God had anointed Him to be King of the whole universe. In His love and grace He was to reign. Even the kings of the earth had to subject themselves to Him and serve Him in His reign of grace. However, they had exalted themselves over against Him and therefore He came for judgment, particularly of these kings.

Suddenly John saw an angel standing in the sun, summoning all the birds of prey. There would now be enough prey for them among the large number of destroyed enemies, both the prominent and the insignificant. A great war broke out between Christ with His army and the antichrist with all the kings of the earth and their armies. The whole earth became a battlefield. Such spiritual warfare between the Spirit of Christ and the spirit of His enemies has been raging on earth throughout history. At His return, however, the decisive moment will come and the war will be brought to an end.

John saw how the antichrist and the false prophet were captured and thrown alive into the lake of fire. The wrath of God is kindled against them for all eternity. And God's judgment is not only upon them but also upon their followers. They will be condemned and put away from the earth forever; their names will perish with them. Judgment came as a great war in which they were all slain and the birds devoured their remains. An honorable burial was not permitted; nothing was left to remember them by.

With all hostility quashed Christ will reign forever on the new earth. And together with Him all His people will enjoy eternal communion with God and reign over all the works of God's hands.

46: The Age to Come

Revelation 21–22

The new Jerusalem is not the church, just as Jerusalem was not the people of Israel. The new Jerusalem indicates the new state in which God's glory will again cover all things; it refers to what the Scripture calls "the coming age" in contrast to "the present age."

The coming age, however, is not purely future; it does not only follow this age but is also above it, ready to be revealed at any moment. In a certain sense that coming age has already become the present. With the outpouring of the Holy Spirit the new and eternal testament (see Hebrews 9:15; 13:20) really has begun; no third dispensation of the covenant is to follow upon the present one. Full communion with God has been granted to us by the indwelling of the Holy Spirit. The effect of that in our lives is still diluted by the sin in us; besides, we are still waiting for the renewal of heaven and earth, which is the result of the outpouring of the Spirit. That renewal of heaven and earth is necessarily connected with the outpouring of the Spirit. For that reason the prophet Joel links them inseparably. The coming age has thus already begun but we are still awaiting the revelation of its glory. As for communion with God through the Spirit, it is already here, but the transformation of heaven and earth and of our life in its relation to heaven and earth is yet to come.

It is therefore out of the question that a new creation is meant when it is said, "Behold, I make all things new." Just as the outpouring of the Spirit did not mean a new creation (but rather sanctification and renewal), so we are not to look for a new creation at the last day (although indeed we should look for renewal and glorification). There is also going to be glorification; this needs to be emphasized. Not only will sin and its effects be removed from the earth, but there is going to be another form of existence, another form of life. However, the original creation had already been structured with that new form of existence in

263

mind, so no new creation is necessary. In redemption God does not deny the work of His hands; He purifies it and glorifies it at the same time.

Little can be said about what will be characteristic of life in the age to come. In these chapters Scripture speaks about it in language borrowed from our present life. I Corinthians 15:44 speaks of the difference between "the psychic" and "the pneumatic": a psychic body is sown; a pneumatic body is raised. The "psychic" is now indeed corrupted by sin and therefore has become the opposite of the "pneumatic," but that's not how it was with the "psychic" as originally created. Once, God created a holy "psychic" life, that He might produce "the pneumatic" out of it. The name "pneumatic" for the new form of existence points to a much more intimate communion between the Spirit of God and our life than was possible with our "psychic" existence. This most intimate communion makes a new fall into sin impossible.

There is something ambiguous about the life of the believer. On the one hand, through the outpouring of the Spirit he participates in the coming age; on the other hand, he still lives in this present age. In the life of the believer too the outpouring of the Spirit cries out for the renewal of all things.

Notice that in the first part of chapter 21 the writer speaks of the new heaven and the new earth and of the new Jerusalem coming down out of heaven from God. Then, in the second part of the chapter this new Jerusalem is described as it is already now prepared in heaven. That is why it is possible for the writer to speak of the ongoing presence of the nations (Gentiles), and to say (22:2) that the leaves of the tree of life are for the healing of the nations.

Main thought: *The future age is about to come.*

The new heaven and the new earth. With His outpouring on Pentecost, the Holy Spirit came to dwell in the hearts of Christ's people and we were given the most intimate communion with God. This intimate communion was to bring with it the glorification (transfiguration) of our life. And because man is the head of the whole creation, the glorification of heaven and earth was necessarily tied to that fact. Accordingly, at the Feast of Pentecost Peter had cited Joel's prophecy, in which the renewal of heaven and earth is most intimately connected with the outpouring of the Spirit. We still are awaiting that renewal. That does not mean it has been postponed. It will come very quickly but there is still so much to be done before that time. Life on earth must have had its full opportunity for renewal.

To John on Patmos the Lord showed in visions what some day will take place. When later John again received such a vision, he saw a new heaven and a new earth, with a new communion between them. Heaven and earth were perfectly united so that on earth men shared the life of heaven.

It certainly must have been a delight for John to see that gloriously new thing which God was going to bring about. It must have been a feast for his eyes. Nothing was left of the old form of the earth, not even the sea with its negative implications about separating the nations of the world.

As he looked he saw a city coming down from God out of the heart of heaven. This was the new Jerusalem, the new life in glory that God had prepared for His people. That new life God had made lovely and glorious for His people, just as a bride is made beautiful for her husband.

At the same moment John heard a clear voice from heaven, saying that God would now dwell forever with His people. That communion brought with it the glorification of their life and of heaven and earth. There would be no more sadness or death. Lapsing into sin was now out of the question because the Spirit of the Lord had taken complete possession of the hearts of the believers. The old state of things was gone forever. John had to write down what God said: "Behold I make all things new." Communion through the Spirit would surely bring this renewal. God pledged His Word to it.

As if everything had already been realized, God said, "It is done." And He called Himself the Alpha and the Omega, the beginning and the end. It was He in His love, from whom were all things, and to whom all things would again return. Because His love was the starting point and goal of all things, He would give the thirsty to drink from the fountain of His love. The thirsty would have the water of life; it would mean eternal life to him, and it would be without cost.

Still, this renewal of all things did not include all men. They who conquer by faith will inherit everything; they will forever be God's children. But they who for fear of the sinful world denied their faith will be put away from the earth and cast into the lake of fire. They will suffer the second death, eternal oblivion.

The new Jerusalem. The new Jerusalem, the glorious new life, will one day come down from God out of heaven. Already the new Jerusalem is being prepared under the direction of the Lord Jesus Christ and He hastens to give it to His own.

John was privileged to see this new Jerusalem. An angel carried him away in the Spirit to a high mountain from where he had a view of the city. And it was indeed a city; believers lived together as in any other city. Properly directed, life in a city can be innovative and exciting. In the new Jerusalem also the life of the believers will come to full development.

Covering the city was the glory of God, producing a radiance that sparkled the way a crystal-clear jasper stone can sparkle. The Spirit of communion brought a shining glory to the city.

The city had a high wall with twelve gates, three on each of the four sides. From each side there was access to the city; however, the entrances were guarded by twelve angels. On the gates the names of the twelve tribes of Israel were inscribed and on the foundations of the wall were the names of the twelve apostles. Believers of the old and the new covenant together found a safe fellowship in that city.

The angel who talked with John measured the city before his very eyes with a golden measuring stick. The city was a cube of enormous proportions, just as once the Holy of Holies in the temple had been in the shape of a cube. The measurements of God's holy dwelling place are of equal and perfect length. And all the people of God were to enjoy His communion in that large city.

When John took a somewhat closer look at the city, he saw that its wall was one crystal-clear jasper stone. The streets were pure gold, smooth and shining as glass. The twelve foundations of the wall were precious stones of various glittering colors. Each of the twelve gates was a single pearl. More wonderful than you could ever imagine anything on earth is the life that God has prepared for His people.

Everlasting reign. Apparently there was no temple in that city as there once had been in Jerusalem. Neither was that necessary since life in the city is one of constant adoration; here God through Christ lives with His elect.

The sun and moon no longer have to shine; the glory of God's communion in the Christ is its light.

The nations that are saved shall walk in this light. Believers of all nations and races will pass through those streets. There they will know a unity they never found on earth. Yet their life on earth will not have been in vain; the fruits will become evident in the new Jerusalem. Kings will lay their glory at the feet of Christ and His people. What did the richest possessions of kings mean compared with the glory of this city? Those possessions will first have to be consecrated in order for them to be accepted there. Still, all the treasures of the earth shall become glorified in the new Jerusalem. From all sides they will enter the city. It will never be necessary to close its gates, for there will be no night there. Not only the glory of the kings, but also the glory and the honor of the nations will be brought in. Believers from all nations will gladly bring their treasures into the new Jerusalem to see them glorified there. Even unbelievers will have contributed to the store of those treasures but only the elect will benefit. Nothing shall enter that city that pollutes or awakens horror but only those who are written in the Lamb's book of life shall enter.

The angel showed John a pure river of the water of life, clear as crystal. This river flowed from the throne of God and of the Lamb. That throne was in the city; the sovereign reign of God's grace is upon it. On each side of the river was a street and on the edge of the water stood the tree of life. Every month that tree bore a new crop of fruit and the leaves of the tree were for the healing of the nations (Gentiles). The river and the tree point to the communion that God will give for the healing of life.

God in His grace shall rule over that city forever. No one will ever be accursed again. Full of joy, its citizens will serve the Lord; daily they will see His face and they will carry His name on their foreheads. With the Lord Jesus Christ they will reign eternally as kings over everything the Lord God has made.

The entire life in that city will be radiant and full of splendor because it is the fruit of the most intimate communion between

God and His people through the Holy Spirit. And because this intimate communion between the Spirit of God and the spirit of man has come, it will never be possible for this life to be disturbed.

Behold, I am coming soon. The Lord Jesus had all these things shown and explained to John by His angel. John was so deeply impressed that he fell down to worship at his feet. This startled the angel who told John to worship only God as he was just a fellow-servant with John and all the believers.

The angel urged John to make the vision known because the time of decision would come soon. Everyone should be prepared for the coming of the new Jerusalem. That involves making a choice: either continue in iniquity or grow in communion with God. Those who choose to live for Him in His communion will enter through the gates into the city and eat the fruit of the tree of life. Outside the city will be all those who turn away from the Lord.

The Lord said that He would come quickly. It has now been many centuries, yet we must not think the Lord delays fulfilling His promise. There is so much to be done but the Lord is hurrying; He hastens the course of events. We shall neither take away from nor add to His Word, but keep it faithfully in our hearts and pray for His coming. If we live close to the Lord His coming will not frighten us; it will be cause for celebration!

Subject Index*

---

*This index is intended to *supplement* the tables of contents. To read about Samson, for example, turn to the chapter in Volume II based on Judges 13-16. The Scripture passages on which the various chapters are based are listed in the tables of contents.

269

regeneration, IV, 25
religion, I, 12-13
   III, 14, 16, 343
   IV, 208
"remnant," I, 108, 418
   II, 213, 217, 223, 226, 227, **232**, 245, 251, **261**, 288, 313, 341, **366**
   III, **101**, 249
   IV, 124
resurrection of Christ, I, 49, 63, 207, **272**, 277
   II, 186, 263, **305**, 345, 382
   III, **14**, 39, 41, 91, 95, 100, **173ff**, 256, **299ff**, 424, **447ff**
   IV, 82, **105ff**, **109-10**, 115, 126, 140, 208, **224**, 235
resurrection of the dead, I, 423
   II, 340-1
   III, **96**, 167-8, 228, **254**, **270**, 272, 328, 330, **442**, 444
   IV, 109, 140, 148, 223-4, 229, 232-3, 235, **257**
return of Christ, I, 247, 251, 279, 283-4
   III, 127, 397, 424
   IV, 124, 252, 261
Ridderbos, Herman, III, 12-13
righteousness and justice of God, I, **121-4, 406-9**
   II, **131**, 271-2, 276, 419, 436
   III, **156-60**, 269, **415-17**
   IV, **59-61**, 248, 251, 253
Roman Catholicism, IV, 160
Rousseau, J.J., I, 12
   III, 15, 18

sabbath, I, **30**, 35, 287, **291**, 309
   II, 454-5
   III, 171, 174, **198ff**, 390, **393**, **394-5**
   IV, **46-7**, 56, 65, 192-3, **218**
sacred vs. secular, I, 242
   III, 245
sacrifice, I, **49-50**, 51-2, 59, 62, 64, 80, **136ff**, 163, **235ff**, **255-6**, 272,
     295-6, 297, **299**, 301, **310-11**, **313-16**, 318, **320-2**, 372
   II, **32**, **36**, 38, 55, 70, **79-80**, 85, **93-4**, **99**, 102, 108-9, 131, 136, 157,
     189-90, 198-9, 207, 209-10, 228, 251, **295**, 300, 354, 360-1, 383,
     385, 391, 430, 433, 455

Index of Scripture References*

Genesis			19:16-18	IV, 137
2	I, 30		22:28	IV, 229
3:15	I, 21		24:8	III, 17
9:25	I, 408		39:24-6	I, 319
12	I, 82, 94			
17	I, 94		Leviticus	
18:10	I, 125		12	III, 327
19:30-7	I, 368		12:2	III, 327
23	IV, 156		26:27-9	II, 316
31:10-13	I, 200			
42:37	II, 32		Numbers	
46	I, 236		3:11-13	III, 327
49:3-4	I, 220		11:16-30	III, 367
49:29—50:13	IV, 156		18:15	III, 327
Exodus			Deuteronomy	
3:12	I, 288		17:14-20	II, 67, 82, 84
13:2	III, 327		18:15-19	IV, 50
13:11-15	III, 327		20:19-20	II, 295
15:11-18	III, 313		21:17	II, 291
18:1-9	I, 263		24:19	II, 60
19:4	I, 287		25:5-6	III, 272
19:5	II, 295			

---

*This index does not include references that fall *within* the Scripture passage or passages being dealt with in a given chapter. To determine whether the author includes a chapter based on the book of Esther, for example, consult the tables of contents.

291